Activate

Question • Progress • Succeed

3

Teacher Handbook

Simon Broadley
Mark Matthews
Victoria Stutt
Nicky Thomas
Assessment Editor
Dr Andrew Chandler-Grevatt

OXFORD
UNIVERSITY PRESS

Contents

Biology B3

Chemistry C3

Introduction

About the series

Activate is designed to match the 2014 Key Stage 3 Programme of Study and to help prepare your students for success in the new GCSEs and equivalent Key Stage 4 qualifications, whether you decide to take a two- or three-year route. Across the Student Books, Teacher Handbooks, and Kerboodle courses *Activate* allows you to track your students' progress through Key Stage 3 using innovative and reliable assessment and learning resources. With our expert author team and Assessment Editor, you can be confident that *Activate* provides the best support for the new curriculum.

About *Activate 3*

Activate 3 offers consolidation and extension of core concepts through engaging contexts, with plenty of practice in the skills required for success at Key Stage 4. Unlike *Activate 1* and *Activate 2*, topics in Biology, Chemistry, and Physics are grouped by themes – New technology, Turning points, and Detection. These themes not only allow students to consolidate knowledge and skills covered in *Activate 1* and *Activate 2* but also give students the opportunity to find out more about how the concepts they have met can be applied in context, at the frontiers of scientific discovery.

Your Teacher Handbook

This Teacher Handbook aims to save you time and effort by offering lesson plans, differentiation suggestions, and assessment guidance on a page-by-page basis that is a direct match to the Student Book.

You can use the Unit Openers to see the knowledge required of students from *Activate 1* and *Activate 2* for each topic at a glance. You can also use the Checkpoint Lessons at the end of each chapter to support students who have yet to grasp a secure knowledge of the outcomes covered in each chapter. Lesson plans are written for 55-minute lessons but are flexible and fully adaptable so you can choose the activities that suit your classes best.

Unit Opener

Overview
The Unit Opener provides an overview of the unit (Biology, Chemistry, or Physics) and how it links to *Activate 1*, *Activate 2*, and Key Stage 4.

Curriculum links
An overview of the chapters in this unit, and the Key Stage 3 topics they link to.

Preparing for Key Stage 4 success
This table provides an overview of the Key Stage 4 skills and underpinning knowledge that are covered in the unit. It also provides details of where Key Stage 4 style assessment questions can be found throughout the unit.

Activate catch-up
This table outlines the knowledge from *Activate 1* and *Activate 2* that is a pre-requisite for this unit. This can be assessed using the automarked Unit Pre-test on Kerboodle.

For each statement, a suggestion for how you can help students to catch up is provided, as well as an index of which topic each statement links to.

Lesson

Curriculum links
This indicates the area of the 2014 Programme of Study this lesson covers. A Working Scientifically link is also given for most lessons. This indicates the main Working Scientifically focus of the lesson.

Differentiated outcomes
This table summarises the possible lesson outcomes. They are ramped and divided into three ability bands. Levels for each outcome are given in brackets. The three ability bands are explained on the following page.

An indication of where each outcome is covered is given in the checkpoint table, helping you to monitor progress through the lesson.

Maths and Literacy
These boxes provide suggestions of how Maths and Literacy skills can be developed in the lesson. They also indicate when a Maths or Literacy activity is given in the Student Book.

Maths and Literacy skills are ramped through *Activate*. A Progression Grid and Progress Tasks are supplied on Kerboodle.

Assessing Pupil Progress (APP)
Opportunities for integration of APP (based on the 2009 APP framework) are included in the APP box.

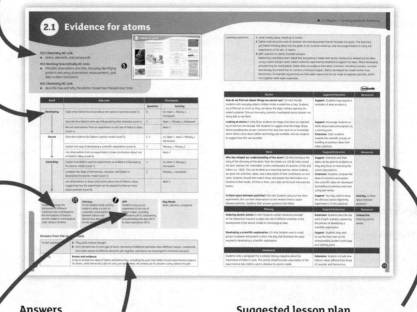

Answers
Answers to the Student Book activities and questions can be found here. For Quality of Written Communication (QWC) questions, only the correct scientific points for marking are given. When marking these questions, attention needs to be given to the quality of the writing in the answer.

Suggested lesson plan
A suggested route through the lesson is provided, including ideas for support, extension, and homework. The right-hand column indicates where Kerboodle resources are available.

Each lesson plan is supported by an editable lesson presentation on Kerboodle.

Checkpoint Lesson

Overview
The Checkpoint Lesson is a suggested follow-up lesson after students have completed the automarked Checkpoint Assessment on Kerboodle. There are two routes through the lesson, with the route for each student being determined by their mark in the assessment. Route A helps students to consolidate what they have learnt through the chapter, whilst Route B offers extension for students who have already grasped the key concepts.

Checkpoint routes
A summary of the two suggested routes through the lesson.

Progression table
This table summarises the outcomes covered in the Revision Lesson, and provides guidance for how students can make progress to achieve each outcome.

The tasks outlined in the table, resources for the Extension Lesson, and detailed Teacher Notes are all available on Kerboodle.

Answers
Answers to the End-of-Chapter questions in the Student Book.

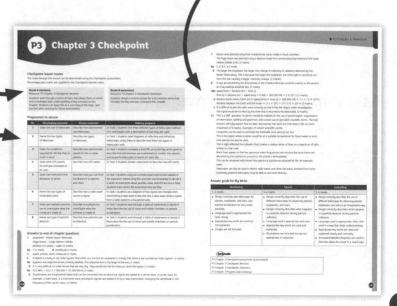

Assessment and progress

About the Assessment Editor

Dr Andrew Chandler-Grevatt has a doctorate in school assessment, and has a real passion for science teaching and learning. Having worked as a science teacher for ten years, of which five was spent as an AST, Andy has a real understanding of the pressures and joys of teaching in the classroom. This stays at the forefront of his mind during all of his work in education.

Alongside his national and international research in school assessment, Andy is a teaching fellow on the PGCE course at the University of Sussex, and is a successful published assessment author.

Welcome

from the Assessment Editor

Welcome to your *Activate 3* Teacher Handbook. The Teacher Handbooks, together with Kerboodle, and the Student Books, provide comprehensive assessment support for the new curriculum.

The new Key Stage 3 curriculum has no prescribed assessment framework. Our assessment model will help your school monitor progress and attainment against the new curriculum, whether you want to continue using levels, or adopt a new model based on curriculum statements. Throughout *Activate*, formative assessment has been made easy, and we have followed a set of guiding assessment principles.

Activate assessment principles

Assessment in *Activate* aims to:

- inform teaching and/or learning directly (have a formative function)
- assess agreed and shared objectives
- provide opportunities for peer- and self-assessment
- provide opportunities for specific feedback to be given to and acted upon by individual students
- provide usable data or information that informs teachers of progress of classes and individuals.

I have been working closely with our expert author teams across all components of *Activate* to ensure consistency in the assessment material, meaning you can be confident when using *Activate* to monitor your students' progress.

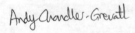

Assessing the new curriculum

The current system of levels will be removed from the National Curriculum. Schools are expected to set their own methods of tracking progress, whilst ensuring students gain a secure level of understanding of each block of content.

The *Activate* assessment model is based on bands; the middle band indicates that students have a *secure* grasp of the content or skills specified in the Programme of Study.

The band working towards *secure* is *developing*, and the band moving past *secure* is *extending*. The bands have been matched to levels and grades, meaning you can adopt a system that works for your school.

Activate bands	Developing		Secure		Extending	
Level equivalent	3	4	5	6	7	8
Grade indicator	To ensure grade indicators are up-to-date with KS4 qualifications, the information is stored on Kerboodle.					
Bloom's Taxonomy links	Remembering & Understanding		Application & Analysing		Evaluation & Creating	

Flexible assessment that works for you

Assessment in *Activate* is designed to be flexible, formative, and summative, allowing you to choose what best suits your students and school. All paper assessments are fully editable for you to adapt to your chosen approach.

All automarked assessments have the option of providing either formative feedback (where students receive feedback on each question and additional attempts) or summative feedback (with one attempt at each question and feedback at the end).

Bands	Levels	Grades	Comment only
All outcomes are banded throughout this book and in progress tasks. Use this model to assess students on their grasp of curriculum statements and set improvement targets, with a focus on ensuring students are always aiming for a *secure* band or higher.	All outcomes are matched to levels in this book and in progress tasks. This means you can continue using levels with *Activate* content, as well as integrating content you already have with *Activate*. This enables progress to be monitored and targets to be set.	Grade indicators are provided on Kerboodle. This enables progress to be monitored with reference to KS4 qualifications.	Some schools have adopted the 'no grades or marks' approach to assessment, opting for comment-only feedback. Interactive assessments provide comments and feedback to facilitate progression, and all paper assessments are fully editable, so banding and levelling can be removed.

The Checkpoint system

At the end of each chapter, there is an automarked online assessment. It will help you to determine if your students have a *secure* understanding of the chapter.

Activities for a follow-up Checkpoint Lesson are provided on Kerboodle. There are two recommended routes through the lesson for students, depending on the percentage they achieve in the assessment. Revision and Extension routes can be followed in the same lesson, allowing students to either consolidate their understanding or attempt an extension task.

Each lesson also includes informal checkpoints to track progress through a lesson.

Follow assessment with learning

Activate includes a Checkpoint assessment system.

1. Use the automarked Checkpoint Assessment at the end of each chapter to determine next steps.

2. Use the Checkpoint Lesson and resources to support and extend your students as needed.

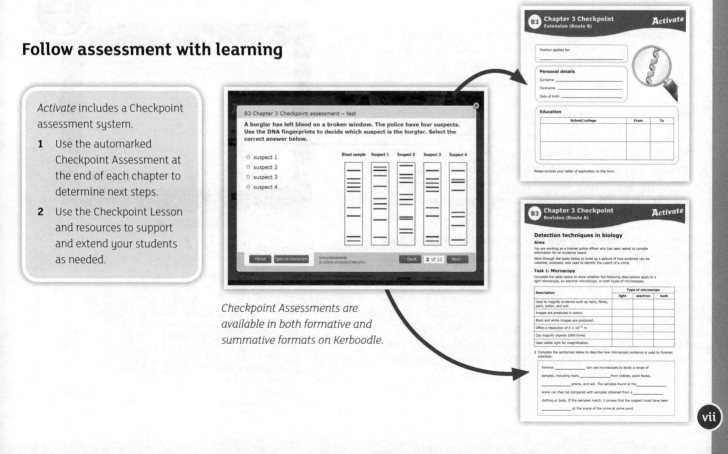

Checkpoint Assessments are available in both formative and summative formats on Kerboodle.

Differentiation and skills

Maths and Literacy skills

Maths and Literacy skills have always been important for science but with the introduction of the new GCSEs, competence in maths and the ability to answer QWC questions and produce extended pieces of writing in scientific contexts will be vital for success.

Key Maths skills for science include quantitative problem solving, use of scientific formulae, and the calculation of arithmetic means. Key Literacy skills include understanding meaning of scientific texts, adapting writing styles to suit audience and purpose, and the organisation of ideas and information. Each skill has been integrated across components in *Activate*, with progress in each skill mapped out. You can view the Progression Grids for Maths and Literacy on Kerboodle.

The **Student Books** contain maths and literacy activities with hints to support and develop Maths and Literacy skills as students work from their books. There are also Maths challenges and Big Writes at the end of most chapters, focussing on quantitative problem-solving skills and extended writing. QWC questions are provided on most spreads, while Key Words and the Glossary help students get to grips with scientific terms.

On **Kerboodle** you will find automarked Skills Interactives and Progress Quizzes that provide formative feedback when assessing Maths and Literacy skills. Maths questions are also incorporated into other assessments where appropriate, and designated Progress Tasks for Maths and Literacy will help you track progress in key skill areas throughout the key stage. In addition, Question-led Lessons offer an alternative approach to one lesson in each chapter, focusing on the Literacy skills needed to answer a Big Question.

In this **Teacher Handbook**, you will find Maths and Literacy suggestions for most lessons, linking to the Student Book where relevant. By using *Activate* resources, students will gain plenty of experience in a range of Maths and Literacy skills that have been identified as vital for success at Key Stage 4.

Working Scientifically

Working Scientifically is new to the 2014 Key Stage 3 Programme of Study and the new GCSE criteria. It is divided into four areas, and is integrated into the teaching and learning of Biology, Chemistry, and Physics. The four areas are **Scientific attitudes**, **Experimental skills and investigations**, **Analysis and evaluation**, and **Measurement**.

Working Scientifically is integrated throughout the **Student Book**, where you will be able to find activities and hints to help students build their investigative skills and understand the process of working scientifically. A dedicated Working Scientifically chapter is also provided in *Activate 1*.

On **Kerboodle** you will find Practicals and Activities, each with their own Working Scientifically objectives, as well as Interactive Investigations, Skills Interactives, Skill Sheets and Progress Tasks that have a specific Working Scientifically focus.

The **Teacher Handbook** lessons often have one Working Scientifically focus in mind for the activities of that lesson. Working Scientifically outcomes are ramped and included as part of the lesson outcomes.

Differentiation

Activate will help you to support students of every ability through Key Stage 3. A variety of support is available, combining opt-in differentiation, ramped questions and tasks, and differentiation by task, as appropriate for each type of activity.

Differentiation using the Checkpoint system
- The end-of-chapter Checkpoint lessons will help you to progress students of every ability.
- The revision tasks are designed to be used with students in need of support. Teacher input will help them grasp important concepts from the chapter.
- The extension tasks provide an opportunity to stretch students who require an extra challenge. Students can work independently.

Teacher Handbook
Lesson outcomes are differentiated, including those for Working Scientifically. Suggestions for activities throughout lesson plans are also accompanied by support and extension opportunities.

Student Book
The Summary Questions and End-of-Chapter Questions in the Student Book are ramped. The level of demand of each question is indicated by the number of conical flasks depicted at the beginning of the question.

Practicals and Activities
Each Practical or Activity includes an extension task. Support Sheets or Access Sheets are available as an extra resource for most Practicals and Activities. Support Sheets offer opt-in differentiation, providing additional support with a difficult area of the task. Access Sheets offer alternative lesson activities where the main Practical or Activity is not accessible by some students.

Skill Sheets may also be used in tandem with Practicals and Activities to provide extra support. These can be found in the Additional support section on Kerboodle.

Interactive Assessments
Interactive Assessments are ramped in difficulty and support is provided in the feedback.

Written assessments
- End-of-Unit Tests and Big Practical Projects have Foundation and Higher versions.
- Progress Tasks each contain two tasks and a progress ladder to cater for all abilities.

Key Stage 4 preparation

Activate 3 is the perfect resource for preparing your students for Key Stage 4 success. It consolidates and extends the skills required for GCSE and equivalent examinations.

- QWC questions
- use of command words
- use of scientific terminology
- extended writing and literacy
- quantitative problem solving
- data handling
- Working Scientifically
- examination-style questions, with a breakdown of the marks given for each part of the question.

Kerboodle

Activate **Kerboodle** is packed full of guided support and ideas for running and creating effective Key Stage 3 science lessons, and assessing and facilitating students' progress. It's intuitive to use, customisable, and can be accessed online.

Activate **Kerboodle consists of**:

- *Activate* Lessons, Resources, and Assessment (includes teacher access to the accompanying Kerboodle Book)
- *Activate* Kerboodle Books.

Lessons, Resources, and Assessment

Activate **Kerboodle** – **Lessons**, **Resources**, and **Assessment** provides hundreds of engaging lesson resources as well as a comprehensive assessment package. Kerboodle offers flexibility and comprehensive support for both the *Activate* course and your own scheme of work.

You can **adapt** many of the resources to suit your students' needs, with all non-interactive activities available as editable Word documents. You can also **upload** your existing resources so that everything can be accessed from one location.

Kerboodle is online, allowing you and your students to access the course anytime, anywhere. Set homework and assessments through the Assessment system, and **track** progress using the Markbook.

Lessons, Resources, and Assessment provide:

- Lessons
- Resources
- Assessment and Markbook
- Teacher access to the Kerboodle Book.

Lessons

Click on the **Lessons tab** to access the *Activate* Lesson Plan and Presentations (with accompanying notes).

Ready-to-play Lesson Plan and Presentations complement every spread in the Teacher Handbook and Student Book. Each lesson presentation is easy to launch and features lesson objectives, settlers, starters, activity guidance, key diagrams, plenaries, and homework suggestions. You can further **personalize** the lessons by adding in your own resources and notes. This means that the Lesson Presentations and accompanying notes sections are 100% customisable. Your lessons and notes can be accessed by your whole department and they are ideal for use in cover lessons.

Every lesson is accompanied by teacher notes that provide additional support and extension opportunities, to fully support lesson delivery.

Resources are built into each lesson presentation so that associated interactive content, practical, or activity worksheets are ready to launch.

FAQs about nanoparticles (40 min)

Students use a range of resources (textbooks and the Internet) to write a newspaper article that answers frequently asked questions from readers about nanoparticles.

An Access Sheet is available where students complete a partially written article on nanoparticles using key words provided.

Fully editable resources and Teacher and Technician Notes (offering further guidance on this activity and answers to the questions on the Activity Sheet) are available from the Resources tab on Kerboodle, under *Activate 3* > Chemistry 3 > C3, 1 New technology.

Resources

Click on the **Resources tab** to access the full list of *Activate* lesson resources.

Fully customisable content to cater all your classes. Resources can be created using the create button.

Existing resources can be uploaded onto the platform using the upload button.

Page navigator shows resources matching to particular pages in the Student Book and Kerboodle Book.

Navigation panel and search bar allow for easy navigation between resources by book, unit, and chapter.

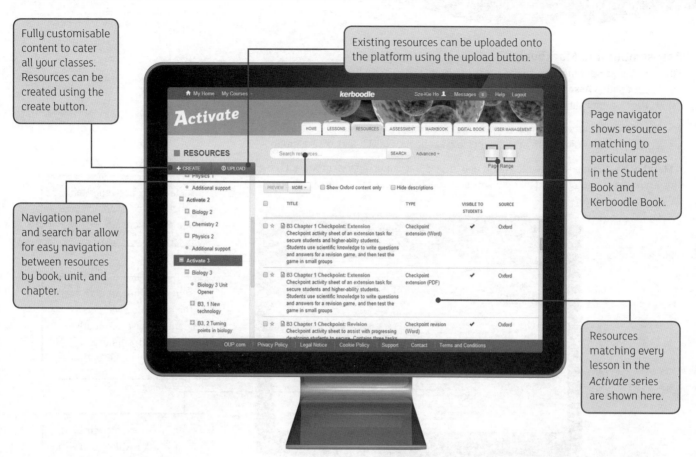

Resources matching every lesson in the *Activate* series are shown here.

The resource section contains:

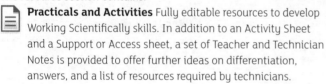 **Practicals and Activities** Fully editable resources to develop Working Scientifically skills. In addition to an Activity Sheet and a Support or Access sheet, a set of Teacher and Technician Notes is provided to offer further ideas on differentiation, answers, and a list of resources required by technicians.

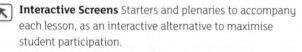 **Interactive Screens** Starters and plenaries to accompany each lesson, as an interactive alternative to maximise student participation.

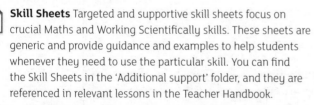 **Skill Sheets** Targeted and supportive skill sheets focus on crucial Maths and Working Scientifically skills. These sheets are generic and provide guidance and examples to help students whenever they need to use the particular skill. You can find the Skill Sheets in the 'Additional support' folder, and they are referenced in relevant lessons in the Teacher Handbook.

Animations Animations focus on explaining difficult concepts using real-life contexts, engaging visuals, and narration. They are structured to clearly support a set of learning objectives and are followed by an Interactive Screen to help consolidate key points.

Videos Videos help students to visualise difficult concepts using engaging visuals and narration. They are structured to clearly address a set of learning objectives.

Skills Interactives Automarked interactive activities with formative feedback that focus on key Maths, Literacy, and Working Scientifically skills. You can use these activities in class to help consolidate key skills relevant to the lesson. They can also be set as homework by accessing them through the Assessment tab.

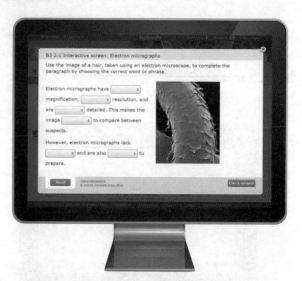

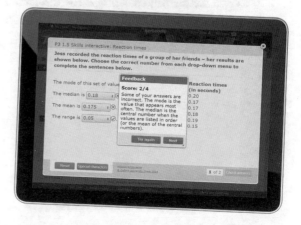

Kerboodle

Assessment and Markbook

All of the Assessment material on Kerboodle has been quality assured by our expert Assessment Editor. Click on the **Assessment tab** to find a wide range of assessment materials to help you deliver a varied, motivating, and effective assessment programme.

It's easy to import class registers and create user accounts for your students. Once your classes are set up, you can assign them assessments to do at home, individually, or as a group.

A **Markbook** with reporting function helps you to keep track of your students' results. This includes both automarked assessments and work that needs to be marked by you.

A Markbook and reporting function help you track your students' progress.

Assign assessments with 'test' in the title if you want your students to have summative feedback, with only one attempt at each question.

Assign assessments with 'practice' in the title if you want your students to get formative feedback on each answer before having another go.

Practice or test?

Each automarked assessment in *Activate* is available in formative or summative versions.

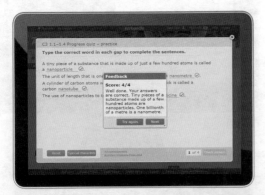

Practice versions of the assessment provide screen-by-screen feedback, focussing on misconceptions, and provide hints for the students to help them revise their answer. Students are given the opportunity to try again. Marks are reported to the Markbook.

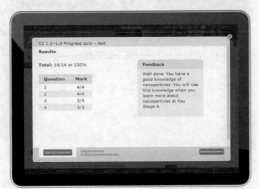

Test versions of the assessment provide feedback on performance at the end of the test. Students are only given one attempt at each screen but can review them and see which answers they got wrong after completing the activity. Marks are reported to the Markbook.

The Assessment section provides ample opportunity for student assessment before, during, and after studying a unit.

Before each unit

 Unit Pre-tests These automarked tests revise and assess students' prior knowledge about the content covered in this unit. Students are given feedback on their answers to help them correct gaps and misconceptions.

After each unit

 End-of-Unit Revision Quizzes These automarked assessments are ramped and focus on revising content from the unit. They can be assigned to students as homework revision ahead of formal end-of-unit testing.

 End-of-Unit Tests These written assessments mimic examination-style questions. They include QWC, Working Scientifically, and quantitative problem-solving questions and are available in two tiers. The Foundation paper contains *developing* and *secure* questions. The Higher paper has a full range of questions, stretching to *extending*. You can use the Raw Score Converter to convert scores to levels, bands, or grades.

 Big Practical Projects These written assessments focus on Working Scientifically and Literacy skills. Students plan and complete an investigation based on a given scenario. The Foundation paper contains *developing* and *secure* questions. The Higher paper has a full range of questions, stretching to *extending*.

Through each chapter

 Progress Quizzes These automarked assessments focus on content midway through a chapter to help you keep track of students as they move through the course.

 Skills Interactives These automarked interactives focus specifically on Maths, Literacy, and Working Scientifically skills.

 Interactive Investigations These automarked assessments are set in the context of an investigation. Each screen assesses a different Working Scientifically skill.

 Progress Tasks These written task-based assessments focus on progress in Maths, Literacy, and Working Scientifically skills. Each task uses a real-life scenario and comes with a progress ladder for students to self- or peer-assess their work.

 Checkpoint Assessments These automarked assessments determine whether students have a *secure* grasp of concepts from the chapter. These assessments are ramped in difficulty and can be followed up by the Checkpoint Lesson revision and extension activities.

 End-of-chapter tests These paper-based tests mimic examination-style questions, and can be used in conjunction with the End-of-Chapter Summary questions in the Student Book to give a comprehensive offline alternative to end-of-chapter assessments.

Kerboodle Book

The *Activate* Kerboodle Book provides a digital version of the Student Book for you to use on your students at the front of the classroom.

Teacher access to the Kerboodle Book is automatically available as part of the Lessons, Resources, and Assessment package. You can also purchase additional access for your students.

A set of tools is available with the Kerboodle Book so you can personalize your book and make notes.

Like all other resources offered on Kerboodle, the Kerboodle Book can also be accessed using a range of devices.

Zoom in and spotlight any part of the text.

Use different tools such as sticky notes, bookmarks, and pen features to personalize each page.

Every teacher and student has their own digital notebook for use within their Kerboodle Book. You can even choose to share some of your notes with your students, or hide them from view – all student notes are accessible to themselves only.

Navigate around the book quickly with the contents menu, key-word search, or page-number search.

Biology 3

Preparing for Key Stage 4 success

Knowledge Underpinning knowledge is covered in this unit for KS4 study of:	• Prokaryotic and eukaryotic cells • Stem cells • Human circulatory system • Health and disease • Infectious diseases • Treating, curing, and preventing disease	• Biodiversity • Reproduction • The genome • Gene expression • Variation and evolution • Selective breeding and genetic engineering

Maths Skills developed in this unit (Topic number).	• Understand number size and scale and the quantitative relationship between units (2.8, 3.1). • Conversion between decimals, fractions, and percentages (1.1, 1.2, 1.9). • Extract and interpret information from charts, graphs, and tables (1.8, 2.2, 2.8, 3.1). • Understand, use, and convert between common units (2.8, 3.5, 3.7). • Carry out calculations involving $+$, $-$, $\times$, $\div$, either singly or in combination (3.1).
Literacy Skills developed in this unit (Topic number).	• Identify meaning in scientific text, taking into account potential bias (1.1, 1.2, 1.9, 3.4, 3.7). • Summarise a range of information from different sources (1.9, 2.8, 3.2, 3.7). • Approach detailed writing tasks by first creating a detailed structural plan (1.2, 1.7, 1.9, 2.3, 2.6, 2.8, 3.1, 3.3, 3.4, 3.7). • Identify ideas and supporting evidence in text (1.3, 1.4, 1.5, 1.9, 2.6, 2.8, 3.6, 3.7). • Arguments are well presented, discussing issues, ethics, and opinions of others (1.4, 1.5, 1.9, 2.2, 2.7, 3.4). • Use largely correct form in a range of writing styles and texts to include information relevant to the audience (1.2, 1.3, 1.4, 1.6, 1.7, 1.9, 2.1, 2.3, 2.4, 2.6, 2.8, 3.4, 3.7). • Take different roles in discussion and show understanding of ideas and sensitivity to others (2.7). • Ideas are organised into well developed, linked paragraphs (1.2, 1.4, 1.5, 1.6, 1.7, 1.9, 2.1, 2.2, 2.3, 2.4, 2.5, 2.6, 2.7, 2.8, 3.1, 3.4, 3.6, 3.7). • Use scientific terms confidently and correctly in discussions and writing (1.3, 1.4, 1.7, 2.1, 2.4, 2.6, 2.7, 3.3, 3.4, 3.5, 3.6).
Assessment Skills	• QWC questions (1.3, 1.4, 1.5, 1.6, 1.7, 1.8, 2.1, 2.2, 2.3, 2.4, 2.5, 2.6, 2.7, 3.1, 3.2, 3.3, 3.4, 3.5, 3.6) (end-of-chapter 1 Q6, end-of-chapter 2 Q6, end-of-chapter 3 Q6) • Quantitative problem solving (1.1, 1.2, 3.1) • Application of Working Scientifically (1.6) (end-of-chapter 1 Q3, end-of-chapter 2 Q4)

	Key concept	Catch-up
Chapter 1	The heredity of characteristics shown by individuals is introduced through the use of dominant and recessive alleles in genetic crosses. This provides students with a firm foundation when tackling further topics in genetics, for example, the **genome, gene expression**, and **variation and evolution**.	B2 3.3 Variation B2 3.4 Continuous and discontinuous B2 3.5 Inheritance

Chapter 1: New technology	**Genetic crosses** are practiced further when discussing the inheritance of genetic disorders, for example, haemophilia, cystic fibrosis, and polydactyly. The drawing of genetic crosses is essential when demonstrating how characteristics can be inherited, showing **variation and evolution** of different species.	B2 3.3 Variation B2 3.4 Continuous and discontinuous B2 3.5 Inheritance
	The benefits, risks, and ethical issues of **selective breeding, genetic engineering,** and **cloning** are introduced in this chapter, serving as a foundation for further study of these topics.	B2 1.1 Competition and adaptation B2 3.2 Adapting to change B2 3.3 Variation B2 3.4 Continuous and discontinuous B2 3.5 Inheritance
	The use of enzymes as catalysts in reactions is covered when discussing their use in the production of food products. This provides students with a good foundation towards understanding of **the mechanism of enzyme action** and the **importance of biotechnology.**	B2 1.5 Bacteria and enzymes in digestion
Chapter 2: Turning points in biology	The way the human body gains immunity is covered in the context of antibiotics, vaccinations, and white blood cells. This serves as an important introduction to **health and disease**, in particular, the **treating**, **curing, and preventing of diseases**.	B2 1.6 Drugs B2 1.7 Alcohol B2 1.8 Smoking
	The structure of DNA is consolidated by discussing the work carried out by scientists prior to Crick and Watson's discovery. This provides students with further foundations towards understanding the **genome** and how it relates to **phenotype**.	B2 3.3 Variation B2 3.4 Continuous and discontinuous B2 3.5 Inheritance
	Darwin's theory of evolution is consolidated by considering his work on the Galapagos Islands and his correspondence with Wallace. This chapter also covers biodiversity and techniques used to prevent extinction. This will aid students in the further study of **biodiversity**, **variation**, and **evolution**.	B2 3.6 Natural selection B2 3.7 Extinction
Chapter 3: Detection	The use of light and electrons in analysing microscopic data is covered in this chapter. This can provide students with the foundation for appreciating how electron microscopy has changed **the understanding of sub-cellular structures**.	B1 1.1 Observing cells B1 1.2 Plant and animal cells
	Techniques used in the identification of suspects, for example, fingerprinting and DNA, are covered in this chapter. These techniques consolidate the **variation** (genetic or otherwise) in humans.	B2 3.3 Variation B2 3.4 Continuous and discontinuous B2 3.5 Inheritance
	Blood groups and the composition of human blood are discussed in the context of a fictitious crime. These concepts are important for the further study of the **human circulatory system**.	B1 1.4 Movement of substances B2 2.5 Aerobic respiration B2 2.6 Anaerobic respiration
	The rate of reactions and insect activity is covered when discussing how time of death can be determined. This serves as an introduction for students when predicting how **temperature and water content affect rate of decomposition** and the **rates of chemical reactions**.	B1 1.4 Movement of substances B2 1.5 Bacteria and enzymes in digestion C1 3.1 Chemical reactions

kerboodle

B3 Unit pre-test	B3 Practical project hints: writing frame	
B3 Big practical project (foundation)	B3 End-of-unit test (foundation)	
B3 Big practical project (higher)	B3 End-of-unit test (foundation) mark scheme	
B3 Big practical project teacher notes	B3 End-of-unit test (higher)	
B3 Practical project hints: graph plotting	B3 End-of-unit test (higher) mark scheme	
B3 Practical project hints: planning		

Answers to Picture Puzzler
Key Words

injection, microscope, mould, ultrasound, nucleus, eye
The key word is **immune.**

Close up
electron micrograph of cotton

1.1 Genetics

KS3 Biology NC Link:
- inheritance, chromosomes, DNA, and genes.

KS3 Working Scientifically NC Link:
- apply mathematical concepts and calculate results.

KS4 Biology NC Link:
- explain the following terms: chromosome, gene, dominant, and recessive
- explain monogenic inheritance
- predict the results of monogenic crosses.

Band	Outcome	Checkpoint	
		Question	Activity
Developing	State what is meant by an allele (Level 4).	A, 1	Main, Plenary 1, Plenary 2
	State that genetics allows us to track alleles from one generation to the next (Level 3).		Starter 1, Starter 2, Main
	Complete a Punnett square to state how many offspring will have a particular characteristic (Level 4).	3	Main
Secure	Describe the difference between dominant and recessive alleles (Level 6).	B, C, 1	Main, Plenary 1, Plenary 2
	Use a Punnett square to show what happens during a genetic cross (Level 6).	3	Main
	Trace characteristics through a family tree using Punnett squares, giving answers as percentages and ratios (Level 6).	3	Main
Extending	Explain how dominant or recessive alleles can be expressed as external features (Level 7).	C, 1	Main, Plenary 1, Plenary 2
	Explain how to use a Punnett square to predict the outcome of a genetic cross (Level 7).	3	Main, Plenary 2
	Trace characteristics through a family tree using Punnett squares, calculating the probability of different outcomes (Level 8).	3	Main, Plenary 2

Maths
Students demonstrate their understanding of probability by using genetic crosses to calculate the ratio and percentage of offspring who demonstrate certain characteristics.

Students are also required to convert between ratios, percentages, and fractions in the student-book activity.

Literacy
Students read scientific text to extract information about a Jack Russell's family tree.

Key Words
allele, dominant, recessive, Punnett square

Answers from the student book

In-text questions	**A** Different forms of the same gene. **B** dominant **C** two		
Activity	**Genetic-cross outcomes** $0 \text{ in } 4 = \frac{0}{4} = 0 = 0\%$ $\quad 2 \text{ in } 4 = \frac{2}{4} \text{ or } \frac{1}{2} = 0.5 = 50\%$ $\quad 4 \text{ in } 4 = \frac{4}{4} \text{ or } 1 = 1 = 100\%$ $1 \text{ in } 4 = \frac{1}{4} = 0.25 = 25\%$ $\quad 3 \text{ in } 4 = \frac{3}{4} = 0.75 = 75\%$		

Summary Questions	**1** alleles, dominant, recessive (3 marks)

2 a black   **b** white   **c** black (3 marks)

3

		father	
		F	f
mother	F	FF	Ff
	f	Ff	ff

3 of 4 offspring will inherit freckles.

$\frac{3}{4} = 0.75 = 75\%$

Only 1 in 4 offspring will not inherit freckles ($\frac{1}{4} = 0.25 = 25\%$).

(6 marks)

kerboodle

Starter	Support/Extension	Resources
Inheriting characteristics (10 mins) Recap the ideas about inheritance from B2. Ask students how they inherit characteristics. If students are comfortable with the idea, you may wish to allow students to trace one characteristic that is present in their family. Introduce the idea that some characteristics are not displayed in every generation.	**Support**: Students may need reminding about characteristics being passed on in the form of genes during the fertilisation of gametes. **Extension**: Students should categorise inherited characteristics as continuous or discontinuous.	
Inheritance (10 mins) Put the following keywords on the board: mother, father, egg, sperm, offspring, fertilisation. Ask students to draw a diagram on a mini-whiteboard to illustrate how these words are linked, and suggest how these key words are linked to inheritance.	**Extension**: Students should include genes and DNA in their diagrams.	

Main	Support/Extension	Resources
Inheriting eye patches (35 mins) Introduce the idea that characteristics are inherited from parents in the form of genes. Explain the importance of alleles (dominant and recessive) using Punnett squares and work through a couple of examples as a class. Students then work through an activity explaining the characteristics displayed in a family of Jack Russell terriers using their scientific knowledge and understanding. Students answer questions based on this family of dogs, using Punnett squares and associated calculations to deduce answers.	**Support**: A formal recap of how genetic material is inherited from gametes at fertilisation may be useful. Some students may also require additional support when converting probabilities between fractions and percentages.	**Activity**: Inheriting eye patches **Skill sheet**: Calculating percentages **Skill sheet**: Calculating probabilities

Plenary	Support/Extension	Resources
Genetic key words (10 mins) The interactive resource asks students to match the correct key word to its definition. You may wish to use mini-whiteboards to increase participation.	**Extension**: Students write a short paragraph linking these words together.	**Interactive**: Genetic key words
Parents and children (10 mins) Pose the question 'Can a child with ginger hair really have parents with brown and blonde hair?' Allow students to pair-share their ideas before discussing this as a class. Be aware of students who are adopted. This may be a sensitive topic.	**Extension**: Students explain the conditions necessary for this to be true (e.g., the ginger-hair allele is recessive) and show this using a Punnett square.	

Homework		
Students research and write a paragraph on the work of Gregor Mendel to describe how his work paved the way to our understanding of genetics today.		

1.2 Inherited disorders

KS3 Biology NC Link:
- inheritance, chromosomes, DNA, and genes.

KS3 Working Scientifically NC Link:
- present observations and data using appropriate methods, including tables and graphs.

KS4 Biology NC Link:
- explain monogenic inheritance
- predict the results of monogenic crosses.

Band	Outcome	Checkpoint	
		Question	Activity
Developing	Name a genetic disorder (Level 3).		Lit, Main, Plenary 1
	State that the chance of inheriting a genetic disorder can be calculated (Level 4).		Lit, Main, Plenary 2
	Draw a Punnett square to show the likelihood of an offspring inheriting a genetic disorder (Level 4).	3	Lit, Main, Plenary 2
Secure	Describe what is meant by a genetically inherited disorder (Level 5).	A, 1	Lit, Plenary 1
	Calculate the probability of a person suffering from an inherited disease (Level 6).	3	Lit, Main
	Use a Punnett square to calculate the probability of an offspring inheriting a genetic disorder (Level 6).	3	Lit, Main, Plenary 2
Extending	Explain how a genetic disorder can be inherited (Level 7).	1, 3	Lit, Main
	Predict possible alleles present in parents given a child with a genetically inherited disorder (Level 8).	3	Lit, Main, Plenary 2
	Use a Punnett square to calculate the probability of an offspring inheriting a genetic disorder, giving answers as percentages, fractions, and decimals (Level 7).	3	Lit, Main, Plenary 2

Maths
Students give the probabilities of offspring suffering from an inherited disorder as percentages, decimals, and fractions.

Literacy
Students research genetic disorders (symptoms and possible treatments) in the student-book activity and in the main lesson activity. Students use their findings to produce a presentation and a coherent, concise report.

APP
Students evaluate the quality of the evidence used in their research, recognising potential bias (AF5).

Key Words
genetically inherited disorder, carrier

Answers from the student book

In-text questions	A A condition passed from parents to their offspring in their genes.
	B A person who has one dominant and one recessive allele for a recessive disorder.
	C Polydactyly is caused by a dominant allele, so you need only one copy of the allele to display the disorder.
Activity	**Genetically inherited disorders** Presentations should include the main symptoms of the disorder, treatments available, and a genetic cross showing the possible offspring from two carriers.

Summary Questions	
	1 inherited, parents, offspring, recessive, carrier (5 marks)
	2 Carriers of a genetically inherited disorder do not display the symptoms of the disorder. This is because they have only one copy of the recessive allele. A person needs both of the alleles to be recessive in order to have the disorder. (3 marks)

3

		father	
		C	c
mother	C	CC	Cc
	C	CC	Cc

Neither parent has cystic fibrosis.
This is because cystic fibrosis is recessive.
You would need to have cc in order to have the disorder.
The offspring of these parents show that there is 0% chance of the offspring suffering from cystic fibrosis.
50% of offspring will have CC, and 50% Cc (carriers of cystic fibrosis).
(6 marks)

Starter	Support/Extension	Resources
What do these have in common? (10 mins) Show students images from the Internet of inherited disorders such as polydactyly, cystic fibrosis, and Huntington's disease. Ask students to suggest what they have in common. **Have you heard of these?** (5 mins) Write the names of some inherited disorders on the board: cystic fibrosis, polydactyly, haemophilia, and sickle cell anaemia. Ask if students know what they are, suggesting how people develop the disorder, and whether they are contagious or not.	**Extension**: Students explain how genes are passed on from one generation to the next.	
Main	**Support/Extension**	**Resources**
Researching inherited disorders (40 mins) Introduce the idea of genetically inherited disorders, and how each of these is related to dominant or recessive alleles. You may wish to allow the class to practice drawing Punnett squares using one or two inherited disorders as examples before starting the research task. Students should then use a variety of sources (textbooks and the Internet) to carry out research on one inherited disorder. They can do this independently or in pairs. Sources can be differentiated by the level of scientific concepts discussed. At the end of the research task, ask groups of students to share their findings so that the whole class can gain a general idea about the different types of inherited disorders. Be aware of students who may have relatives with inherited disorders.	**Support**: The support sheet has a research evidence table for cystic fibrosis. It includes a row for how the information may be used by a genetic counsellor. You may also wish to limit the number of sources students look through in this task. **Extension**: Encourage students to research more complex genetic disorders such as sickle cell anaemia and haemophilia.	**Activity**: Researching inherited disorders **Skill sheet**: Calculating probabilities **Skill sheet**: Calculating percentages
Plenary	**Support/Extension**	**Resources**
Genetic disorders (10 mins) Students complete a crossword on the key words from this lesson using clues provided on the interactive resource. **Practising Punnett squares** (5 mins) Students draw Punnett squares on mini-whiteboards when given different scenarios.	**Extension**: Students write sentences that use the key words from the crossword. **Support**: Students offer probabilities in the form of X out of Y. **Extension**: Students give probabilities as percentages, fractions, and decimals.	**Interactive**: Genetic disorders
Homework		
Students use the evidence table completed during the main activity to produce a report about the genetically inherited disorder researched. An alternative WebQuest homework activity is available on Kerboodle where students research sickle cell anaemia.	**Support**: Students should use the headings provided in the evidence table to structure their reports.	**WebQuest**: Sickle cell anaemia

KS3 Biology NC Link:

- inheritance, chromosomes, DNA, and genes.

KS3 Working Scientifically NC Link:

- understand that scientific methods and theories develop as earlier explanations are modified to take account of new evidence and ideas, together with the importance of publishing results and peer review.

KS4 Biology NC Link:

- describe the impact of selective breeding on food plants and domesticated animals.

Band	Outcome	Checkpoint	
		Question	Activity
Developing	State what is meant by selective breeding (Level 3).	A	Main
	State one advantage and disadvantage of selective breeding (Level 4).	B, D, 2	Lit, Main, Plenary 2
	State one way in which selective breeding has changed over time (Level 3).		Main, Homework
Secure	Describe the process of selective breeding (Level 5).	1	Lit, Main, Plenary 1, Homework
	Describe some advantages and disadvantages of selective breeding (Level 6).	2, 3	Main, Plenary 2
	Describe how scientists have discovered problems with early selective breeding methods (Level 6).		Main
Extending	Explain how the process of selective breeding is carried out (Level 7).	3	Main, Plenary 1, Homework
	Evaluate the advantages and disadvantages of selective breeding (Level 8).		Main, Plenary 2, Homework
	Explain how scientific understanding has improved the process of selective breeding (Level 7).		Main

Literacy

In the student-book activity students adapt writing styles to produce an information leaflet explaining to farmers how to selectively breed cows for milk production.

Students also extract information from scientific text to answer the questions on their activity sheet.

APP

Students consider the development of scientific ideas over time and the role of the scientific community in the development of these ideas (AF1).

Key Words

selective breeding

Answers from the student book

In-text questions	
	A Choosing the best plants/animals to breed.
	B Offspring are more likely have the desired characteristics.
	C Variation is reduced/smaller gene pool.
	D Reduces variation/useful genes lost/species could become extinct.

Activity	**Milk production** Information leaflet should include steps involved in selective breeding of cows for milk production. The farmer selects the cow with the highest milk production. He breeds this with his best bull. From the offspring the farmer chooses the cow with the highest milk production and breeds again with the best bull. This process continues over several generations. Eventually all the cows will have the desired characteristic of high milk production.
Summary Questions	**1** Choose a desirable characteristic. Select parents that show high levels of the required characteristic. Breed these individuals. Select the best offspring and breed again. Repeat the process for many generations. (5 marks) **2** Advantage: high proportion of offspring exhibiting desired characteristic, for example, Dalmatians with clearly defined spots. Disadvantage: often suffer health problems, for example, Labradors suffer hip problems. Selectively bred dogs are at higher risk of inheriting a genetic disorder and have lower life expectancies. (2 marks) **3** QWC question (6 marks). Example answers: The farmer should choose tomato plants that produce tomatoes of the desired characteristics (large and sweet). Select the plant that produces the biggest tomatoes. Select another plant that produces the sweetest tomatoes. Breed these together. Choose from the offspring using the same criteria. Breed these two offspring together. Continue this method of breeding over many generations. This reduces the gene pool so that tomato plants with large and sweet tomatoes are produced.

Starter	Support/Extension	Resources
Selecting desired characteristics (10 mins) Ask students how they would solve the problem over time of having two types of grapes – one that is sweet but poor yielding, and one that produces good yield but is sour. Students pair-share ideas before a class discussion. **Domestic farm animals** (5 mins) Show students images of different varieties of animal, for example, breeds of cattle. Ask them how we can produce different varieties of the same species. Students justify answers in terms of genetic inheritance and variation.	**Extension**: Students demonstrate the process of selective breeding using an appropriate prop, for example, marbles.	
Main	**Support/Extension**	**Resources**
Selective breeding in dogs (40 mins) Formally introduce the idea of selective breeding in the context covered by the chosen starter. Summarise the stages involved in selective breeding. (This is available from the corresponding student-book spread.) Students read through the passage provided on the activity sheet and use this information, together with their own knowledge, to answer the questions that follow. You may wish to discuss what the simplified evolutionary tree of wolves and dogs shows with the class before beginning this activity.	**Support**: Write out the steps of selective breeding for a different organism, for example, dairy cows, and leave this on the board for the duration of the lesson for students to refer to. **Extension**: Encourage students to include ideas about ethics in their discussions.	**Activity**: Selective breeding in dogs
Plenary	**Support/Extension**	**Resources**
The sequence of selective breeding (5 mins) Interactive resource where students reorder sentences to describe the process of selective breeding to produce racing dogs. **Advantages and disadvantages of selective breeding** (10 mins) Read out advantages and disadvantages of selective breeding. Students indicate using mini-whiteboards or thumbs up/down whether the statement is an advantage or disadvantage. Students justify their answers and come up with other suggestions.	**Extension**: Encourage students to explain in terms of genetics how selective breeding works.	**Interactive**: The sequence of selective breeding
Homework		
Students research the selective breeding of a crop (wheat, corn, and so on) or an animal. They write a paragraph explaining how the selective breeding was carried out in the past, and if this has now changed.	**Extension**: Students evaluate selective breeding using the examples in their research.	

KS3 Biology NC Link:
- inheritance, chromosomes, DNA, and genes.

KS4 Biology NC Link:
- describe the main stages of the process of genetic engineering
- explain some of the possible benefits of using genetic engineering in modern agriculture and medicine
- recognise some of the practical and ethical issues of using genetic engineering in modern agriculture and medicine
- describe possible biological solutions, including those using new biotechnologies, to the problems of the growing human population.

Band	Outcome	Checkpoint	
		Question	Activity
Developing ↓	State what is meant by genetic engineering (Level 4).	A, 1	Main, Homework
	Name a product produced by genetically engineered organisms (Level 4).	C, 1	Lit, Main, Homework
Secure ↓	State how a product is produced using genetic engineering (Level 5).	3	Lit, Main, Homework
	Describe some advantages of producing products through genetic engineering (Level 6).	B, 2	Main, Plenary 1, Plenary 2, Homework
Extending ↓	Describe how a product is produced using genetic engineering (Level 7).	3	Lit, Main, Homework
	Analyse advantages and disadvantages of producing products through genetic engineering (Level 8).		Main, Plenary 1, Plenary 2, Homework

Maths

Some students may use numerical sources of data during their research about genetic engineering that they will interpret before using in their discussion.

Literacy

Students draw a cartoon strip about one example of genetic engineering in the student-book activity and write associated captions for each cartoon entry.

Students collate and summarise information and evidence from a range of scientific texts when researching the advantages and disadvantages of genetic engineering.

APP

Students demonstrate teamwork during their research task, presenting their arguments using scientific evidence during the class discussion on the advantages and disadvantages of genetic engineering. (AF3)

Key Words

genetic engineering

Answers from the student book

In-text questions	**A** Altering the genes of an organism to display desired characteristics.
	B Very precise/much quicker than selective breeding.
	C vaccines and antibiotics
Activity	**Genetic engineering cartoon strip**
	Cartoon strip should include the following:
	Select an organism (plant or animal) and identify a characteristic to alter.
	Take genes from another organism that shows this characteristic. These are known as foreign genes.
	Insert the foreign genes into the plant/animal cells at the early stages of the organism's development.
	As the organism develops, it will display the characteristics of the foreign genes.

Summary Questions	1 foreign, characteristics, genetic, vaccines/antibiotics/insulin (4 marks)
	2 Genetic engineering is much more precise than selective breeding, it is a much quicker process, and it can alter characteristics more dramatically, for example, making fish glow in polluted water. (3 marks)
	3 QWC question (6 marks). Example answers:
	Genes that produce Factor VIII are identified and isolated. These genes are cut from a cell in that organism. These are then inserted into bacteria. The bacteria now produce Factor VIII. The bacteria multiply many times, producing a large amount of Factor VIII. The bacteria can then be removed, for example, by killing them using high temperatures. This leaves behind large amounts of pure Factor VIII. This can then be administered to sufferers of haemophilia.

Starter	Support/Extension	Resources
Useful combinations (5 mins) Discuss as a class characteristics that students would transfer into a crop or animal. They should identify an organism with the characteristic, and justify why it would be useful to the organisms targeted.	**Extension**: Students suggest how this characteristic can be transferred to the crop or animal.	
Fact or fiction? (10 mins) Display newspaper headlines and photos with sensational examples of genetic engineering, for example, cats that glow in the dark. (These examples are readily available on the Internet.) Ask the class to discuss the plausibility of these stories and suggest how genetic engineering can be carried out.	**Extension**: Encourage students to evaluate the reliability of the sources shown.	

Main	Support/Extension	Resources
Researching genetic engineering (40 mins) Introduce students to the theory behind genetic engineering. It is important that students appreciate the differences between selective breeding (a process involving the same species, over several generations of offspring) and genetic engineering (the transfer of desirable genes from one organism to another). Split students into small groups of three or four and ask groups to carry out research into the advantages and disadvantages of genetic engineering. Approximately half the class should research the advantages and the other half the disadvantages of genetic engineering for this activity to work successfully. Students must fill in four entries in their table during their research time (20 min) and complete the rest of the table using the findings of other groups during the class discussion (20 min). Students should then summarise their thoughts on genetic engineering using the evidence obtained.	**Support**: The accompanying support sheet provides a table where students are already given four advantages and three disadvantages of genetic engineering to focus their research. **Extension**: Sources of information can be ramped in such a way that students are given more complex scientific texts, with additional numerical data to analyse.	**Activity**: Researching genetic engineering

Plenary	Support/Extension	Resources
Advantages of genetic engineering (10 mins) Interactive resource where students identify the advantages of genetic engineering from a list of advantages and disadvantages. Mini-whiteboards can be used to increase class participation.	**Extension**: Ask students to suggest other advantages and disadvantages, or to extend ideas.	**Interactive**: Advantages of genetic engineering
Genetic engineering continuum (5 mins) Set up the classroom as a continuum from strong advantage to strong disadvantage. Ask students to give statements on genetic engineering and to stand on the continuum where they think the statement fits in best. This can be done on paper if movement around the classroom is restricted.	**Extension**: Students should be able to justify their position and argue their case if necessary.	

Homework		
Students write a short report on what genetic engineering is and how genetic engineering is used in a different scenario, for example, in golden rice. Students should include the advantages and disadvantages of genetic engineering in this context.	**Extension**: Students should include more advanced ideas such as the use of restriction enzymes to cut sections of DNA.	

1.5 Cloning

KS3 Biology NC Link:

● inheritance, chromosomes, DNA, and genes.

KS3 Working Scientifically NC Link:

● use appropriate techniques, apparatus, and materials during laboratory work, paying attention to health and safety.

KS4 Biology NC Link:

● recognise the advantages and disadvantages of asexual and sexual reproduction in animals and plants.

Band	Outcome	Checkpoint	
		Question	**Activity**
Developing	Give one example of cloning (Level 3).	B	Starter 1, Starter 2, Main, Plenary 1
	State one advantage and one disadvantage of cloning an organism (Level 3).	C	Main, Plenary 2, Homework
	Follow part of a method to set up an experiment involving plant cuttings (Level 3).		WS, Main
Secure	Describe what is meant by a clone (Level 5).	A, 1	Main, Plenary 1
	Describe some advantages and disadvantages of cloning (Level 6).	3	Main, Plenary 2, Homework
	Use appropriate techniques to take cuttings from a plant (Level 5).		WS, Main
Extending	Explain in terms of genetics the differences between sexual and asexual reproduction (Level 8).	2	Starter 1, Starter 2, Main, Plenary 1
	Compare the advantages and disadvantages of cloning (Level 7).	3	Main, Plenary 2, Homework
	Use appropriate techniques to take cuttings from a plant, suggesting how risks can be minimised during the experiment (Level 7).		WS, Main

Literacy
Students summarise their views about cloning when they argue for or against cloning using advantages and disadvantages of this technique.

APP
Students identify a hazard in their experimental procedure and suggest how the risk can be minimised. (AF4)

Key Words
clone, asexual reproduction

Answers from the student book

In-text questions	**A** An organism that is genetically identical to its parent.
	B When offspring are produced from one parent, and there is no mixing of genetic material.
	C Reduces gene pool/increases risk of disease and extinction.
Activity	**Plant cuttings**
	The simplest way to take a cutting is to remove a branch from the parent plant.
	Its lower leaves should be removed and the stem planted in damp compost.
	To encourage new roots to develop the stem can be dipped in 'rooting powder' containing plant hormones prior to planting.
	The cutting needs to be kept moist and warm.
	After a few weeks, new roots should develop and a new plant (that is genetically identical to the parent) is produced. This is the practical in the lesson plan.

Summary Questions	1 identical, clones, asexual (3 marks)
	2 Asexual reproduction involves one parent whilst sexual reproduction requires two.
	There is no genetic variation in asexual reproduction whereas sexual reproduction involves the mixing of genetic material from the two parents.
	This means that there is variation between parents and different offspring in sexual reproduction whereas the offspring in asexual reproduction are identical to the parent. (3 marks)
	3 QWC question (6 marks). Example answers:
	Students must give an example of cloning, for example, plant cuttings, and use this example to illustrate the advantages and disadvantages they give.
	Examples of advantages include:
	Offspring can be reproduced quickly. Cloning is cheap (in plant reproduction). Desired characteristics are replicated in offspring. Cloning of a species can prevent extinction. Cell cloning allows scientists access to human cells for research into diseases. Tissue cultures allow new skin and cartilage to be grown.
	Examples of disadvantages include:
	Ethical concerns. Reduction of gene pool. This increases the risk of disease. If an external change affects one individual, the whole population of clones will be affected due to a lack of genetic variation. This increases the likelihood of extinction.

Starter	Support/Extension	Resources
Identical plants (10 min) Show students a photograph of a tray of identical plants. Ask students to suggest how these plants may have been reproduced. Allow students time to discuss their ideas before revealing the answer. Students should then compare the similarities and differences between this type of reproduction (asexual) and human reproduction (sexual).	**Extension**: Students should offer advantages and disadvantages of asexual reproduction.	
Types of reproduction (5 min) Recap the key points of human (sexual) reproduction met in B1. Ask students how they think bacteria reproduce. Introduce the term asexual reproduction and encourage students to suggest a possible definition of this.	**Extension**: Students should explain how plants are able to produce sexually (cross-pollination) and asexually (self-pollination).	

Main	Support/Extension	Resources
Plant cuttings (40 min) Formally introduce the concept of sexual and asexual reproduction before linking this to cloning. It is important that students understand why cloning is carried out in different scenarios, and that advantages and disadvantages of cloning are covered before starting this practical. Students then work in small groups to take plant cuttings from suitable plants and answer the questions that follow.	**Support**: Compost can be set up in small trays/ice-cream tubs ready for each group to take a cutting.	**Practical**: Plant cuttings

Plenary	Support/Extension	Resources
Defining cloning (5 min) Students match key words form this lesson with their definitions using the interactive resource. Students can then write a sentence using each key word on a mini-whiteboard.		**Interactive**: Defining cloning
Advantage or disadvantage of cloning? (10 min) Students take turns to offer a statement about cloning that is either an advantage or disadvantage. The rest of the class then decides in which category the statement falls (using thumbs up/down, coloured cards, or mini-whiteboards). Students can then be asked to justify their choice.	**Extension**: Students compare the advantages with the disadvantages given, and offer a concluding statement about cloning overall.	

Homework		
Design a poster that summarises the key similarities and differences between selective breeding, genetic engineering, and cloning. This can be done in the form of a visual summary. A list of advantages and disadvantages of each technique should be included.		

1.6 Biotechnology 1

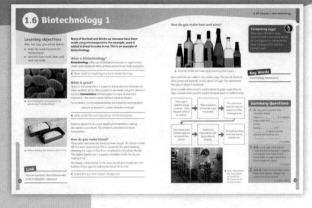

KS3 Biology NC Link:
- cellular respiration.

KS3 Working Scientifically NC Link:
- make and record observations and measurements using a range of methods for different investigations; and evaluate the reliability of methods and suggest possible improvements.

KS4 Biology NC Link:
- describe some anabolic and catabolic processes in living organisms including the importance of sugars, amino acids, fatty acids, and glycerol in the synthesis and breakdown of carbohydrates, lipids, and proteins
- describe possible biological solutions, including those using new biotechnologies, to the problems of the growing human population.

Band	Outcome	Checkpoint	
		Question	Activity
Developing	State what is meant by fermentation (Level 4).	1	Starter 1, Homework
	Name the organism used to make bread, beer, and wine (Level 3).	1	Starter 1, Main, Homework
↓	Make observations about the rising of bread dough in an investigation (Level 3).		Main
Secure	Write the word equation for fermentation (Level 5).	B	Main, Plenary 2
	Describe how bread, beer, and wine are made (Level 6).	1, 3	Plenary 1, Homework
↓	Carry out an investigation to investigate the effect of temperature on fermentation, recording measurements and drawing a conclusion (Level 6).		Main
Extending	Explain how the process of fermentation works in relation to the word equation (Level 7).		Main, Plenary 1, Homework
	Explain why temperature is important in the making of bread, beer, and wine (Level 8).		Main, Plenary 2, Homework
↓	Carry out an investigation to investigate the effect of temperature on fermentation, using results to draw a conclusion, and suggest one way to minimise error (Level 7).		Main

Maths

Students demonstrate their understanding of the number scale when reading values from a measuring cylinder, carry out simple subtractions, and extract information from graphs.

Literacy

In the student-book activity students write out an investigation that they can carry out to determine the ideal temperature for yeast.

APP
Students plan an investigation to determine the ideal temperature for yeast to ferment sugar in the student-book activity (AF4), present data obtained from the experiment in a table (AF3), and use these results to draw a conclusion (AF5).

Key Words
biotechnology, fermentation

Answers from the student book

In-text questions	A The use of biological processes or organisms to create useful products.
	B glucose → ethanol + carbon dioxide (+ energy)

C carbon dioxide

Activity	**Fermenting sugar** Students can study this reaction by using boiling tubes of sugar solution that have been kept in a water bath at different temperatures. The rate of the fermentation reaction can be measured by counting how many carbon dioxide bubbles are produced per minute. This task can be used to introduce the accompanying interactive investigation for this chapter.
Summary Questions	**1** microorganism, alcoholic, fermentation, enzymes, carbon dioxide (5 marks) **2** Bread made without yeast will be flatter in appearance and will not contain air bubbles. This is because fermentation will not have occurred, so carbon dioxide is not made. This means that the bread will not rise. (3 marks) **3** QWC question (6 marks). Example answers: Apples are squeezed/crushed (to release the juice). Yeast is added. The container with the juice and yeast is sealed. This keeps out oxygen and microorganisms. Yeast ferments the sugar in the apple juice. The mixture is left until the sugar has fermented into alcohol/cider. Sediment is removed from the liquid (by filtration). The liquid is bottled or put into barrels.

Starter	Support/Extension	Resources
Biotechnology crossword (5 min) Students complete a crossword using the clues supplied on the interactive resource. This activity recaps respiration from B2 and introduces some new key words for this lesson. **Biotechnology products** (10 min) Show images of beer, bread, and wine. Ask students to suggest what these products are made from and how they are made. Students are often surprised to find that these products are made using living microorganisms.	**Extension**: Students should supply the word equation of anaerobic respiration and fermentation met in B2.	**Interactive**: Biotechnology crossword
Main	**Support/Extension**	**Resources**
The effect of temperature on fermentation (40 min) Introduce the idea of fermentation and how this is used in the production of bread, beer, and wine. Some students should be able to link this to the anaerobic respiration of yeast (the transfer of energy and the release of waste gases from food, in the absence of oxygen), and that it is the waste gases that cause the bread to rise. Show students the word equation for fermentation. Students then focus on how temperature affects the fermentation process in bread making. They carry out an investigation involving fermenting bread dough, and answer the questions that follow. Note that each group should be assigned one temperature value to investigate, as there will not be enough time for groups to investigate all three temperatures.	**Support**: The accompanying support sheet includes a suggested table of results. **Extension**: The extension questions touch on the denaturing of enzymes. This concept can be discussed further if time. Students should also predict the changes in rate of fermentation if the amount of glucose is reduced at the start of the experiment.	**Practical**: The effect of temperature on fermentation **Skill sheet**: Recording results
Plenary	**Support/Extension**	**Resources**
Fermentation treasure hunt (10 min) Write the steps of fermentation on sheets of paper and scatter these statements around the room. In groups, students find the sentences, remember them, and then return to their group scribe who writes these down. (The scribe must not leave their seat and sentences cannot be removed.) The groups then put the sentences in the correct order. The first group to do so wins. **Equations** (5 min) Ask students to write the word equations for aerobic respiration, anaerobic respiration, and fermentation on mini-whiteboards.	**Extension**: Encourage students to explain to the rest of their group the science behind each step in fermentation. **Extension**: Students can explain why temperature is important in fermentation.	
Homework		
Students write a recipe for making bread. This should include the ingredients list, a method, and an explanation of why each step is carried out using scientific knowledge.	**Extension**: Students could include a labelled diagram of the yeast cell, and discuss why temperature should be strictly monitored during the cooking process.	

1.7 Biotechnology 2

KS3 Biology NC Link:
- cellular respiration.

KS3 Working Scientifically NC Link:
- evaluate risks.

KS4 Biology NC Link:
- describe some anabolic and catabolic processes in living organisms including the importance of sugars, amino acids, fatty acids, and glycerol in the synthesis and breakdown of carbohydrates, lipids, and proteins
- describe possible biological solutions, including those using new biotechnologies, to the problems of the growing human population.

Band	Outcome	Checkpoint	
		Question	Activity
Developing	Name the type of microorganism responsible in the production of cheese and yoghurt (Level 3).	1	Lit, Main, Plenary 1, Plenary 2
	Name the main substance that cheese and yoghurt are made from (Level 3).		Lit, Plenary 1, Plenary 2
	Complete a risk assessment to identify the main risks in yoghurt production (Level 4).		Main
Secure	Describe the role of bacteria in fermentation (Level 5).	1	Lit, Main, Plenary 1, Plenary 2
	Describe how cheese and yoghurt are made (Level 5).	3	Lit, Main, Plenary 1, Plenary 2
	Produce a risk assessment for the main risks in yoghurt production (Level 6).		Main
Extending	Explain the role of lactic acid in cheese and yoghurt production (Level 7).	2	Main, Plenary 1, Plenary 2
	Compare the similarities and differences between cheese and yoghurt production (Level 7).	3	Main, Plenary 1, Plenary 2
	Produce a comprehensive risk assessment for all the risks and hazards in yoghurt production (Level 8).		Main

Literacy
Students summarise information given on how one food or drink product is made using fermentation to produce an infographic in the student-book activity.

APP
Students carry out a practical to investigate yoghurt production, which includes preparing a risk assessment (AF4) and presenting observations appropriately (AF3).

Key Words
pasteurised

Answers from the student book

In-text questions	**A** lactic acid
	B To add enzymes to the mixture that curdles the milk.
	C Milk that has been heated to a high temperature to kill bacteria.
Activity	**Fermentation products**
	Students should use the information contained in the flow diagrams shown on the corresponding student-book spread, adding illustrations to create the infographic.

Summary Questions	**1** bacteria, ferment, yoghurt, lactose (4 marks)
	2 The lactic acid curdles the milk turning it into yoghurt and prevents the growth of harmful bacteria. (2 marks)
	3 QWC question (6 marks). Example answers:
	Similarities between cheese- and yoghurt-making:
	both made using bacteria
	both made using milk
	both involve fermentation
	lactose is fermented to lactic acid
	Differences between cheese- and yoghurt-making:
	rennet is required to manufacture cheese (to provide the enzymes required to curdle the milk)
	cheese (curds) needs to be separated from the resulting liquid (whey)
	yoghurt needs to be kept warm during its production
	the milk used for making yoghurt is pasteurised beforehand

Starter	Support/Extension	Resources
Friendly bacteria? (10 min) Ask students the question 'Do all bacteria cause disease, or are there useful products we can get from bacteria?' Allow students to share their ideas in small groups before opening up as a class discussion.	**Support**: Prompts may be required to start this discussion. You may wish to show students an advert for a probiotic yoghurt (or similar) from the Internet.	
More biotechnology products (5 min) Ask students if they know of other products (of biotechnology) related to bread, beer, and wine. Show students images of cheese and yoghurt, and ask students to suggest how these products are made.		

Main	Support/Extension	Resources
Making yoghurt (40 mins) Introduce how cheese and yoghurt can also be made using microorganisms (this time, using bacteria). Describe to students the steps necessary to make each product, including the similarities and differences, before moving onto the practical. It is important for students to recap the elements required in a risk assessment before beginning their practical task. A summary of the contents of a risk assessment is provided on the practical sheet. Students write a risk assessment for making yoghurt in the classroom before carrying out this practical and answering the questions that follow. You may wish to prepare a sample of yoghurt in advance, 24 hours before the experiment, so that students may use this sample to test the pH 'after'.	**Support**: The accompanying support sheet includes a partially filled risk-assessment grid. This grid includes one example of a hazard fully filled in for students to use as an example.	**Practical**: Making yoghurt

Plenary	Support/Extension	Resources
Comparing yoghurt and cheese (5 mins) Students use the interactive resource to categorise steps in cheese and yoghurt production that are unique to one product or common to both. Students then sort the statements in order to describe how cheese and yoghurt are made.	**Extension**: Students should explain why some steps are required in making one product and not the other.	**Interactive**: Comparing yoghurt and cheese
Making cheese or yoghurt (10 mins) Provide students with a set of cards, with each card containing a statement describing one step in the production of yoghurt or cheese. Students arrange the statements in order, and identify whether the process they have been given produces yoghurt or cheese. The steps in the production of yoghurt and cheese can be found on the corresponding student-book spread.	**Extension**: Students justify the order of statements for the production of their product, and explain why this process cannot be used to make the other product discussed in this lesson.	

Homework		
Students write an explanation of how to make cheese on toast from the very beginning. They need to explain how to make both bread and cheese, and include general equations for anaerobic respiration and fermentation.	**Extension**: Students include balanced formula equations in their work.	

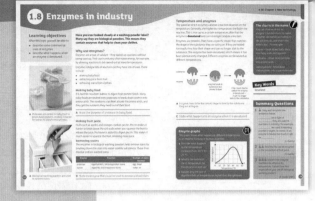

KS3 Biology NC Link:
- nutrition and digestion.

KS3 Working Scientifically NC Link:
- evaluate the reliability of methods and suggest possible improvements.

KS4 Biology NC Link:
- explain the mechanism of enzyme action including the active site and enzyme specificity.

KS4 Chemistry NC Link:
- recall that enzymes act as catalysts in biological systems.

Band	Outcome	Checkpoint	
		Question	Activity
Developing	Name a commercial product produced by enzymes (Level 3).	1, 2	Starter 1, Main, Homework
	State the effect of temperature on enzyme action (Level 4).	C	Maths, Starter 1, Starter 2, Homework
	Identify a possible error in the method (Level 4).		Main
Secure	Describe some commercial uses of enzymes (Level 5).	A, B, 1, 2, 3	Starter 1, Main, Plenary 1, Plenary 2, Homework
	Describe what happens when an enzyme is denatured (Level 6).	C, 3	Maths, Main, Plenary 2, Homework
	Identify an error in the method and describe the effect it may have on results (Level 6).		Main
Extending	Explain the advantages of the commercial use of enzymes (Level 7).	2, 3	Main, Plenary 1, Plenary 2, Homework
	Explain what happens to an enzyme when it denatures, and why this slows the speed of reaction (Level 8).	3	Maths, Main, Homework
	Identify an error in the method, describing its effect on results, and suggest a way to minimise this error (Level 7).		Main

Maths
In the student-book activity students extract and interpret information from a graph showing the relationship between temperature and the speed of an enzyme-catalysed reaction.

Literacy
In the student-book activity students learn about the origin of different names of enzymes.

APP
Students present results from their practical in an appropriate table (AF3), evaluate their method (AF5), and suggest possible improvements to it (AF4).

Key Words
denatured

Answers from the student book

In-text questions	A To break down proteins into amino acids, making it easier for babies to absorb the nutrients.
	B protease C It changes shape permanently (so it can no longer catalyse a reaction).
Activity	**Enzyme graphs**
	A speed of reaction increases B approximately 40°C
	C Enzyme is denatured so can no longer catalyse the reaction.

Summary Questions	1 enzymes, catalyst, lipases, denatured (4 marks)
	2 Pectin is present in cell walls of fruit and makes the cell walls harder to break down.
	The addition of pectinase/enzyme breaks down the pectin.
	This breaks the cell wall and makes fruit easier to squeeze. (3 marks)
	3 QWC question (6 marks). Example answers:
	In general, as you increase the temperature the speed of reaction increases. This happens until an optimum point/temperature. Further heating will result in the denaturing of the enzyme. This is when the enzyme changes shape irreversibly so it can no longer catalyse the reaction. Different enzymes have different denaturing temperatures. Biological washing powers contain enzymes. This means that washing cycles must be carried out at low temperatures, below the temperature that will denature enzymes. Lower temperatures in washing machines save fuel.

Starter	Support/Extension	Resources
An alternative question-led lesson is also available.		**Question-led lesson**: Enzymes in industry
Enzymes so far (5 min) Ask students to work in pairs or in threes to come up with as many facts as possible about enzymes that they have learnt so far. Discuss findings as a class. A common misconception in this topic is to confuse enzymes (for making bread) with the addition of bacteria (for making cheese and yoghurt). This should be corrected accordingly.		
Temperature and enzymes (10 mins) Draw a labelled graph to show the relationship between temperature and speed of reaction for an enzyme-catalysed reaction. Label the upward slope 'A', the peak 'B', and the drop down 'C'. Ask students to describe the shape of the graph and, in particular, suggest what could be happening at points A, B, and C.	**Extension**: Some students may be able to link this graph to the extension carried out in the practical for B3 1.6 – The effect of temperature on fermentation.	

Main	Support/Extension	Resources
Enzymes in washing powders (40 mins) Recap the uses of enzymes in industry that students have met in this chapter (bread, wine, and beer) and introduce new uses of enzymes such as in the production of baby foods, fruit juices, and washing powders. Before the start of the experiment, it is important to relate the denaturing of enzymes to the limitations of their uses. Students then set up an experiment to investigate the effect of biological and non-biological washing powders on egg white and answer the questions that follow.	**Support**: Allow students to work in small groups to discuss possible errors that they may see in any experiment, in order to help them answer the questions on the practical sheet.	**Practical**: Enzymes in washing powders

Plenary	Support/Extension	Resources
Using enzymes in industry (10 min) Interactive resource where students complete a paragraph on some of the uses of enzymes in industry. Students then write down similar sentences to describe the uses of other enzymes, such as pectin and yeast, on mini-whiteboards.	**Extension**: Encourage students to suggest other scenarios in which enzymes may be used, for example, in the disposal of waste.	**Interactive**: Using enzymes in industry
Advantages of enzymes in industry (5 mins) Say a series of statements about the use of enzymes in industry, for example, 'stains are removed from clothes', or 'do not function at high temperatures'. Students then indicate whether this is an advantage or disadvantage of using enzymes, explaining the answers given. This can be done using thumbs up/down.	**Extension**: Students should suggest additional statements to describe the use of enzymes in industry.	

Homework		
Produce an advertising poster for a new biological washing powder. The advert should contain as many scientific facts about enzymes as possible.		

Checkpoint lesson routes

The route through this lesson can be determined using the Checkpoint assessment.

Percentage pass marks are supplied in the Checkpoint teacher notes.

Route A (revision)
Resource: B3 Chapter 1 Checkpoint: Revision

Students work through a series of tasks that allows them to revisit and consolidate their understanding of key concepts in this chapter. Students can keep this as a summary of the topic, and use this when revising for future assessments.

Students can then join in with the board game activity offered in Route B if time.

Route B (extension)
Resources: B3 Chapter 1 Checkpoint: Extension

Students write questions and accompanying answers for a KS3 revision board game that includes the key concepts covered in this chapter, before testing the game out for themselves. To test the game students will require access to counters and dice.

Progression to *secure*

No.	Developing outcome	Secure outcome	Making progress
1	State what is meant by an allele.	Describe the difference between dominant and recessive alleles.	In Task 1 students describe the difference between dominant and recessive alleles in the context of offspring produced between parent plants with red and white flowers respectively.
2	State that genetics allows us to track alleles from one generation to the next.	Use a Punnett square to show what happens during a genetic cross.	In Task 1 students complete a Punnett square to show what happens when a plant with red flowers is bred with a plant with white flowers.
3	Name a genetic disorder.	Describe what is meant by a genetically inherited disorder.	In Task 1 students complete a word fill to describe what genetic disorders are.
4	State that the chance of inheriting a genetic disorder can be calculated.	Calculate the probability of a person suffering from an inherited disease.	In Task 1 students draw Punnett squares to show what happens when two parents of Pp alleles produce offspring, calculating the chance that their offspring will have polydactyly.
5	State what is meant by selective breeding.	Describe the process of selective breeding.	In Task 2 students link halves of statements together to describe the process of selective breeding.
6	State one advantage and one disadvantage of selective breeding.	Describe some advantages and disadvantages of selective breeding.	In Task 2 students complete a table to describe some advantages and disadvantages of selective breeding.
7	State what is meant by genetic engineering.	State how a product is produced using genetic engineering.	In Task 2 students use the statements given to fill in a table that compares genetic engineering with cloning.
8	Name a product produced by genetically engineered organisms.	Describe some advantages of producing products through genetic engineering.	In Task 2 students use the statements given to fill in a table that compares genetic engineering with cloning.
9	Give one example of cloning.	Describe what is meant by a clone.	In Task 2 students use the statements given to fill in a table that compares genetic engineering with cloning.
10	State one advantage and one disadvantage of cloning an organism.	Describe some advantages and disadvantages of cloning.	In Task 2 students use the statements given to fill in a table that compares genetic engineering with cloning.
11	State what is meant by fermentation.	Write the word equation for fermentation.	In Task 3 students are asked to write the word equation for fermentation.
12	Name the organism used to make bread, beer, and wine.	Describe how bread, beer, and wine are made.	In Task 3 students select the correct words to complete a paragraph that describes how bread is made. Students then reorder statements provided to describe how beer and wine are made.
13	Name the type of microorganism responsible in the production of cheese and yoghurt.	Describe the role of bacteria in fermentation.	In Task 3 students are asked to describe the role of bacteria in fermentation given information about fermentation in the production of various products.

14	Name the main substance that cheese and yoghurt is made from.	Describe how cheese and yoghurt are made.	In Task 3 students complete missing words on flow charts given to describe how cheese and yoghurt are made.
15	Name a commercial product produced by enzymes.	Describe some commercial uses of enzymes.	In Task 3 students link commercial uses of enzymes with descriptions provided.
16	State the effect of temperature on enzyme action.	Describe what happens when an enzyme is denatured.	In Task 3 students choose from a list of possible answers the correct description of what happens to enzymes when they denature.

Answers to end-of-chapter questions

1   Milk is placed into a large container. Bacteria are added to convert the lactose into lactic acid by fermentation. Rennet is added. Enzymes curdle the milk. Milk separates into curds. The curds are pressed to make a solid cheese. The cheese is left to mature. (6 marks)

2a yeast (1 mark)   **c** carbon dioxide (1 mark)

b ethanol (1 mark)   **d** Ethanol evaporates when the bread is cooked. (1 mark)

3a Any two from: wear goggles, tie hair back, sterilise equipment, wash hands (2 marks)

b The heating of milk to high temperatures to kill harmful bacteria. (1 mark)

c By using an incubator/water bath. (1 mark) *Credit other sensible suggestions.*   **d** yoghurt (1 mark)

e Probiotic yoghurts aid digestion. They also replace useful bacteria in the intestines that are killed by antibiotics. (2 marks)

4a Any two from: to speed up reactions, to reduce temperatures required, to save fuel (2 marks)

b Graph should show an increase of reaction rate as temperature increases until the optimum temperature (peak) is reached. After this the enzyme becomes denatured and the reaction rate decreases rapidly after this point. (4 marks)

c The enzyme pectinase is added when producing fruit juice. This breaks down the pectin (a substance that is found in cells walls). This makes the fruit much easier to squeeze, releasing more juice. (3 marks)

5a longer shelf life (1 mark) *Credit other sensible suggestions.*   **b** Any from: size/colour/taste (1 mark)

c Genes for a desired characteristic are taken from another organism. These are inserted into tomato cells at an early stage of their development. The tomatoes will then display the desired characteristics. (3 marks)

d Genetic engineering is more accurate a process. Genes are inserted directly into the cell. Characteristics are shown in one generation rather than after several generations in selective breeding. (2 marks)

6   This is a QWC question. Students should be marked on the use of good English, organisation of information, spelling and grammar, and correct use of specialist scientific terms. The best answers will fully explain the chance of a person inheriting sickle cell anaemia (maximum of 6 marks).
Examples of correct scientific points:

To suffer from a recessive disorder you must have both copies of the allele.

Carriers do not have the disorder.

Parents are carriers and will have the alleles Ss.

Possible alleles in the offspring are SS, Ss, and ss.

This occurs in the ratio 1SS: 2Ss: 1ss.

Only the offspring with ss will inherit the disorder.

This is 25% or $\frac{1}{4}$.

Award marks for an annotated Punnett square if used.

Credit the use of other letters to denote the alleles.

Answer guide for Big Write

Developing	Secure	Extending
1–2 marks	3–4 marks	5–6 marks
• The article is not presented in a logical way. • However, the student has stated an application of a relevant biological technique. • An attempt has been made to describe the scientific basis for the application. • No diagrams or images have been used. • No discussion of risks and benefits of this technique have been included.	• The article is clearly presented. • The student has stated an application of a relevant biological technique. • An attempt has been made to explain the scientific basis for the application. • At least one risk or benefit of this technique has been discussed. • Images and diagrams have been included but are not necessarily relevant or clearly labelled.	• The article is engaging and has been presented in the style of a magazine. • The student has clearly stated and explained an application of a relevant biological technique. • At least one risk and one benefit have been discussed. • Images and labelled diagrams have been included to good effect.

kerboodle

B3 Chapter 1 Checkpoint assessment (automarked)	B3 Chapter 1 Checkpoint: Extension
B3 Chapter 1 Checkpoint: Revision	B3 Chapter 1 Progress task (Maths)

2.1 Vaccines 1

KS3 Working Scientifically NC Link:

- understand that scientific methods and theories develop as scientists modify earlier explanations to take account of new evidence and ideas, together with the importance of publishing results and peer review.

KS4 Biology NC Link:

- recall that bacteria, viruses, protoctista, and fungi can cause infectious disease in animals and plants
- explain how the spread of infectious diseases may be reduced or prevented in animals and plants
- describe the use of vaccines and medicines in the prevention and treatment of disease.

Band	Outcome	Checkpoint	
		Question	Activity
Developing	State what is meant by a vaccine (Level 3).	B, 1	Lit, Main, Plenary 1, Homework
	State how Jenner reduced the spread of smallpox (Level 3).		Lit, Main, Plenary 1
	State Jenner's hypothesis about smallpox that he tested (Level 3).		Main
Secure	Describe the role of vaccines in fighting disease (Level 5).	1, 2	Lit, Main, Plenary 1, Homework
	Describe how Jenner developed the smallpox vaccine (Level 6).	4	Lit, Main, Plenary 1
	Describe how scientific methodology was used to develop the vaccine for smallpox (Level 6).		Main, Plenary 2
Extending	Explain how a vaccine works (Level 8).		Lit, Main, Plenary 1, Homework
	Explain why it is important for scientists like Jenner to study the spread of a disease (Level 7).	3	Main, Plenary 2
	Explain how modern scientists have built on Jenner's work (Level 8).		Main

Literacy
Students present arguments for the risks and benefits of Jenner's experiment, and adapt their language to a cartoon strip to describe this story.

Students collate and interpret scientific texts to describe the importance of Jenner's work and how this has affected our understanding and control of the spread of diseases.

APP
Students make links between abstract ideas to explain the vaccination process and the eradication of smallpox (AF1).

Key words
immunisation, vaccine, immune system

Answers from the student book

In-text questions	**A** A method of inserting a vaccine into the body.
	B Something that contains dead or inactive disease-causing microorganisms (or antibodies).
	C Edward Jenner
Activity	**Human experiments** Students should provide a balanced argument based on the risks and benefits of Jenner's experiment. Students may wish to discuss the ethical issues surrounding Jenner's experiment. Risks: James Phipps could have caught smallpox/could have died. Benefits: The vaccine saved many lives.

22

	Smallpox vaccine Cartoons should include the following steps (with captions): Jenner took some pus from a milkmaid's blisters. This was the vaccine. He inserted the pus into a cut on the arm of a boy - James Phipps. A few days later, Jenner injected Phipps with smallpox. Phipps became ill but after a few days he made a full recovery. The cowpox vaccine had prevented James from getting smallpox.
Summary Questions	**1** diseases, immunisations, vaccines, microorganisms (4 marks) **2** Because they cannot cause disease but will trigger the immune system to act against the vaccine/cause antibodies to be produced. (2 marks) **3** Any three from: Jenner's work was extremely important in understanding how vaccinations work. By doing this, scientists have been able to develop other vaccines to prevent epidemics. Diseases such as smallpox have been completely eradicated, whereas others such as polio are slowly being wiped out. There are now procedures in place for outbreaks in certain (notifiable) diseases, allowing officials to predict future recurrences or the end of an outbreak. **4** QWC question (6 marks). Example answers: Jenner observed that milkmaids did not get smallpox. Instead, milkmaids suffered from a weaker version of the disease called cowpox. He took pus from cowpox blisters and inserted this into a cut of a boy. The boy contracted cowpox. A few days later, he injected the boy with smallpox. The boy made a full recovery. Jenner realised that cowpox pus was the vaccine to smallpox.

kerboodle

Starter	Support/Extension	Resources
Immunisation (10 min) Ask students if they've had immunisations before, and whether they can remember what they were for. Students pair-share ideas about how vaccines work before being given the explanation. **What's the link?** (5 min) Show students a short video about cowpox and smallpox. (These are readily available on the Internet.) Ask students to suggest any similarities and differences they can see between the two. Can students spot a link between these two diseases?	**Support**: Students need to understand the difference between immunisations (the insertion of a vaccine) and the vaccine itself (substance containing inactive or dead pathogens).	

Main	Support/Extension	Resources
The discovery of vaccines (40 min) Introduce the key words vaccines and immunisations, ensuring that students are confident about the difference between the two terms. Students then read the information sheet that relates what they have just learnt to cowpox, smallpox, and Jenner's discovery of the smallpox vaccine, before answering questions that follow.	**Support**: You may wish to read the information sheet about Edward Jenner as a class. **Extension**: Students apply their knowledge of smallpox to the spread of measles in Wales.	**Activity**: The discovery of vaccines

Plenary	Support/Extension	Resources
Edward Jenner (5 min) Interactive resource where students complete a crossword on the work of Edward Jenner. Students use the key words to summarise the role of vaccines and how Jenner discovered the smallpox vaccine. **The road to discovery** (10 min) Students work in groups to discuss how the scientific discovery of vaccines developed with time. Would Edward Jenner be allowed to test his smallpox vaccine on a boy in today's society? Ask students to produce a simple flow chart on mini-whiteboards to show this road of discovery. Students should be able to explain their flow charts.	**Extension**: Students should be able to explain how a vaccine works. **Support**: The following key words may aid discussion: ideas, trials, analysis, improvements, scientific explanations, peer review, and publication.	**Interactive**: Edward Jenner

Homework		
Students write a small paragraph about the benefits and risks of vaccinations. This may be approached using a case study.		

2.2 Vaccines 2

KS3 Working Scientifically NC Link:
- interpret observations and data, including identifying patterns and using observations, measurements, and data to draw conclusions.

KS4 Biology NC Link:
- describe the use of vaccines and medicines in the prevention and treatment of disease
- describe the non-specific defence of the human body against pathogens
- describe the role of the immune system in defence against disease.

Band	Outcome	Checkpoint	
		Question	Activity
Developing	State one method of gaining immunity to a disease (Level 3).	1	Main, Plenary 1, Homework
	Give one advantage and one disadvantage of receiving a vaccine (Level 3).	C, D	Starter 2, Main, Plenary 2
	Use the data to state whether vaccinations affect the number of cases of a disease (Level 4).		Maths, Main
Secure	Describe how a person develops immunity (Level 5).	1, 2	Plenary 1, Homework
	Compare the advantages and disadvantages of receiving a vaccine (Level 6).	3	Maths, Starter 2, Main, Plenary 2
	Interpret data to describe the effect of using vaccines on the number of cases of a disease (Level 5).		Maths, Main
Extending	Explain how a person becomes immune to a disease (Level 8).		Main, Plenary 1, Homework
	Evaluate the advantages and disadvantages of receiving a vaccine, and draw a conclusion (Level 8).		Main, Plenary 2
	Suggest reasons for and against continuing vaccinations against a disease using data provided (Level 7).		Main

Maths
Students extract and interpret information from graphs to explain if there is a link between the MMR vaccine and autism in children for the student-book activity.

Students then use graphical data in the activity to discuss the effectiveness of vaccines regarding the number of cases of TB in England and Wales.

Literacy
Students extract information from scientific text when reading through the information sheet on vaccinations. They summarise this information when planning and drawing their comic strips to explain how a person gains immunity to a disease for homework.

APP
Students interpret data presented in a variety of formats (AF5).

Key Words
immune, pathogen, antibody

Answers from the student book

In-text questions	**A** They attack and destroy pathogens/harmful microorganisms. **B** white blood cells
	C Possible side effects or concerns about the safety of some vaccines.
	D Any two from: temperature, sickness, swollen glands, a small lump at the site of the injection.

24

Activity	**MMR and autism** Vaccination rate is approximately constant across the 15-year period. Autism rate in children increased significantly in the same period of time. The evidence does not therefore suggest a link between the rate of vaccination and the rate of occurrence of autism.
Summary Questions	**1** microorganism/pathogen, antibodies, white blood cells, immunity (4 marks) **2** Any four from: Vaccine contains dead/inactive harmful microorganisms/pathogens (or antibodies). These pathogens cannot cause disease. However they do trigger the white blood cells in the immune system to produce antibodies. These antibodies destroy the pathogen. If the same pathogen enters the body in the future, antibodies are made much faster. The pathogen is destroyed before the person becomes ill. **3** QWC question (6 marks). Example answers: Advantages of immunisation: Stops a person from getting the disease. This happens without the person having experienced the disease previously. Immunisations also stop diseases spreading. This is because the microorganisms cannot survive in as many people since most are immune. Immunisations can also eradicate diseases, for example, smallpox. Disadvantages of immunisation: There are concerns over the safety of some vaccines. For example, some people have argued that the MMR vaccine has increased the number of cases of autism in children. This has since been disproven. There are also side effects associated with some vaccines, for example, a temperature, sickness, swollen glands, and a small lump at the site of the injection.

kerboodle

Starter	Support/Extension	Resources
What are vaccines? (5 min) Students recap the work of Edward Jenner in the discovery of the smallpox vaccine. Students should describe how vaccines trigger an immune response in the body. **Are vaccinations always good?** (5 min) Ask students whether they think vaccination is always good. Students discuss possible side effects of immunisation.		

Main	Support/Extension	Resources
Vaccines and their effect on disease (40 min) Introduce the two ways in which a person can gain immunity from a disease (natural immunity versus immunisation) and discuss the advantages and disadvantages of immunisations. Students then read a piece of scientific text about how vaccines work. Using this information, together with a graph showing the number of cases of tuberculosis (TB) in England and Wales since 1930, students must answer the questions that follow. You may wish to describe briefly what TB is to give students some background before they begin the activity.	**Support**: Allow students to read the information in small groups, or even as a class, to support weaker readers.	**Activity**: Vaccines and their effect on disease

Plenary	Support/Extension	Resources
How do vaccines work? (10 min) Students reorder sentences provided on the interactive resource to describe how vaccines work. They should add more detail and explanations where appropriate. **Advantage or disadvantage?** (10 min) Give statements that are advantages and disadvantages of vaccines and have students categorise them. For each disadvantage students explain why it is a disadvantage and evaluate how much of a risk this poses.	**Extension**: Students compare immunity by vaccinations with natural immunity. **Extension**: Present the activity as a case study of MMR, with students evaluating the vaccine.	**Interactive**: How do vaccines work?

Homework		
Students draw a cartoon strip (with captions and annotations) to explain the process of vaccination. For example, they may choose to depict white blood cells as white knights, illustrating how these defend our bodies.	**Support**: Give students key words to include, with a simple structure to use for their cartoons.	

2.3 Antibiotics 1

KS3 Working Scientifically NC Link:
- evaluate data, showing awareness of potential sources of random and systematic error.

KS4 Biology NC Link:
- recall that bacteria, viruses, protoctista, and fungi can cause infectious disease in animals and plants
- outline the discovery and development of new medicines, including preclinical and clinical testing.

Band	Outcome	Checkpoint	
		Question	**Activity**
Developing	State what is meant by an antibiotic (Level 3).	B, 1	Main, Plenary 1, Homework
	Name the discoverer of penicillin (Level 3).	C, 1	Plenary 1, Homework
	Identify one source of error in the antibiotic experiment (Level 3).		Main
Secure	Describe the use of antibiotics (Level 5).	1, 2	Main, Plenary 1, Homework
	Describe how Fleming discovered penicillin (Level 5).	3	Plenary 1, Homework
	Identify one source of error and suggest how this can be minimised (Level 6).		Main
Extending	Explain why antibiotics are used to treat infections (Level 7).		Main, Plenary 1
	Explain how the effectiveness of different antibiotics against different diseases can be tested (Level 7).	4	Plenary 1, Homework
	Evaluate the accuracy of the results obtained in this experiment, identifying sources of error and how these can be minimised (Level 8).		Main

Maths
Students calculate arithmetic means from measurements of the radii of different zones of inhibition obtained from experimental results.

Literacy
Students adapt their writing style to suit primary-school children when describing how Fleming discovered penicillin for homework.

APP
Students present observations in an appropriate table (AF3), draw conclusions, and evaluate data (AF5).

Key Words
antibiotic

Answers from the student book

In-text questions	**A** prevent, cure, or treat the symptoms of a disease
	B Antibiotics kill bacteria.
	C Alexander Fleming
Summary Questions	**1** antibiotics, drug, bacteria, penicillin, mould (5 marks)
	2 Viruses are not affected by antibiotics/only bacteria are killed by antibiotics. Therefore the pathogen causing the cold will not be destroyed/removed from the body. (2 marks)
	3 Fleming was undertaking research into how bacteria can be killed by growing them on agar plates. He had left a number of plates with live bacteria when he went on holiday. On his return he found mould growing on the plates. The mould seemed to kill bacteria. The mould produced an antibiotic substance. Fleming named this substance penicillin. (4 marks)

4 QWC question (6 marks). Example answers:

A sample of the bacteria is collected and placed on agar plates.

Different antibiotic discs are placed on the agar plates.

The plates are placed in an incubator for a certain period of time.

Clear circles will be seen around the antibiotic discs where bacteria have been inhibited from growing.

The antibiotic with the largest zone of inhibition (largest clear circle) is the most effective against the specific species bacteria.

This antibiotic should then be prescribed to the patient.

Starter	Support/Extension	Resources
When you have a cold... (10 min) Ask students about the last time they had a cold. Did they go and see a doctor? Was the doctor able to prescribe them medicine? Ask students to discuss these questions in pairs before opening up as a class discussion. **The work of Fleming** (5 min) Show a short film from the Internet about Fleming's discovery of penicillin. Ask students to discuss briefly what they have seen.		

Main	Support/Extension	Resources
The effectiveness of antibiotics (40 min) Introduce the role of antibiotics in medicine and how penicillin was accidentally discovered by Alexander Fleming. Tell students that different types of antibiotics have now been discovered, and that some are more effective than others in destroying different species of bacteria. Ask students to suggest how they can investigate this before giving them the answer on the practical sheet. Students then carry out a practical where they investigate the effectiveness of different antibiotics for themselves, setting up an experiment that will result in zones of inhibition of different sizes, before answering the questions that follow. Since this experiment requires at least 24 hours for results to be obtained, you may wish to prepare several samples in advance, so students may use these samples for immediate results. This practical also focuses on the possible sources of error in an experiment, ways to minimise them, and the evaluation of results.	**Support**: An access sheet is available where students are given a results table to fill in. They are not required to calculate the arithmetic means for the different zones of inhibition. Questions given are also much simpler. **Extension**: Students may plot their results on bar chart if time.	**Practical:** The effectiveness of antibiotics **Skill sheet**: Recording results

Plenary	Support/Extension	Resources
How antibiotics work (5 min) Students complete the description of Fleming's discovery on the interactive resource using the words provided. Students should then describe the role of antibiotics in modern medicine. **Hazards and risks** (10 min) Discuss the potential hazards of this experiment, in particular when using live cultures. You may wish to show a template of a risk assessment to guide the discussion. Focus on precautions that should be taken, and ask students to wash their hands before leaving the classroom.	**Extension**: Students explain why antibiotics are given to treat infections. **Support**: Prompts should be given to students to aid discussion, for example, what may happen if a fully grown bacterial culture is opened?	**Interactive**: How antibiotics work

Homework		
Students write a story for primary-school children to describe how Fleming discovered penicillin, explaining what antibiotics are.	**Extension**: Students should explain in simple terms how antibiotics work.	

2.4 Antibiotics 2

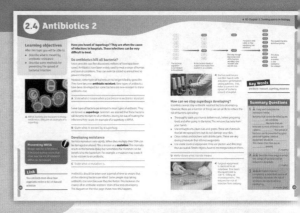

KS4 Biology NC Link:

- show understanding of how infectious diseases are spread in animals and plants
- evaluate the evidence for evolution including antibiotic resistance in bacteria.

Band	Outcome	Checkpoint	
		Question	Activity
Developing ↓	State the meaning of antibiotic resistance (Level 3).	A, 1	Starter 1, Main, Plenary 1, Homework
	List some methods used to prevent the spread of bacterial infections (Level 4).	1	Lit, Main, Plenary 1, Plenary 2
Secure ↓	Describe what is meant by antibiotic resistance (Level 5).	1	Main, Plenary 1, Homework
	Describe some methods for preventing the spread of bacterial infection (Level 6).	1, 2	Lit, Main, Plenary 1, Plenary 2
Extending ↓	Explain how bacteria develop resistance to antibiotics (Level 8).	3	Main, Plenary 1, Homework
	Explain in detail one method of preventing the spread of bacterial infection (Level 7).		Lit, Main, Plenary 1, Plenary 2

Literacy

In the student-book activity, students design a poster aimed at patients in hospital waiting rooms, explaining how the risks of spreading MRSA can be reduced.

Students design a leaflet to explain how bacteria have become antibiotic resistant using the example of MRSA.

APP

Students make explicit links between abstract concepts (AF1) and communicate scientific ideas in an appropriate manner (AF3).

Key Words

antibiotic resistant, superbug, mutation

Answers from the student book

In-text questions	**A** A bacterium that is no longer affected/killed by antibiotics.
	B A type of bacteria that is resistant to most types of antibiotics.
	C A mutation occurs when DNA is damaged/altered (during the replication process in reproduction).
	D Sterile objects have no microorganisms on them.
Activity	**Preventing MRSA**
	Posters should include ways of reducing the risk of spreading MRSA, for example:
	washing hands thoroughly before meals, before preparing food, and after going to the toilet
	using antiseptics to clean cuts and grazes
	cleaning toilets and kitchens with disinfectants
	using sterile medical equipment, including plasters and dressings.

Summary Questions	
	1 antibiotic, resistant, superbug, sterilised, microorganisms (5 marks)
	2 Use of antiseptic gels to kill bacteria on hospital workers' hands when moving from one patient to another.
	Use of disinfectants to kill bacteria on surfaces, for example, the toilet.
	Use sterilised equipment that has no living microorganisms on it. (3 marks)
	3 QWC question (6 marks). Example answers:
	When a course of antibiotics is not completed, some bacteria are not killed in the patient.
	These multiply quickly.
	Bacterial reproduction increases the chance of mutations.
	Mutations occur when DNA is damaged/altered during replication.
	Most mutations result in death of the bacterium.
	However, some mutations allow bacteria to become antibiotic resistant.
	Eventually the whole population of bacteria will become antibiotic resistant.

Starter	Support/Extension	Resources
Defining resistance (5 min) Students match key words for this lesson with their definitions using the interactive resource. Each key word will be introduced in more detail during the course of this lesson.		**Interactive**: Defining resistance
Are antibiotics super medicines? (10 min) Ask students to discuss whether penicillin is still widely used. Why do they think other antibiotics are necessary? This discussion is a useful introduction to the term antibiotic resistance.	**Support**: Prompt students by asking them if they've heard the term superbug. How does this term relate to the use of antibiotics?	

Main	Support/Extension	Resources
Antibiotic resistance (35 min) Introduce how some bacteria have mutated during reproduction to gain antibiotic resistance. Discuss precautions we can take to minimise this risk. Students then work in small groups to carry out an activity where they must rearrange a pack of cards to explain the story of antibiotic resistance and the rise of superbugs such as MRSA. Students use this information to answer the questions on the activity sheet.	**Support**: You may wish to go through the correct ordering of the sort cards before allowing students to attempt the questions. **Extension**: As an added challenge, ask students to deal cards out to one another but they cannot show the contents of their cards to each other. This encourages further discussion and the activity can then be treated as a mystery game.	**Activity**: Antibiotic resistance

Plenary	Support/Extension	Resources
Is penicillin still used today? (15 min) Students use knowledge from this lesson to pair share ideas about whether penicillin is still used today, before opening up as a class discussion. Students explain how bacteria become antibiotic resistant, and precautions we can take to minimise this risk.	**Extension**: Students can include in their explanation why it is important patients finish a full course of antibiotics.	
Limiting the spread of bacterial infections (10 min) Ask students why it is important to wash our hands, especially after using the toilet or blowing our nose. Ask them to suggest statements that may or may not help to reduce the spread of infections. For each statement given, students should use thumbs up/thumbs down, coloured cards, or mini-whiteboards to categorise the statement as one that aids or reduces the spread of infections.	**Extension**: Encourage students to suggest statements for this activity. Students should be able to justify their statements with explanations.	

Homework		
Students design a leaflet for a doctor's waiting room that explains how bacteria have become resistant, using the example of MRSA.		

2.5 DNA

KS3 Biology NC Link:
- inheritance, chromosomes, DNA, and genes.

KS3 Working Scientifically NC Link:
- understand that scientific methods and theories develop as earlier explanations are modified to take account of new evidence and ideas, together with the importance of publishing results and peer review.

KS4 Biology NC Link:
- describe DNA as a polymer made up of two strands forming a double helix
- recall that DNA is made from four types of nucleotides
- describe the genome as the entire DNA of an organism
- explain the following terms: chromosome, gene
- describe the work of Mendel in discovering the basis of genetics.

Band	Outcome	Checkpoint	
		Question	Activity
Developing ↓	Build a model of the DNA molecule (Level 4).		WS, Main
	Name four scientists who worked on the structure of DNA (Level 3).		Starter 1, Main, Homework
Secure ↓	Describe the structure of DNA (Level 5).	B, C, 1	Starter 1, Main, Plenary 2, Homework
	Describe how scientists worked together to discover the structure of DNA (Level 5).	3	Starter 1, Main, Plenary 1, Homework
Extending ↓	Explain how the structure of DNA allows it to achieve its function (Level 8).	2	Main, Plenary 2, Homework
	Explain why it is important for scientists to work together (Level 7).	3	Main, Plenary 1, Homework

Literacy
Students identify meaning in scientific text, collating and summarising information from a range of sources when carrying out the activity to describe the structure and function of DNA, and the order of events leading up to the discovery of its structure.

APP
Students make models of the DNA molecule (AF1) and communicate to a variety of audiences when describing the structure and function of DNA in the activity and for homework (AF3).

Key Words
DNA

Answers from the student book

In-text questions	A A short section of DNA that codes for a characteristic. B DNA is made of two strands that are joined together by bonds between bases. The strands are twisted to form a double helix. C A (adenine), T (thymine), C (cytosine), and G (guanine).
Activity	**DNA model** Credit sensible models for the structure of DNA, for example, different coloured jelly sweets for the bases, held together by a toothpick, and linked to two liquorice strands.

Summary Questions	1 strands, helix, bases, C (4 marks)
	2 DNA contains four different bases.
	The order of the bases leads to the production of a specific/particular protein. (2 marks)
	3 QWC question (6 marks). Example answers:
	Early work by Mendel led to the discovery that certain characteristics can be passed from parents to offspring.
	Miescher identified 'nuclein' in the nucleus of the cell. Nuclein is now called DNA.
	Avery transferred DNA between bacteria, transferring characteristics in the process. This proved that genes are sections of the DNA molecule.
	Chargaff's work showed that all DNA molecules contain equal quantities of bases in their respective pairs (number of A = number of T, number of C = number of G).
	Wilkins and Franklin then used X-rays to take an image of DNA crystals.
	Watson and Crick built on the evidence gathered by a number of other scientists. This helped them to produce the double helix model of the DNA molecule.

kerboodle

Starter	Support/Extension	Resources
What do you remember about DNA? (10 min) Ask students to work in small groups of three or four. Issue each group with a large sheet of paper and marker pens. Ask students to produce a list of facts or a visual summary from what they can remember about DNA from B2. Discuss the results with the class. **DNA ladder** (5 min) Show students an image of the DNA molecule and ask them to suggest what the image may show. Students should justify their suggestions using scientific knowledge.	**Support**: Give students the following key areas to focus their discussion: genes, inheritance, and discovery of the DNA molecule.	

Main	Support/Extension	Resources
The structure and function of DNA (40 min) Recap the discovery of DNA based on the work of Franklin, Wilkins, Watson, and Crick. Students will have done this in B2. Add other scientists to the discussion using the timeline supplied in the corresponding student-book spread. At this stage it is important that students are able to identify the key features of a DNA molecule, as well as the relationship between DNA, the nucleus, chromosomes, and genes. Students carry out an activity where they use the template provided to build a DNA model, and use the corresponding student-book spread to answer the questions that follow.	**Support**: You may wish to provide students with diagrams of the DNA molecule to annotate. **Extension**: More advanced textbooks are required for students to examine the detailed structure of DNA and how it relates to its function.	**Activity**: The structure and function of DNA

Plenary	Support/Extension	Resources
DNA Timeline (5 min) Students rearrange sentences provided on the interactive resource in chronological order to describe events leading up to the discovery of the structure of DNA. **Annotating diagrams** (10 min) Give students a diagram of a DNA molecule to annotate as much as they can in three minutes. Ask students to share their ideas in a class discussion to describe the structure and function of DNA.	**Extension**: Students should explain why it is important for scientists to work together. **Extension**: Encourage students to link the structure of DNA to its function.	**Interactive**: DNA timeline

Homework		
In 1953 Francis Crick wrote a letter to his young son telling him that he had made a fantastic discovery, which was the structure of DNA. This letter was sold for £3.45 million at an auction in 2013. Students pretend to be Crick to write a letter to his son. In this letter students should describe the structure of DNA as well as the journey of its discovery.		

2.6 Charles Darwin

KS3 Biology NC Link:
- relationships in an ecosystem
- inheritance, chromosomes, DNA, and genes.

KS3 Working Scientifically NC Link:
- the importance of publishing results and peer review.

KS4 Biology NC Link:
- describe evolution as a change in the inherited characteristics of a population over time through a process of natural selection
- describe how evolution occurs through natural selection of variants best suited to their environment
- evaluate the evidence for evolution to include fossils and antibiotic resistance in bacteria
- describe the work of Darwin and Wallace in the development of the theory of evolution by natural selection.

Band	Outcome	Checkpoint	
		Question	Activity
Developing ↓	State what is meant by peer review (Level 3).	C	Main, Plenary 2
	Name the process by which organisms evolve (Level 3).	A, 1	Lit, Starter 1, Starter 2, Main
Secure ↓	Describe the process of peer review (Level 5).	3	Main, Plenary 2
↓	Describe the evidence that Darwin used to develop his theory of natural selection (Level 6).	2	Lit, Starter 1, Starter 2, Main, Plenary 1
Extending ↓	Explain the importance of peer review to scientists (Level 7).		Main, Plenary 2
↓	Explain how Darwin used the evidence from finches to develop his theory of natural selection and evolution (Level 7).	4	Lit, Main

Literacy
In the student-book activity students organise and summarise scientific ideas to explain the theory of evolution to the general public.

Students demonstrate how effectively they can communicate in discussions throughout the lesson.

APP
Students explain how different pieces of evidence support accepted scientific ideas and how scientific views and ideas are developed as new evidence is found (AF1).

Key Words
peer review

Answers from the student book

In-text questions	A natural selection
	B finch
	C Where a scientist's work is reviewed by another scientist working in a similar field.
Activity	**Natural selection**
	Students should present their ideas in the form of a newspaper article, with a catchy title, and information that is organised into columns.
	There should be a short introduction to explain who Darwin is but the main content should be explaining the concept of evolution.

	For example: Darwin's theory states that organisms evolve as a result of natural selection. Darwin realised that organisms best suited to their environment are more likely to survive and reproduce, passing on their characteristics to their offspring. Gradually, a species changes over time. We now know that these characteristics are passed on through genes.
Summary Questions	**1** Darwin, evolution, selection, peer review (4 marks) **2** The fossil record provides evidence that organisms have changed over time. Changes have been observed in microorganism populations, for example, the development of antibiotic-resistant bacteria. Species that have not adapted to environmental changes have become extinct. (3 marks) **3** This is the checking of work before it is published. This is often carried out by another scientist who works in a similar area of science. (2 marks) **4** QWC question (6 marks). Example answers: Each island has a different food supply. Finches that hatch with adaptations suited to the food supply of their habitat are more likely to live longer and survive. Other finches are unlikely to find enough food to survive, so die before mating. Well-adapted finches will reproduce. These offspring are likely to share their parents' characteristics. These offspring are also well-adapted so will also produce offspring of their own. Over time, the whole population will gain the advantageous adaptation.

Starter	Support/Extension	Resources
An alternative question-led lesson is also available. **Recapping natural selection** (5 min) Students complete statements provided on the interactive resource to recap basic ideas of adaptation and natural selection. Students have studied variation, adaptation, and natural selection in B2. **Peer marking and peer review** (10 min) As a recap of natural selection (and evolution) that students have met in B2, split students into groups of three or four. Ask each group to write down as many ideas as they can in three minutes about how a particular characteristic may have evolved in a given organism. Groups then swap their answers for peer marking, before opening a class discussion about evolution and the importance of peer review.		**Question-led lesson**: Charles Darwin **Interactive**: Recapping natural selection

Main	Support/Extension	Resources
Darwin's finches (40 min) Students carry out an activity where they play a game to match different types of finch with their habitats based on information cards. Students then interpret a flow chart that explains briefly the modern process of peer review before answering questions about natural selection and peer review.	**Support**: Limit students to the three finches on the top row of the information sheet (medium ground finch, vegetarian tree finch, and mangrove finch).	**Activity**: Darwin's finches

Plenary	Support/Extension	Resources
Evidence for evolution (5 min) Display the following terms on the board: fossils, antibiotic resistance, and extinction. Ask students to pair share ideas about how these terms are linked before inviting a class discussion. **The importance of peer review** (10 min) Ask students to imagine what might have happened if Watson and Crick had never found out about Photo 51 from Franklin and Wilkins, or if Darwin and Wallace had never communicated with each other.	**Extension**: Students should explain how antibiotic resistance links to natural selection. **Extension**: Discuss external pressures, for example, in Darwin's time an overwhelming proportion of people believed in creationism.	

Homework		
Students design a poster to explain the theory of natural selection and evolution. The poster should include case studies/fact files about three animals and how these have adapted/evolved.	**Extension**: Challenge students to discuss case studies from Wallace's travels.	

Preventing extinction

KS3 Biology NC Link:
- inheritance, chromosomes, DNA, and genes.

KS3 Working Scientifically NC Link:
- interpret observations and data, including identifying patterns and using observations, measurements, and data to draw conclusions.

KS4 Biology NC Link:
- explain what is meant by biodiversity and discuss the challenges
- recognise both positive and negative human interactions with ecosystems and their impact on biodiversity
- discuss benefits of maintaining local and global biodiversity.

Band	Outcome	Checkpoint	
		Question	Activity
Developing	State what is meant by extinction (Level 3).	A	Starter 1, Main, Homework
	Name one way of protecting endangered species (Level 4).	C, 1	Starter 1, Plenary 1, Plenary 2, Homework
	Identify a general increase or decrease in the data provided (Level 3).		Main
Secure	Describe how animals become extinct (Level 5).	2	Starter 2, Main, Homework
	Describe some techniques used to prevent extinction (Level 6).	D, 1	Main, Plenary 1, Plenary 2, Homework
	Use data from a graph to describe the effect of Project Tiger on the local tiger population (Level 6).		Main
Extending	Explain some of the causes of extinction (Level 7).	4	Starter 2, Main, Homework
	Explain how the techniques used to prevent extinction work (Level 7).		Main, Plenary 1, Plenary 2, Homework
	Link ideas given in the text to explain data presented in a graph (Level 7).		Main

Maths
Students use data provided to plot an appropriate graph, interpreting the data presented to answer questions.

Literacy
Students organise their understanding and opinions of captive breeding to debate these schemes in the student-book activity.

Students extract information and ideas from text about a government initiative in India to stabilise the population of tigers.

APP
Students weigh up evidence presented to construct arguments and explanations (AF1).

Key Words
endangered species, conservation, captive breeding, seed bank

Answers from the student book

In-text questions	**A** No organisms of a species are alive anywhere in the world. **B** Loss of habitat and threat of poachers **C** The protection of a natural environment/habitat. **D** Create stable, healthy population of a species and gradually re-introduce species into its natural habitat.
Activity	**Captive-breeding debate** The debate should cover advantages and disadvantages of captive-breeding programs. Advantages include: creates a stable and healthy population, can gradually re-introduce the species back into its natural habitat to repopulate in the wild, helps to prevent extinction, enables scientists to study the organisms, protects the organisms from poachers.

	Disadvantages include: can be perceived as cruel, animals have less space, animals have less choice of partners, reduces gene pool, increases the risk of inherited disorders, encourages organisms to display unnatural behaviours, organisms may not be able to cope with re-introduction to the wild.
Summary Questions	**1** endangered, extinct, banks, captivity, conservation (5 marks) **2** When a species can no longer adapt to changes in the environment and compete effectively for resources, its population decreases and it becomes endangered. This continues until no individuals of that species are left alive anywhere in the world (extinction). (3 marks) **3** The advantages are that populations of endangered species can be stabilised/increased and endangered species can then be re-introduced into their natural habitat. The disadvantages are that it is difficult to maintain genetic diversity and organisms bred in captivity may not survive in the wild. (4 marks) **4** QWC question (6 marks). Example answers: Positive effects by humans: Populations of species can be maintained using a range of techniques, for example, conservation, captive breeding, and seed/gene banks. Conservation is where humans protect natural habitats of engendered species. This reduces disruption to food chains and food webs. Captive breeding can stabilise/increase the population of endangered species before re-introducing them to the wild. Gene banks provide a back-up against the extinction of species by preserving their genetic material. Negative effects by humans: Human activity has caused many organisms to become extinct or endangered, for example, hunting/poaching of animals in the case of the rhino. Deforestation leads to the loss of animal habitat. There is also general competition with animals (for food, space, and water).

kerboodle

Starter	Support/Extension	Resources
Revising key words (5 min) Interactive resource to revise key words from B2 where students link the key words with their definitions.		**Interactive**: Revising key words
Spot the difference (5 min) Display images of endangered (giant panda, snow leopard) and extinct (woolly mammoth, dinosaur) species. Ask students to spot the difference. Students describe how organisms become extinct or endangered. Students met these terms in B2.		

Main	Support/Extension	Resources
Project Tiger (40 min) Students read a case study about how tigers have become endangered, and a government initiative that has begun in India to try and save them. Students then use the information provided and their own knowledge about this topic to answer the questions that follow.	**Support**: The support sheet includes simplified data and text for students to access.	**Activity**: Project Tiger **Skill sheet**: Drawing graphs **Skill sheet**: Choosing scales

Plenary	Support/Extension	Resources
Local conservation (10 min) Ask students what is meant by the term conservation, giving an example of a local conservation programme if possible. Discuss why conservation is important (preserve habitats and limit disruption to food webs). Can students think of other ways to prevent extinction?	**Extension**: Students suggest advantages and disadvantages of different methods used to prevent extinction.	
Saving for the future (10 min) Ask students what is the purpose of zoos. Guide students to seed banks at places like Kew Gardens. Students describe how these operate, suggesting other methods of preventing extinction.	**Extension**: Students evaluate advantages and disadvantages of seed banks and other techniques used to prevent extinction.	

Homework		
Students summarise how one organism became extinct. (They should be discouraged from researching dinosaurs as this was covered in B2.) Ask students to describe how extinction can be prevented today.		
An alternative WebQuest homework activity is also available on Kerboodle where students research an endangered species and the conservation efforts for it.		**WebQuest**: Endangered species

Checkpoint lesson routes

The route through this lesson can be determined using the Checkpoint assessment.

Percentage pass marks are supplied in the Checkpoint teacher notes.

Route A (revision)

Resource: B3 Chapter 2 Checkpoint: Revision

Students work through a series of tasks that allow them to revisit and consolidate their understanding of key concepts in this chapter. Students can keep this as a summary of the topic, and use this when revising for future assessments.

Route B (extension)

Resource: B3 Chapter 2 Checkpoint: Extension

Students work as a scientific director to plan six documentaries in a series entitled 'Turning points in Biology'. This series covers all the key concepts in this chapter (vaccines, antibiotics, DNA, preventing extinction, and peer reviews). Students produce an outline of the scenes for each of the six episodes.

Progression to *secure*

No.	Developing outcome	Secure outcome	Making progress
1	State what is meant by a vaccine.	Describe the role of vaccines in fighting disease.	In Task 1 students complete a flow chart to describe how vaccines help people to develop immunity against disease.
2	State how Jenner reduced the spread of smallpox.	Describe how Jenner developed the smallpox vaccine.	In Task 1 students reorder statements to describe how Jenner discovered the relationship between cowpox and smallpox to develop the smallpox vaccine.
3	State one method of gaining immunity to a disease.	Describe how a person develops immunity.	In Task 1 students complete a flow chart to describe how vaccines help people to develop immunity against disease.
4	Give one advantage and one disadvantage of receiving a vaccine.	Compare the advantages and disadvantages of receiving a vaccine.	In Task 1 students summarise the opinions of different people to compare the risks and benefits of vaccinations.
5	State what is meant by an antibiotic.	Describe the use of antibiotics.	In Task 2 students complete a word fill to describe how Fleming discovered penicillin and how antibiotics are used.
6	Name the discoverer of penicillin.	Describe how Fleming discovered penicillin.	In Task 2 students complete a word fill to describe how Fleming discovered penicillin and how antibiotics are used.
7	State the meaning of antibiotic resistance.	Describe what is meant by antibiotic resistance.	In Task 2 students label diagrams to show how bacteria can become antibiotic resistant, adding extra annotations to describe this process.
8	List some methods used to prevent the spread of bacterial infections.	Describe some methods for preventing the spread of bacterial infection.	In Task 2 students read a description of a typical day for Doctor Lizzy, suggesting ways to improve her day in order to minimise the spread of bacterial infection.
9	Build a model of the DNA molecule.	Describe the structure of DNA.	In Task 3 students describe the structure of DNA using key words provided before drawing a labelled diagram of the DNA molecule using the descriptions written.
10	Name four scientists who worked on the structure of DNA.	Describe how scientists worked together to discover the structure of DNA.	In Task 3 students complete missing entries in a timeline to describe how different scientists worked towards the discovery of DNA structure.
11	State what is meant by peer review.	Describe the process of peer review.	In Task 4 students describe the process of peer review using key words provided.
12	Name the process by which organisms evolve.	Describe the evidence that Darwin used to develop his theory of natural selection.	In Task 4 students use information provided about Darwin's work on the Galapagos Islands to complete a word fill that describes how Darwin's theory of evolution is supported using evidence from finches.
13	State what is meant by extinction.	Describe how animals become extinct.	In Task 5 students are asked to describe how animals such as the woolly mammoth became extinct.
14	Name one way of protecting endangered species.	Describe some techniques used to prevent extinction.	In Task 5 students link techniques used to prevent extinction with the descriptions provided.

Answers to end-of-chapter questions

1 Darwin – theory of evolution by natural selection   Watson and Crick – structure of DNA
Fleming – penicillin   Jenner – smallpox vaccine   (4 marks)

2a captive breeding – animals, seed bank – plants, conservation – both (3 marks)

b An endangered species is one with only small numbers of organisms left in the world.
A species that is extinct has no organisms of that species alive anywhere in the world. (2 marks)

3 A vaccine is inserted into the body. White blood cells make antibodies against the dead or inactive microorganism. Antibodies destroy the microorganism. White blood cells 'remember' the microorganism. If the live microorganism enters the body, antibodies are made very quickly. Microorganisms are destroyed before you get ill. (6 marks)

4a bacteria (1 mark)   **b** Any two from: wash hands, wear gloves, sterilise equipment (2 marks)

c sterilisation (1 mark)

d Antibiotic B should be used because it created the largest zone of inhibition. This means that it was the most effective of the three antibiotics at killing bacteria/stopping bacterial growth. (3 marks)

5a MRSA is a type of bacteria that has mutated to become antibiotic resistant. This means that MRSA is no longer affected/killed by antibiotics, hence becoming a superbug. (2 marks)

b Any two from: washing hands thoroughly, using antiseptics to clean cuts and grazes, regular cleaning of surfaces using disinfectants, sterilising medical equipment. (2 marks)

c Any two from: washing hands thoroughly using antiseptics to clean cuts and grazes, and cleaning kitchen surfaces and toilets using disinfectants. (2 marks)

6 This is a QWC question. Students should be marked on the use of good English, organisation of information, spelling and grammar, and correct use of specialist scientific terms. The best answers will fully explain the importance of the discoveries of vaccines, antibiotics, DNA, and evolution (maximum of 6 marks). Examples of correct scientific points:

These discoveries are extremely important because without them, we would not understand how organisms have shaped the world around us.

Vaccines were important in treating diseases that were previously incurable, for example, Jenner's discovery successfully eradicated smallpox in the 1970s. Without it, many would die from the disease, and those who survived it would have been left badly scarred and often blind.

Like immunisations, Fleming's discovery of penicillin also saved many lives. Penicillin is an antibiotic that works by killing bacteria. Antibiotics helped to treat bacterial infections and diseases such as meningitis and scarlet fever.

The structure of DNA was discovered by Crick and Watson in 1953 (with significant contribution from other scientists, for example, Wilkins and Franklin). Without this discovery, we would not know how hereditary diseases work, and would not be able to carry out research on the human genome to attempt to treat these disorders. We would also not be able to increase food production for an ever-increasing population with genetically engineered food.

Finally, Darwin's discovery of natural selection has helped us understand how different species have evolved, and how different species are related to each other.

Answer guide for Big Write

Developing	Secure	Extending
1–2 marks	3–4 marks	5–6 marks
• The article is not presented in a magazine style. • The student has stated at least one scientist and their discovery. • An attempt has been made to describe the science behind the discovery. • No attempt has been made to include explanations of scientific terms.	• The article is clearly presented in a magazine style. • The student has stated at least two scientific discoveries, and named the scientists behind these advances. • An attempt has been made to explain the science behind the discoveries. • Some scientific terms have been included and explained.	• The article is engaging and has been presented in a magazine style. • The student has clearly described at least two scientific discoveries, and has named the scientists behind these advances. • The science behind the discoveries has been clearly explained. • All scientific terminology in the article has been clearly explained.

kerboodle

B3 Chapter 2 Checkpoint assessment (automarked)
B3 Chapter 2 Checkpoint: Revision
B3 Chapter 2 Checkpoint: Extension
B3 Chapter 2 Progress task (Handling data)

3.1 Microscopy

KS3 Working Scientifically NC Link:
- make and record observations and measurements using a range of methods for different investigations and suggest possible improvements.

KS4 Biology NC Link:
- evaluate the impact of electron microscopy.

Band	Outcome	Checkpoint	
		Question	Activity
Developing	Name two different types of microscope (Level 3).	B, 1	Starter 1, Starter 2, Main, Homework
	Name one piece of microscopic evidence used by a forensic scientist (Level 4).	C, 1	Main, Homework
	Record observations from an investigation to analyse hair samples (Level 4).		Main
Secure	Describe the main differences between a light microscope and an electron microscope (Level 5).	2	Main, Plenary 2, Homework
	Describe how microscopic evidence is used by forensic scientists (Level 5).	3	Main, Plenary 2, Homework
	Record and interpret observations from an investigation to draw conclusions (Level 6).		Main
Extending	Suggest with an explanation the microscope that should be used in a given scenario (Level 8).		Main, Homework
	Explain how microscopic evidence is used in a court case (Level 7).	3	Plenary 2, Homework
	Analyse results obtained from an investigation analysing hair samples, suggesting one method of improving the accuracy of the observations (Level 7).		Main

Maths
Students convert between cm, mm, and µm in the student-book activity.

APP
Students present observations in a results table (AF3), draw conclusions from their results, and suggest possible improvements to the method (AF5).

Key Words
forensic science, magnification, resolution

Answers from the student book

In-text questions	**A** The study of objects/materials/situations/evidence that relate to a crime.
	B electron and light microscopes
	C Any three from: hairs, fibres, paint flecks, pollen grains, soil.
	D Wool fibres have overlapping scales whereas cotton fibres are made from continuous strands, or wool fibres have a regular shape whereas cotton fibres appear twisted.
Activity	**Converting units**
	a 8 cm = 8 × 10 = 80 mm
	b 6 mm = 6 × 1000 = 6000 µm
	c 3500 µm = 3500 ÷ 1000 ÷ 10 = 0.35 cm

Summary Questions	**1** forensic, law, microscope, electron (4 marks)
	2 Any three from:
	Electron microscopes use electrons, light microscopes use light.
	Electron microscopes have greater magnification.
	Electron microscopes have better resolution.
	Light microscopes produce colour images whereas electron microscopes produce images in black and white.
	3 QWC question (6 marks). Example answers:
	Samples are taken from a crime scene, for example, hairs, fibres, paint flecks, pollen grains, and soil. Microscopes help forensic scientists to compare evidence to known samples that are too small to see with the naked eye. They use microscopes to identify unique features of individual samples from the magnified images. There are two types of microscopes that can be used (light and electron). Samples obtained from a suspect can be compared with evidence taken from a crime scene. Samples that match provide evidence that the suspect was present at the crime scene. However, this does not always mean that they were there when the crime was committed.

Starter	Support/Extension	Resources
Seeing tiny objects (5 min) Ask students to suggest ways we can see small objects, for example, examining features of a human hair. Students should then explain the steps required to use a light microscope. **Magnification and resolution** (10 min) Show students a diagram of the light microscope and ask them to label it. Students should explain, using an example, what is meant by magnification. Introduce the idea of resolution in the context of measurement and ask students to link this to the light microscope.	**Extension**: Encourage students to discuss other types of microscopes. Some will remember the electron microscope from C2.	

Main	Support/Extension	Resources
Analysing hair samples (40 min) Introduce the electron microscope, and how it is different to a light microscope. Show students the same object magnified using a light microscope and an electron microscope to highlight the difference. These images can then be used to explain magnification and resolution. (Images of chloroplasts in a moss cell are shown in the student book.) Explain the role of forensic scientists (many students will already have an idea about this due to TV programmes) and how microscopes are indispensable in forensic investigations. Students then carry out a practical to examine hair samples from a crime scene microscopically and answer the questions that follow. If animal hairs are used, please be aware of potential allergies within the group.	**Support**: If time is short, you may wish to prepare the sample slides in advance. Students can also be provided with hairs that are more obviously different. **Extension**: Hair samples should have subtle differences. Observations must therefore be accurate in order to find a match between the sample from the crime scene and one of the suspects.	**Practical**: Analysing hair samples

Plenary	Support/Extension	Resources
SOCO – Scene of crime officers (5 min) Show an image of a forensic scientist in a SOCO overall. Discuss the various parts of the overall and how it helps prevent contamination of the crime scene and evidence, as well as protecting the SOCOs themselves. **Electron micrographs** (5 min) Students study an electron micrograph shown in the interactive resource and complete the sentences that accompany it to compare light and electron micrographs.	**Extension**: Students should explain how micrographs are used as evidence in court.	**Interactive**: Electron micrographs

Homework		
Give students the following scenario: You are a forensic scientist who has been invited to give a talk at your school. Explain to a KS3 audience how forensic scientists use microscopes to provide evidence in court, and explain the similarities and differences between the two types of microscopes.	**Extension**: Give examples of evidence that would require each type of microscope.	

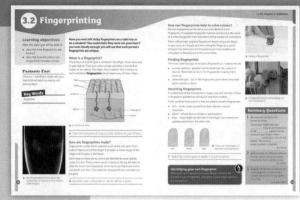

KS3 Working Scientifically NC Link:

- use appropriate techniques, apparatus, and materials during fieldwork and laboratory work, paying attention to health and safety.

KS4 Biology NC Link:

- explain that the genome interacts extensively with the environment to influence the development of the phenotype.

Band	Outcome	Checkpoint	
		Question	Activity
Developing	State whether one person's fingerprint is likely to be the same as another person's fingerprint (Level 3).		Starter 2, Main, Plenary 1, Homework
	Name one surface on which a fingerprint can be left (Level 3).	B	Starter 1, Plenary 2, Homework
	Use appropriate techniques to collect fingerprints (Level 4).		WS, Main
Secure	Describe how fingerprints are formed (Level 6).	B, 1	Main, Plenary 1, Homework
	Describe how the police use fingerprints to solve crimes (Level 5).	2, 3	Main, Plenary 1, Plenary 2, Homework
	Use appropriate techniques to collect fingerprints for analysis (Level 5).		WS, Main
Extending	Explain the different methods of retrieving fingerprints at a crime scene (Level 7).	3	Main, Plenary 1, Plenary 2, Homework
	Explain how police use the unique patterns on fingerprints to solve crimes (Level 7).	3	Main, Plenary 1, Plenary 2, Homework
	Use appropriate techniques to collect fingerprints for analysis, suggesting possible methods of collecting other types of fingerprints (Level 8).		WS, Main

Literacy
For homework students adapt their writing style to produce an instruction manual on fingerprinting for forensic science trainees to use.

APP
Students collect fingerprints during the practical activity (AF4), presenting results and observations in an appropriate manner (AF3).

Key Words
fingerprint

Answers from the student book

In-text questions	**A** They allow us to grip objects.
	B Oils left behind after sweat evaporates from the finger form an impression when they touch the glass.
	C arch, whorl, loop
Activity	**Identifying your own fingerprint**
	Different fingers have different prints, even if the prints all come from the same person.
	Students should make an impression of their fingerprints using ink and identify features such as arches, whorls, and loops.

Summary Questions	
	1 unique, ridges, sweat, fingerprint (4 marks)
	2 Powder dusting – powders are brushed over the surface of objects. The powder sticks to the oil in the fingerprint.
	Ultraviolet light – oils in the fingerprints glow in UV light. (3 marks)
	3 QWC question (6 marks). Example answers:
	Fingerprints are collected from a crime scene. This can be done by dusting with a powder or by using ultraviolet light.
	A suspect's fingerprints are collected. This is done by taking an impression from an inkpad onto paper/card. The suspect's prints are compared to those from the crime scene.
	Fingerprints are unique to the individual. There is only a 1 in 64 000 000 000 change that one person's fingerprints will match up with another person's fingerprints.
	This means that, where a match occurs, the suspect was at the crime scene (at some point).

Starter	Support/Extension	Resources
An alternative question-led lesson is also available.		**Question-led lesson**: Fingerprinting
Sticky fingers (10 min) Ask students to pair share ideas about fingerprints. They may have many preconceptions based on crime dramas on TV. Ask students to suggest when they would get good fingerprints at a scene of crime, and when they would get poor prints. Ask them to consider the state of the hands (dirty, clean, or gloved) and the nature of the surface (prints best left on smooth surfaces). Summarise a few of these points in a class discussion.		
Fingerprint patterns (5 min) Show students a short video on fingerprints. (These are readily available on the Internet.) Students should summarise why fingerprints are unique to the individual, and how this allows the police to solve crimes.		

Main	Support/Extension	Resources
Taking fingerprints (40 min) Introduce how fingerprints are formed (from how ridges on the fingers are made during the development of the fetus, to how fingerprints can be left on different surfaces due to the oils present on our skin). Explain how the unique nature of fingerprints allows the police to solve crimes. Students then carry out a practical where they take their own fingerprints and collect a latent fingerprint, before answering questions that follow.		**Practical**: Taking fingerprints

Plenary	Support/Extension	Resources
Forming fingerprints (10 min) Students complete the paragraph given on the interactive resource to explain how fingerprints are formed. Students should then elaborate on how the police can use fingerprints to solve crimes.	**Extension**: Encourage students to explain the different ways in which fingerprints can be collected at a crime scene.	**Interactive**: Forming fingerprints
Collecting evidence (5 min) Ask students to summarise the types of evidence they have met so far (microscopic and fingerprints). Students should explain where and how they would collect these pieces of evidence, and how police may use the observations from evidence to solve a crime.		

Homework		
Give students the following scenario: You are a senior forensic scientist who has been asked to produce a training manual for new trainees. Your manual must explain how fingerprints are formed, where trainees may find them at a crime scene, how to obtain fingerprint samples, and what use these have in court as evidence.		

3.3 DNA fingerprinting

KS3 Biology NC Link:
- inheritance, chromosomes, DNA, and genes.

KS3 Working Scientifically NC Link:
- use appropriate techniques and apparatus during laboratory work, paying attention to health and safety.

KS4 Biology NC Link:
- discuss the potential importance for medicine of our increasing understanding of the human genome.

Band	Outcome	Checkpoint	
		Question	Activity
Developing	Name one type of sample that can be used for DNA fingerprinting (Level 3).	B	Lit, Starter 2, Main
	Give one example where two people share the same genetic information (Level 3).	1	Lit, Starter 1, Main
↓	Use appropriate techniques to isolate DNA (Level 4).		Main
Secure	State what is meant by DNA fingerprinting (Level 5).	A, 1	Lit, Main, Plenary 1
	Describe some uses of DNA fingerprinting (Level 6).	3	Lit, Main, Plenary 1, Plenary 2
↓	Use an appropriate technique to isolate DNA and give reasons why this is useful (level 5).		Main
Extending	Describe how to carry out DNA fingerprinting (Level 7).	2	Lit, Main
	Explain uses of DNA fingerprinting (Level 8).	3	Lit, Main, Plenary 1
↓	Use appropriate techniques to isolate DNA and interpret results from DNA fingerprinting to identify a suspect (Level 7).		Main

Literacy
In the student-book activity students adapt their writing to write a short presentation for Year 7 students to describe DNA fingerprinting and its uses.

APP
Students carry out a practical to extract DNA from kiwi fruit (AF4), presenting observations in an appropriate manner (AF3).

Key Words
DNA fingerprinting

Answers from the student book

In-text questions	**A** The analysis of DNA to identify individuals from body samples. **B** Any two from: white blood cells/blood, hair, cheek cells.
Activity	**Presentation** Presentations should include a description of how DNA fingerprinting works, and how this can be used for solving crimes and in medicine, for example, matching suspects to crime scenes, in maternity and paternity testing, in the identification and treatment of genetic disorders, and in genetic counselling.
Summary Questions	**1** fingerprinting, DNA, fragments, identical, unique (5 marks) **2** DNA is extracted from cells and cut into fragments using enzymes. These sections of DNA are placed into a gel that is part of an electric circuit, so current passes through the gel. The fragments of DNA move different distances depending on their size, and the resulting pattern is the DNA fingerprint. (3 marks)

	3 QWC question (6 marks). Example answers (maximum of two marks for each example): Identifying a suspect from a crime: DNA samples taken from a suspect and compared to evidence/DNA taken from crime scene. If the DNA fingerprints match, it proves that the suspect was at the crime scene (at some point). Maternity/paternity testing: Samples of a child's DNA are compared with that of the mother/father. The child's DNA is made of fragments that match the DNA of the mother and father. Genetic counselling: Allows people to discover if they are carriers of a genetic disorder. This allows them to make an informed choice as to whether or not to have a baby. Identification and treatment of genetic disorders: Allows genetic disorders to be identified in patients early in life. This increases the effectiveness of treatment.

Starter	Support/Extension	Resources
Barcodes (10 min) Show students a few examples of product barcodes on the board. Ask students to describe the patterns they see and what they are for. Discuss how barcodes are unique to each product. Can students think of other codes that may be unique? (Students will hopefully talk about fingerprints and DNA. This can then prompt the discussion of whether DNA will always be unique amongst individuals.) **Sources of DNA at a crime scene.** (5 min) Ask students to write down on a mini-whiteboard all the possible sources of DNA evidence at a crime scene. Students will probably only mention one or two sources, for example, blood. You may wish to introduce other DNA sources such as skin, hair, and saliva.	**Extension**: Students consider how much we have in common with other organisms given information about the proportion of DNA we share with them, for example: chimpanzees – 98% zebrafish – 85% bacteria – 7%	

Main	Support/Extension	Resources
Extracting DNA from cells (40 min) Introduce sources of DNA at a crime scene, and why they are useful in solving crimes. Describe how DNA fingerprinting is carried out in laboratories and discuss its other uses, for example, in maternity and paternity testing, genetic counselling, and the identification and treatment of genetic disorders. Students then carry out a practical where they extract DNA from kiwi fruits, answering the questions that follow. (Strawberries and onions can also be used for this experiment.) This is a lengthy practical so questions should be completed for homework.	**Support**: Some students may find the pouring of ice-cold ethanol down the side of a test tube tricky. For this reason you may wish to demonstrate this step prior to the start of the practical.	**Practical**: Extracting DNA from cells

Plenary	Support/Extension	Resources
DNA fingerprinting key words (5 min) Students use the clues provided on the interactive resource to complete a crossword that includes key words from this lesson. Students should describe how each key word relates to the lesson. **DNA fingerprinting results** (10 min) Show students an image of the banding pattern produced after electrophoresis. Discuss how the bands are made. Ask students to describe possible uses of this result before presenting other DNA fingerprints for students to compare. This can then be introduced as a game to identify the suspect.	**Extension**: Students should explain how results from DNA fingerprinting can be used. **Extension**: For an added challenge, other bands can be presented as maternity/paternity tests. (Only a subset of the bands will be similar between the mother/father and the child.)	**Interactive**: DNA fingerprinting key words

Homework		
Students complete questions on the practical sheet for homework.		
An alternative WebQuest homework activity is also available on Kerboodle where students research DNA fingerprinting.		**WebQuest**: DNA fingerprinting

KS3 Biology NC Link:

- inheritance, chromosomes, DNA, and genes.

KS3 Working Scientifically NC Link:

- use appropriate techniques and apparatus during laboratory work, paying attention to health and safety.

KS4 Biology NC Link:

- recognise the main components of the blood as red blood cells, white blood cells, platelets, and plasma and explain the functions of each.

Band	Outcome	Checkpoint	
		Question	Activity
Developing	Name the components of blood (Level 3).	B, 1	Lit, Main, Plenary 2
	Name the possible blood groups in humans (Level 3).	C, 2	Lit, Main, Homework
	Use appropriate techniques to carry out an experiment on blood typing (Level 4).		Main
Secure	Describe the structure and function of blood components (Level 5).	1, 3	Lit, Plenary 1, Plenary 2
	Describe what is meant by a blood group (Level 5).	2	Lit, Main, Homework
	Use appropriate techniques to determine the blood group of samples supplied (Level 5).		Main
Extending	Compare the structure of two types of blood cells and relate them to their function (Level 7).	3	Main, Plenary 1, Plenary 2
	Explain the similarities and differences between different blood groups (Level 8).	2	Lit, Main, Homework
	Use appropriate techniques to determine the blood group of samples supplied, suggesting a limitation to this technique (Level 7).		Main

Literacy

Students write a TV advert to encourage more people to give blood in the student-book activity. This requires students to explain the functions of the different components of blood, adapting their language to suit their audience.

APP

Students carry out an experiment to determine blood groups of the artificial samples supplied (AF4), presenting results in an appropriate manner (AF3).

Key Words

blood group, plasma, platelets

Answers from the student book

In-text questions	**A** Analysis of a blood sample to determine its blood group.
	B red blood cells, white blood cells, plasma, platelets
	C A, B, AB, O
Activity	**Giving blood** TV adverts should include examples or reasons why people may require blood transfusions, what is meant by a blood group, a simple description of the four blood groups, and the dangers of receiving the wrong type of blood. Students may also include a description of the different components in blood and why each component is so important.

Summary Questions	
	1 Red blood cells transport oxygen. White blood cells fight disease. Plasma transports blood cells, digested food, waste, hormones, and antibodies around the body. Platelets clot the blood. (4 marks)
	2 Each blood group contains red blood cells that carry different combinations of antigens (except the red blood cells in Group O, which do not carry antigens). If blood from a different blood group (with different antigens on the red blood cells) enters the body, the immune system will identify the foreign antigens, triggering an immune reaction that produces antibodies to destroy them. This means that receiving the wrong blood group in a blood transfusion would be life threatening. (3 marks)
	3 QWC question (6 marks). Example answers: Red blood cells are smaller. They are disc shaped with no nucleus. This shape increases the surface area for effective diffusion of oxygen into and out of the cell. The transport of oxygen is done by haemoglobin, a chemical found in red blood cells that binds to oxygen. Haemoglobin (when bound to oxygen) gives red blood cells their distinctive red colour. White blood cells are much larger. They have a nucleus. Some white blood cells can change shape (to engulf pathogens). Other white blood cells can produce antibodies. White blood cells protect our bodies against disease, destroying pathogens and foreign bodies.

kerboodle

Starter	Support/Extension	Resources
Blood smear (10 min) Show an image of a blood smear at a crime scene. Ask students to suggest how this piece of evidence can be used (in DNA fingerprinting). Continue to discuss how blood samples can also be examined using a light microscope. What can students see? Can they name any components of the blood? **Blood function** (5 min) Ask students to discuss what they know about blood. Do they know what blood groups are possible in humans? What does it mean to have a different blood group?	**Extension**: Encourage students to suggest functions of different components of blood.	

Main	Support/Extension	Resources
Identifying blood groups (40 min) Introduce the main components of blood and the nature of different blood groups. Explain how the body is able to recognise foreign antigens (carried by red blood cells) in our bodies and ask students to explain why it is dangerous to give a blood transfusion of the wrong blood group. (Is the idea of blood group a continuous or discontinuous variable?) Can students give examples of where knowledge of blood groups is beneficial? Students then carry out a practical to determine blood groups of five different samples (of artificial blood). Students use their observations to determine the correct blood groups of the samples and answer the questions that follow.	**Support**: You may wish to demonstrate how the procedure is carried out using the sample from the crime scene. This will allow students to see how blood groups can be determined using real results.	**Practical**: Identifying blood groups

Plenary	Support/Extension	Resources
Blood function (5 min) Students match the components of blood with functions supplied on the interactive resource. Students then suggest possible uses of blood typing (forensic science, transfusions). **Facts about blood** (10 min) Divide the class into groups of five or six and give each group four envelopes, each with a component of blood written on. Each student writes at least one fact about each component and puts these into the correct envelopes. Gather the facts to be discussed as a class in order to identify missing information or correct misconceptions.	**Extension**: Students compare the different components and relate their structure to their function. **Support**: Allow students to work through their ideas together, while still offering on average one idea per person.	**Interactive**: Blood function

Homework		
Students draw a poster to describe what is meant by a blood group and explain where knowledge about different blood groups is important, for example, in forensic science and blood transfusions.	**Extension**: Students explain the similarities and differences between different blood groups.	

KS3 Working Scientifically NC Link:

- interpret observations and data, including identifying patterns and using observations, measurements, and data to draw conclusions.

KS4 Biology NC Link:

- predict the effect of factors such as temperature and water content on rate of decomposition.

Band	Outcome	Checkpoint	
		Question	Activity
Developing	State one factor that scientists use to determine the time of death of an animal (Level 3).	A, 1	WS, Main, Plenary 1, Homework
	State one limitation to a technique used in determining the time of death (Level 4).		Main, Plenary 2
	Interpret one observation that can be used to estimate the time of death (Level 4).		Main
Secure	Describe how time of death can be determined (Level 5).	2	WS, Main, Plenary 1, Homework
	Describe some of the difficulties in determining time of death (Level 6).	3	Main, Plenary 2
	Interpret observations to determine the time of death (Level 5).		Main
Extending	Explain why different methods are used to determine the time of death (Level 7).	4	Main, Plenary 1
	Explain advantages and disadvantages of using different techniques for estimating time of death (Level 8).	4	Main, Plenary 2
	Explain how observations of the sequence of changes in the body can be used to determine the time of death (Level 7).		Main

Literacy
Students extract meaning from and summarise scientific texts.

APP
Students identify limitations to the different methods of determining time of death that may result in uncertainties (AF4) and apply observations to draw valid conclusions (AF5).

Key Words
rigor mortis

Answers from the student book

In-text questions	**A** body temperature, body appearance, presence of insects
	B The process where the body gradually becomes rigid/muscles in the body stiffen after death.
	C cockroaches
Activity	**Insect identification key**
	Credit sensible keys that can correctly identify blowflies, fly larvae, cockroaches, and mites.
	You may wish to prompt weaker students towards a possible first question, for example, 'Does it have legs?'.

Summary Questions	
	1 temperature, insects, rigor mortis (3 marks)
	2 Any three from:
	Body will be at room temperature.
	No rigor mortis/body not stiff.
	Skin will have a marble-like appearance or a greenish tone.
	Presence of blowflies and fly larvae (maggots) on the body.
	3 Any three from:
	Reduces the time taken for body temperature to match the temperature of the environment.
	The means that body temperature data will only be useful for a short amount of time after death.
	Warmer conditions will accelerate the decay of the body, so the abdomen inflates quicker than normal.
	Insect activity will also increase, for example, insects can reduce a body to skeleton in less than two weeks.
	4 QWC question (6 marks). Example answers:
	Scientists can record the body temperature. This is because core body temperature drops by around 1.5 °C every hour. This occurs until the temperature of the body matches the temperature of its environment (thermal equilibrium).
	Scientists can also use the appearance of the body and the presence/absence of rigor mortis to identify the time of death. Rigor mortis occurs in the first 48 hours after death. This is due to the lack of blood and oxygen in the muscles.
	After 48 hours, skin colour becomes green because of the bacteria growing on the skin. Between 4–7 days after death, the skin appears marble-like as the veins come closer to the surface of the body. The abdomen also starts to inflate because of the gases produced as the body decays.
	Finally, scientists also use the presence of insects at different stages in their life cycle. This can help scientists estimate time of death up to 4 weeks, for example, the presence of blowflies indicates death 0–3 days prior.

Starter	Support/Extension	Resources
Need to know? (5 min) Ask the students why they think detectives need to know the time of death. They could discuss cases they may have seen on TV (including crime dramas, if appropriate). Continue the discussion to ask how they think forensic scientists determine the time of death.		
Changes after death (10 min) Pose the question 'What happens to a body after death?'. Students pair-share ideas before discussing as a class. (Students may be aware of rigor mortis and should have some ideas about decay.)	**Extension**: Encourage students to suggest reasons for these changes in the body.	

Main	Support/Extension	Resources
Determining the time of death (40 min) Introduce briefly the changes in the body that occur after death, and how time of death can be determined using observations. Students then work through an activity where detailed descriptions of each method that can be used to determine time of death is discussed. Students summarise the information provided and answer questions that follow.	**Support**: The accompanying support sheet provides students with a framework to summarise their research. Research is also limited to three methods, rather than five.	**Activity**: Determining the time of death

Plenary	Support/Extension	Resources
Order of events (10 min) Students match the different methods of determining time of death with the correct time frames using the interactive resource. Students then draw their own timelines in their books to summarise what they have learnt this lesson using the answers provided.	**Extension**: Students explain why it is important to use several methods of determining time of death, rather than relying on one method.	**Interactive**: Order of events
Difficult cases (10 min) Give students a scenario, for example, a cold day with snow. Ask students how these conditions may affect scientists' estimate for the time of death. Students should suggest limitations to each technique.	**Extension**: Students should offer reasons for their suggestions.	

Homework		
Students design a crossword with accompanying clues that summarises key words covered in this topic so far.		

KS3 Working Scientifically NC Link:

- interpret observations and data, including identifying patterns and using observations, measurements, and data to draw conclusions.

Band	Outcome	Checkpoint	
		Question	Activity
Developing	State what is meant by a pathologist (Level 3).	A, 1	Main, Plenary 2
	State one way in which dental records are useful (Level 3).		Main, Plenary 1, Homework
	Record observations from an experiment (Level 4).		Main
Secure	Describe the role of a pathologist (Level 5).	1	Main, Plenary 2
	Describe how dental records can be used to help solve crimes (Level 6).	2	Main, Plenary 1, Homework
	Interpret results recorded from an experiment (Level 5).		Main
Extending	Explain how a pathologist determines the cause of death or disease (Level 7).	3	Plenary 2
	Explain why up-to-date and accurate dental records are important to correctly identify a body (Level 7).		Main, Plenary 1, Homework
	Interpret observations recorded from an experiment to draw conclusions (Level 7).		Main

APP

Students list safety precautions a pathologist should take to minimise risks when working with body samples in the student-book activity (AF4).

Students carry out a practical where they produce a cast from a model skull (AF4), present their observations using a dental record (AF3), and draw conclusions to identify a victim given reference dental records for comparison (AF5).

Key words
pathologist

Answers from the student book

In-text questions	**A** A pathologist is a doctor who specialises in understanding the nature and cause of disease. A forensic pathologist may be asked to determine if a person's death is suspicious or not.
	B blood, urine, and feces
	C By comparing the teeth of a victim to dental records.
Activity	**Protecting yourself**
	Credit suitable suggestions for safety precautions taken by a pathologist, for example:
	work in a sterile environment
	tie hair back
	wear eye protection/protective clothing
	wear gloves
	disinfect benches regularly
	sterilise all equipment after use.

Summary Questions	1 pathologist, samples, post mortems (3 marks)
	2 Any three from: The teeth of a corpse can be examined/studied using X-rays. This can be compared with existing dental records. The corpse can then be identified from broken/missing/chipped/jagged teeth, or by the presence of fillings/false teeth. Dental records can also be used in bite-mark analysis. Impressions left on the bite mark can be used to link a suspect to a (violent) crime. **3** QWC question (6 marks). Example answers: Pathologists are doctors who specialise in understanding the nature and cause of disease. They can check body tissues for the presence of cancerous cells. They can also perform tests on blood to detect anaemia, urine to detect diabetes, or feces to detect food poisoning. Forensic pathologists can be asked to take part in criminal investigations. They perform post mortems to establish the cause of death. This can determine whether a suspicious death was an accident or not. Pathologists can also identify unidentified bodies through the use of dental records/DNA fingerprinting. Dental records can be used because the teeth of a corpse can be compared with existing dental records/X-rays. The corpse can then be identified from broken/missing/chipped/jagged teeth, or by the presence of fillings/false teeth. Dental records can also be used in bite-mark analysis. Impressions left on the bite mark can be used to link a suspect to a (violent) crime.

Starter	Support/Extension	Resources
The role of a pathologist (10 min) Ask students whether they know what a pathologist does. They may have ideas from TV programmes. Show a short film clip from the Internet that highlights the work of a pathologist. Discuss briefly some of the points raised in the film. How does the role of a forensic pathologist differ? **Cause of death?** (5 min) We now know methods of determining time of death but what other information must forensic scientists find out about the victim? (Prompt students towards cause of death if necessary.) Students should suggest methods forensic pathologists use to determine cause of death.	**Extension**: Students should suggest how clues can be gathered from the victim, and methods used to determine cause of death.	

Main	Support/Extension	Resources
Investigating dental records (40 min) Introduce the role of forensic pathologists in identifying cause of death and the importance of dental records in the identification of a victim, particularly for cold cases and victims of fire. Students then carry out a practical where they make a cast of a model skull, record results as a dental record, and answer questions based on their observations.	**Support**: You may wish to demonstrate to students how observations in a cast can be transferred to a dental record using a different cast before the start of the activity.	**Practical**: Investigating dental records

Plenary	Support/Extension	Resources
Use of dental records (5 min) Students fill in the missing words in the paragraph provided on the interactive resource to describe how dental records may be obtained and used by forensic pathologists for solving crimes. **A day in the life of a forensic pathologist** (10 min) Students describe what a forensic pathologist does in a typical day. This can be done as a role play. Students should explain how the findings of the pathologist can be used to identify victims of crime and the cause of death.	**Extension**: Students explain why up-to-date dental records are so important.	**Interactive**: Use of dental records

Homework		
Students design a crime scene, mapping out as many pieces of evidence as possible. They explain how the crime can be solved using the evidence available, giving a brief description of each technique required. Students should use as many forensic techniques as possible to summarise this topic.		

Checkpoint lesson routes

The route through this lesson can be determined using the Checkpoint assessment.

Percentage pass marks are supplied in the Checkpoint teacher notes.

Route A (revision)

Resource: B3 Chapter 3 Checkpoint: Revision

Students work through a series of tasks that allow them to revisit and consolidate their understanding of key concepts in this chapter. Students can keep this as a summary of the topic, and use this when revising for future assessments.

You may wish students to further apply their understanding to the crime scene evidence board (Task 6) for homework.

Route B (extension)

Resource: B3 Chapter 3 Checkpoint: Extension

Students write an application letter for a trainee scene of crime officer, an apprentice forensic technician, or a junior pathologist. This activity covers all the key concepts in this chapter. Students produce an application letter that must not only cover the techniques used in the role they have applied for but also how these techniques fit in with the techniques used by others in the forensics team.

Progression to *secure*

No.	Developing outcome	Secure outcome	Making progress
1	Name two different types of microscope.	Describe the main differences between a light microscope and an electron microscope.	In Task 1 students decide if the statements provided correctly describe light microscopes, electron microscopes, or both types of microscopes.
2	Name one piece of microscopic evidence used by a forensic scientist.	Describe how microscopic evidence is used by forensic scientists.	In Task 1 students complete a word fill to describe how microscopic evidence can be used by forensic scientists.
3	State whether one person's fingerprint is likely to be the same as another person's fingerprint.	Describe how fingerprints are formed.	In Task 2 students reorder statements to describe the origin of fingerprints and how these are formed.
4	Name one surface on which a fingerprint can be left.	Describe how the police use fingerprints to solve crimes.	In Task 2 students use the stimulus image and key words provided to describe how fingerprints can be used by the police.
5	Name one type of sample that can be used for DNA fingerprinting.	State what is meant by DNA fingerprinting.	In Task 3 students describe how DNA fingerprinting differs from the fingerprinting described in Task 2.
6	Give one example where two people share the same genetic information.	Describe some uses of DNA fingerprinting.	In Task 3 students decide if the statements given about uses of DNA fingerprinting are true or false.
7	Name the components of blood.	Describe the structure and function of blood components.	In Task 4 students link the different components of blood with their functions.
8	Name the possible blood groups in humans.	Describe what is meant by a blood group.	In Task 4 students read statements describing blood groups to decide if they are true or false. Students then correct statements that are false.
9	State one factor that scientists use to determine the time of death of an animal.	Describe how time of death can be determined.	In Task 5 students annotate a scaled-timeline to describe different ways in which time of death can be determined.
10	State one limitation to a technique used in determining the time of death.	Describe some of the difficulties in determining time of death.	In Task 5 students describe how abnormally cold weather may affect different methods used to determine time of death.
11	State what is meant by a pathologist.	Describe the role of a pathologist.	In Task 5 students identify statements provided that correctly describe the role of a pathologist.
12	State one way in which dental records are useful.	Describe how dental records can be used to help solve crimes.	In Task 5 students describe one method a pathologist can use to identify the identity of a victim after the body has been buried for many years.

Answers to end-of-chapter questions

1 red, white, platelets, groups (4 marks)

2a to magnify an object/image (1 mark)   **b** light and electron microscopes (2 marks)

c Any two from: hair/fibre/fingerprint/paint flecks/pollen grains/soil (2 marks)

3a Powders can be brushed over the surface of objects. These stick to the oils in fingerprints. Alternatively, ultraviolet light can be used that make fingerprints glow. (2 marks)

b Any from: quicker/cheaper/technology and knowledge of technology not required/identical twins will have different fingerprints despite sharing the same DNA. (1 mark)

c The fingertips are pressed onto an ink pad/digital scanner. If ink is used, the fingers are pressed onto paper. Impressions of the ridges of the fingertips are left on the paper/digital scanner. (3 marks)

4 Fingerprint can be compared to a suspect. Matching fingerprints show that a suspect was present at the crime scene. DNA from blood/hair sample can also be compared to the suspect. If the two sources of DNA match, then the suspect must also have visited the crime scene. (4 marks)

5a Any from: blood/hair/semen/saliva (1 mark)

b Suspect 3 – because the number and position of the bands match the sample taken from the crime scene. (2 marks)

c Enzymes cut DNA into smaller fragments. (1 mark)

d Electricity is used to move DNA fragments across the gel.
Different fragments are moved different distances by the electric current. (2 marks)

6 This is a QWC question. Students should be marked on the use of good English, organisation of information, spelling and grammar, and correct use of specialist scientific terms. The best answers will fully explain how the processes of microscopy, fingerprinting, DNA fingerprinting, blood typing, and time-of-death estimates can be used to solve a violent crime (maximum of 6 marks).
Examples of correct scientific points:
Many different types of evidence can be found at scenes of violent crime. Different techniques can be used to analyse each piece of evidence. Microscopy can be used to analyse hairs, fibres, fingerprints, paint, pollen, or soil, amongst other things. These samples can be compared to samples from known locations to determine where these pieces of evidence came from. Fingerprints obtained from the crime scene can also be compared to the fingerprints of suspects to show whether a suspect has visited the crime scene before. Blood-typing and DNA fingerprinting can also be used to identify a suspect's presence at a crime scene, and narrow down the field of suspects. If a murder has been committed, a pathologist can narrow down the time of death using the presence of insects found on the body. This can then inform investigators roughly when the crime occurred. Results from all these techniques can be used to build up a picture of exactly how the crime occurred, and may be used to identify one suspect from a field.

Answer guide for Case Study

Developing	Secure	Extending
1–2 marks	3–4 marks	5–6 marks
• The factsheet is poorly organised. • The student has stated at least one relevant piece of evidence that a forensic scientist could collect. • An attempt has been made to explain how the results could be used to identify a suspect. • Annotated image of the crime scene is missing.	• The factsheet is presented in a logical manner but lacks detail. • The student has stated at least two pieces of evidence that can be collected from the crime scene. • A brief explanation is included for how the evidence can be analysed and how results can be used. • An annotated image of the crime scene has been attempted, although some details are missing.	• The factsheet is presented in a logical and detailed manner. • The student has stated at least three pieces of evidence that can be collected from the crime scene. • The student has explained clearly how the evidence can be analysed and how results can be used. • A detailed annotated image of the crime scene has been included.

kerboodle

B3 Chapter 3 Checkpoint assessment (automarked)
B3 Chapter 3 Checkpoint: Revision
B3 Chapter 3 Checkpoint: Extension
B3 Chapter 3 Progress task (Literacy)

Chemistry ③

Preparing for Key Stage 4 Success

Knowledge Underpinning knowledge is covered in this unit for KS4 study of:	• A simple model of the atom • Properties of transition metals • Bulk and surface properties of matter • Chemical equations • Reactions of acids • Neutralisation reactions • Common atmospheric pollutants and their sources • The principles underpinning the modern Periodic Table • Identification of ions and gases by chemical and spectroscopic means	• The pH scale • The reactivity series of metals • Carbon compounds as fuels • Chemical cells and fuel cells • Factors that influence the rate of reaction • Naturally occurring and synthetic polymers • Separation techniques for mixtures of substances • Carbon dioxide and methane as greenhouse gases
Maths Skills developed in this unit. (Topic number)	• Quantitative problem solving (1.1, 1.7, 3.1). • Understand the idea of probability (1.4). • Use of, calculations with, and conversion between fractions, percentages, and ratios (1.5). • Extract and interpret information from charts, graphs, and tables (1.3, 1.7, 3.1, 3.3, 3.4). • Understand number size and scale and the quantitative relationship between units. (1.2, 2.3, 2.4, 2.5). • Substitute numerical values into simple formulae and equations using appropriate units. (1.6). • Carry out calculations involving $+$, $-$, $\times$, $\div$, either singly or in combination (2.2).	
Literacy Skills developed in this unit. (Topic number)	• Predicting, making inferences, and describing relationships (1.3, 1.4, 2.1, 2.3, 3.1, 3.2, 3.4, 3.7). • Accessing information to ascertain meaning, using word skills and comprehension strategies (1.1). • Communicating ideas and information to a wide range of audiences and a variety of situations (1.8, 2.2, 3.1). • Use of scientific terms (1.1, 1.2, 1.6, 2.2, 2.5, 3.1, 3.2, 3.3, 3.4, 3.6). • Organisation of ideas and information (1.2, 1.3, 1.5, 1.6, 1.7, 1.8, 2.1, 2.2, 2.3, 2.4, 3.1, 3.2, 3.3, 3.5, 3.7). • Collaboration and exploratory talk (3.7). • Identifying main ideas, events, and supporting details (3.6). • Attention to the 'rules' of the particular form of writing (e.g., news article, scientific report) (2.5). • Legibility, spelling, punctuation, grammar, and sentence structure (1.5).	
Assessment Skills	• QWC questions (1.1, 1.2, 1.5, 1.6, 2.1, 2.3, 2.5, 3.2, 3.4, 3.6, 3.7) (end-of-chapter 1 Q5, end-of-chapter 2 Q4, end-of-chapter 3 Q7) • Quantitative problem solving (1.1, 1.5, 1.6, 1.7, 2.2, 3.4) (end-of-chapter 1 Maths challenge, Q4) • Application of Working Scientifically (1.4, 1.5, 2.1, 2.4, 3.1, 3.3, 3.5, 3.6) (end-of-chapter 1 Q3, end-of-chapter 2 Case study, end-of-chapter 3 Case study)	

	Key concept	Catch-up
Chapter 1: New technology	The particulate nature of matter is consolidated by considering how particles are arranged within nanoparticles using particle diagrams. This provides a foundation for **nanoparticle** properties, **patterns in physical properties for Groups 1, 7, 0,** and for **transition metals**.	C1 Chapter 1: Particles and their behaviour C2 1.3 The elements of Group 1 C2 1.4 The elements of Group 7 C2 1.5 The elements of Group 0
	Complete and incomplete combustion of fuels is revisited using balanced formula equations, whilst introducing the word hydrocarbon. These are important concepts when considering **carbon compounds as fuels** and **organic chemistry**.	C1 3.3 Burning fuels C1 3.5 Conservation of mass C1 3.6 Exothermic and endothermic
	Fossil fuels, renewable fuels, and the waste products of their combustion are discussed in terms of vehicles fuels and their impact on the environment. This provides students with a foundation for understanding **greenhouse gases, carbon capture and storage,** and **atmospheric pollutants**.	C1 3.3 Burning fuels C2 4.1 The Earth and its atmosphere C2 4.5 The carbon cycle C2 4.6 Climate change
	Catalysts are introduced for the first time in a chemical sense. Catalysts will be revisited when studying **rates of reactions** and **properties of transition metals**.	C1 3.1 Chemical reactions B2 1.5 Bacteria and enzymes in digestion
	Writing and balancing of formula equations are used throughout this chapter car fuels and exhausts. This allows students to practice **using chemical symbols and formulae** and **writing chemical equations.**	C1 2.4 Chemical formulae C1 3.2 Word equations C1 3.5 Conservation of mass C2 3.2–3.5: Metals and acids
Chapter 2: Turning points in chemistry	Atoms, elements, and compounds are consolidated throughout this topic. This is important for understanding **atomic structure** and the **changes in the atomic model**.	C1 2.1 Elements C1 2.2 Atoms
	Mendeleev's thinking behind the organisation of the Periodic Table is discussed in this chapter, providing students with the foundations required for describing **trends in the Periodic Table**, and **how chemical properties and reactivity can be predicted** using the Periodic Table.	C1 2.1 Elements C2 Chapter 1: The Periodic Table
	The formation of sedimentary rock is consolidated by looking at fossils. This topic also examines the evidence provided by fossils in support of the evolution of different species. These are important concepts when considering **changes in the Earth's climate and landscape** over geological timescales, and when looking at **Darwin's theory of evolution** by natural selection.	C2 4.2 Sedimentary rocks C2 4.3 Igneous and metamorphic rocks C2 4.4 The rock cycle B2 3.3 Variation B2 3.5 Natural selection
Chapter 3: Detection	This chapter consolidates the concept of pure and impure substances using a fictional crime scenario. Students practice their understanding of the **particle model** in relation to **how mixtures can be separated**. This can be applied towards the **identification of ions and gases using chemical and spectroscopic means**.	C1 1.1 The particle model C2 Chapter 2: Separation techniques
	Properties of different substances are considered when discussing how different materials will react under different conditions. This serves as a foundation for distinguishing between **naturally occurring and synthetic polymers** and **the reactivity series of metals**. This can then be applied towards the **extraction of metals**.	C2 3.4–3.8: Metals and acids
	Acid–base neutralisations are considered in this chapter in terms of hazards. Students also practice writing word and formula equations, using **acid–base general equations** to help them. This topic can help students understand **H^+ and OH^- ions, concentration of acids and alkalis**, and **the pH scale**.	C1 3.1 Chemical reactions C1 3.2 Word equations C1 Chapter 4: Acids and alkalis C2 3.1 Acids and metals

kerboodle

C3 Unit pre-test	C3 Practical project hints: writing frame
C3 Big practical project (foundation)	C3 End-of-unit test (foundation)
C3 Big practical project (higher)	C3 End-of-unit test (foundation) mark scheme
C3 Big practical project teacher notes	C3 End-of-unit test (higher)
C3 Practical project hints: graph plotting	C3 End-of-unit test (higher) mark scheme
C3 Practical project hints: planning	

Answers to Picture Puzzler
Key Words

firefighter, oil rig, sheep, spade, ink, litmus paper
The key word is **fossil**.

Close Up
ammonite fossil

1.1 Nanoparticles

KS3 Chemistry NC Link:
- the particulate nature of matter.

KS4 Chemistry NC Link:
- relate 'nano' to typical dimensions of atoms and molecules
- relate surface area to volume for different-sized particles and describe how this affects properties.

Band	Outcome	Checkpoint	
		Question	Activity
Developing ↓	State what nanoparticles are (Level 3).	B, 1	Main
	State a property of nanoparticles (Level 3).	C, 1, 2	Main, Plenary 1, Plenary 2
Secure ↓	Explain what nanoparticles are (Level 6).	1	Main, Plenary 2
	Describe the properties of nanoparticles (Level 5).	C, 1, 2, 3	Main, Plenary 1
Extending ↓	Apply the properties of nanoparticles to one of their uses (Level 7).		Main, Plenary 2
	Compare the properties of nanoparticles and normal-sized particles (Level 7).	3	Plenary 1, Plenary 2

Maths
In the student-book activity students calculate the number of nanoparticles found across an average strand of hair, converting between m, μm, and nm.

Literacy
Students identify meaning in scientific text, summarising this in well-organised paragraphs, and adapting their language for an article in a newspaper for the general public to answer some frequently asked questions about nanoparticles.

APP
Students collate information from secondary sources and present it in an appropriate manner as a newspaper article (AF3). Students also discuss evidence for and against the use of nanoparticles in sunscreen (AF1).

Key Words
nanoparticle, nanometre

Answers from the student book

In-text questions	**A** Bandages to kill bacteria, lightweight bullet-proof vests, and materials that capture carbon dioxide. **B** A tiny piece of a substance made up of a few hundred atoms. Its diameter is between 1 and 100 nanometres. **C** 1 g of gold nanoparticles
Activity	**How small?** Mean diameter of human hair = (20 μm + 100 μm) ÷ 2 = 60 μm 1 nm = 0.000 000 001 ÷ 0.000 001 = 0.001 μm So 30 nm = 0.001 μm × 30 = 0.030 μm So the number of nanoparticles of diameter 30 nm that fit across an average human hair = 60 ÷ 0.030 = 2000
Summary Questions	**1** hundred, 100, 0.000 000 001, different, bigger (5 marks) **2** The 1 g sample of silver nanoparticles has a greater surface area, because there are more atoms on the surface of the 1 g of nanoparticles. (2 marks)

3 QWC question (6 marks). Example answers:

1 g of gold nanoparticles has a greater surface area than 1 g of normal gold.

This is because there are more atoms on the surface of the gold nanoparticles.

Each gold nanoparticle contains only hundreds of atoms whereas a block of gold contains millions of atoms.

Gold in its normal form is yellow-coloured.

This will not dissolve in/mix with water.

Gold nanoparticles can mix with water.

The resulting solution looks red in colour.

Starter	Support/Extension	Resources
Where are nanoparticles found? (10 min) Have a selection of products containing nanoparticles around the room for students to observe, for example, sunscreen, water-repellent material, plasters, and bandages. Ask students to suggest what these materials have in common.	**Extension**: Students should suggest how nanoparticles differ from regular particles. This can be done in a discussion of unit conversions between m, cm, and nm.	
How big is a nanometre? (5 min) Ask students to look on a metre ruler and compare the size of 1 cm with the whole length of the ruler. 1 cm = 1/100 m. Now move down one measurement, to mm, then μm, and finally nm. Students should then practice the conversion between these units with some examples on the board. Animations, such as 'The scale of the universe', are readily available on the Internet and may be useful for this exercise.	**Support**: To help students grasp the mathematical nature of this task, analogies will be helpful. **Extension**: Have students go through units in the opposite direction, from kilo to mega and giga?	

Main	Support/Extension	Resources
FAQs about nanoparticles (40 min) Introduce the idea of nanoparticles to students. It is extremely important that students understand just how small a nanoparticle is, and that they will not be able to see nanoparticles, even when looking through a school light microscope. A scanning electron microscope is required to see nanoparticles. You may wish to discuss the uses of nanoparticles using tangible examples to explain how properties of nanoparticles differ from bulk properties. Students then use a range of textbooks and the Internet to write a newspaper article that answers frequently asked questions about nanoparticles.	**Support**: An access sheet is available where students complete a partially written article on nanoparticles. The access sheet can be completed using the Student Book alone. **Extension**: Students can be given higher-level texts that explore the properties of nanoparticles in more detail.	**Activity**: FAQs about nanoparticles

Plenary	Support/Extension	Resources
Describing molecular models (10 min) Show molecular models of diamond and a carbon nanotube. Explain that both models show atoms of carbon in different arrangements and one is a nanoparticle. Ask students to predict which model represents the nanoparticle, how they can tell this, and to explain the ways in which the two models differ.	**Support**: Remind students that in nanoparticles, the majority of particles appear on the surface. **Extension**: Encourage students to explain the difference in properties between the two models, for example, in the carbon nanotube none of the atoms are 'hidden', unlike in diamond.	
Nanoparticle statements (5 min) Students categorise statements given on the interactive resource as true or false. Students should correct the statements that are false.	**Extension**: Students should be able to justify why each statement is true or false, and offer other statements to add to the list.	**Interactive**: Nanoparticle statements

Homework		
Make a poster to show the number scale from large objects (up to 1 m) to nanoparticles.	**Extension**: Students may wish to start from km and work downwards.	

1.2 Using nanoparticles

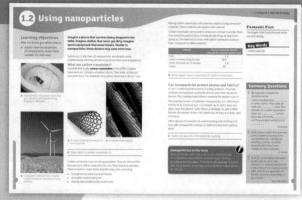

KS3 Chemistry NC Link:
- the particulate nature of matter.

KS4 Chemistry NC Link:
- write 'nano' in standard mathematical form
- relate the properties of nanoparticulate materials to their uses.

Band	Outcome	Checkpoint	
		Question	**Activity**
Developing ↓	Give three properties of carbon nanotubes (Level 3).	B, 1	Lit, Main 1, Main 2, Plenary 1, Plenary 2, Homework
Secure ↓	Explain how the properties of nanoparticles make them suitable for their uses (Level 6).	2	Lit, Main 1, Plenary 1, Plenary 2, Homework
Extending ↓	Compare the properties of nanoparticles and normal materials, explaining how these properties relate to their uses (Level 8).	3	Lit, Main 2, Plenary 2, Homework

Maths
The interactive resource allows students to revise the numerical relationship between nm and m, using standard form to show the relationship $1\,\text{nm} = 1 \times 10^{-9}\,\text{m}$.

Literacy
In the student-book activity students must organise ideas clearly and concisely, adapting their writing style to a general audience when writing a newspaper article on one exciting use of nanoparticles.

APP
Students design models of carbon nanotubes, and use these to explain the properties of nanoparticles (AF1).

Key Words
carbon nanotube

Answers from the student book

In-text questions	**A** A cylinder of carbon atoms that can have walls just one atom thick.
	B strong, stiff, low density, excellent conductors of heat
	C Waterproofing objects, for example, electronic devices and clothes.
Activity	**Nanoparticles in the news**
	Articles should include a description of the innovation to grab attention, and an explanation of how the properties of the material make it suitable for this use, for example, using nanoparticles to protect a phone from water damage.
Summary Questions	**1** cylinders, atom, nanometre, stiff, energy (5 marks)
	2 Carbon nanotubes are strong, stiff, and light (low-density). (1 mark)
	3 QWC question (6 marks). Example answers:
	Thermal conductivity is a measure of how well a substance conducts heat.
	The best thermal conductor in the table is the carbon nanotube, in the direction along the tube.
	Their thermal conductivity is almost nine times that of the next best thermal conductor, copper.
	Brick has the lowest thermal conductivity of the substances in the table.
	This means that it is the best insulator of heat.
	However, the thermal conductivity of carbon nanotubes depends on direction.
	Thermal conductivity is more than 2000 times greater in the direction along the tube than across the tube.

Starter	Support/Extension	Resources
Considering the size of nanoparticles (5 min) Students identify the statements that correctly describe the relationship between metres and nanometres.		**Interactive**: Considering the size of nanoparticles
Uses of nanoparticles (10 min) Show students a range of materials/objects that use nanoparticles again. This time, ask students to compare the samples with nanoparticles to those without. For example, stain-repellent carpet with ordinary carpet. Can students see/feel/observe any differences? Discuss as a class why it is important that claims about such properties can be tested.		

Main	Support/Extension	Resources
Carbon nanotubes and their uses (15 min) Discuss the structure of carbon nanotubes, show illustrations of them, and explain that the walls are usually only one atom thick, with an average diameter of 1 nm. Explain that they are one of the stiffest materials known to man, and that they are very strong but have a very low density. Ask students to suggest what carbon nanotubes may therefore be used in, discussing actual uses of carbon nanotubes on their own, as well as combining with polymers to form composite materials. Students should make notes in their books to summarise their learning.	**Support**: Students can answer Summary Question 1 in the corresponding student-book spread for their summary.	
Carbon nanotube models (25 min) Allow students access to a range of textbooks with illustrations of carbon nanotubes. Students design a model of a carbon nanotube, annotating their diagram and adding explanatory notes to accompany their model. Students can make their own models if time.	**Support**: A support sheet is available where five properties of carbon nanotubes are provided for students to use as a starting point when designing their models. **Extension**: Students calculate the scale of their model compared to a real carbon nanotube.	**Activity**: Carbon nanotube models

Plenary	Support/Extension	Resources
Recapping nanoparticles (10 min) Ask students to design a quick quiz (of three questions) on the size, properties, and uses of nanoparticles. Students should include the number of marks available for each question. They should then swap their quizzes with a partner.	**Extension**: Students should be able provide the mark scheme to questions when required.	
Carbon nanoparticles and their uses (5 min) Students list as many uses of carbon nanoparticles as they can recall. Students should link the properties of nanoparticles to their particular uses.	**Extension**: Students compare the differences in properties between nanoparticles and normal materials.	

Homework		
Students complete their plan of models and make these at home using everyday materials. OR Students research other uses of nanoparticles and write a short paragraph about their research, relating the properties of nanoparticles to their uses.		

1.3 Nanoparticles in medicine

KS3 Chemistry NC Link:
- the particulate nature of matter.

KS3 Working Scientifically NC Link:
- interpret observations and data, including identifying patterns to draw conclusions.

KS4 Chemistry NC Link:
- relate the properties of nanoparticulate materials to their uses.

Band	Outcome	Checkpoint	
		Question	Activity
Developing ↓	State one use of nanoparticles in medicine (Level 3).	1	Lit, Plenary 1, Homework
	State what results given for a nanoparticle test shows (Level 4).		Main
Secure ↓	Describe how nanoparticles are used in medical treatments (Level 5).	1, 2	Lit, Main, Plenary 1, Plenary 2 Homework
	Describe in detail what results given for a nanoparticle test show (Level 6).		Main
Extending ↓	Explain how and why nanoparticles are useful in medical treatments (Level 7).	2, 3	Lit, Main, Plenary 1, Plenary 2 Homework
	Use results given for a nanoparticle test to suggest further investigations to confirm experimental data (Level 7).		Main

Maths
Students interpret and extract information from graphs to draw conclusions.

Literacy
In the student-book activity students organise scientific ideas and adapt their writing style to write a leaflet explaining to potential patients one use of nanoparticles in medicine.

APP
Students interpret graphs to draw conclusions and suggest further investigations that can be carried out (AF5).

Key Words
nanomedicine

Answers from the student book

In-text questions	**A** The use of nanoparticles to treat disease.
	B Infections can be detected and treated immediately without the need to remove the bandages, which can be painful and slow down healing.
	C The drugs are enclosed in nanoparticle structures. The nanoparticles travel through the body to the cancer cell. The cancer cell absorbs the nanoparticles. Inside the cell the nanoparticles break up and release their medicine.
Activity	**Your treatment explained...** Leaflets should include clear descriptions of what will happen to the patient and how the treatment works. Students should choose from: bandages that detect and treat infections, cancer drugs with targeted delivery, or magnetising tumours to kill cancerous cells.

Summary Questions	
	1 nanomedicine, detect, treat, deliver, heat, kill (6 marks)
	2 Doctors will inject magnetic iron oxide nanoparticles into a tumour and apply a magnetic field near this site, repeatedly changing the direction of the field. This heats the nanoparticles and warms up the tumour. At 5 °C above normal body temperature, tumour cells die. Healthy cells nearby are not affected by the magnetic field and therefore are not harmed. (3 marks)
	3 Poster should include a detailed explanation of the uses of nanoparticles in six scenarios (6 marks). Examples include: bandages that detect and treat infections cancer drugs with targeted delivery magnetising tumours to kill cancerous cells carbon nanotubes in sports equipment carbon nanotubes in bullet-proof vests waterproofing of electronic equipment.

kerboodle

Starter	Support/Extension	Resources
What is nanomedicine? (5 min) Ask students to recap what nanoparticles are. These descriptions should include size, properties, and uses of nanoparticles. Ask students to suggest what nanomedicine is, and if they know any applications of this. **Nanomedicine animation** (5 min) Show students an animation or video of nanomedicine in action. Clips are readily available on the Internet. Introduce how nanotechnology can be used in medicine and discuss how the chosen example of nanomedicine works.		

Main	Support/Extension	Resources
The impact of nanomedicine (40 min) Introduce nanomedicine as the use of nanoparticles to treat disease. This can be done using examples such as targeted drug delivery for cancer cells and the use of magnetic nanoparticles to destroy tumours. These examples are found in the corresponding spread in the student book. Students then move onto nanoparticle plasters in the activity, where they interpret a graph of results from an investigation and answer the questions that follow.	**Support**: A support sheet is available where students complete a paragraph to describe the patterns shown by the graphs. **Extension**: Students suggest additional investigations that can be carried out to test conclusively whether nanoparticle films reduce bacterial growth.	**Activity**: The impact of nanomedicine

Plenary	Support/Extension	Resources
Modelling nanomedicine (10 min) Students work in small groups to role play one example of nanomedicine in action. Students should then evaluate each other's role plays when these are performed. **Nanoparticles in bandages** (10 min) Students rearrange sentences provided on the interactive resource to describe how nanoparticles work in bandages. Students could then produce similar descriptions for another use of nanoparticles in medicine.	**Extension**: Students should include an explanation in the narration of role plays.	**Interactive**: Nanoparticles in bandages

Homework		
Students draw a visual summary showing what they have learnt about nanoparticles so far. The visual summary should include branches on the following topics: • what are nanoparticles • properties of nanoparticles • uses of nanoparticles in industry and in medicine.		

1.4 Nanoparticle safety

KS3 Chemistry NC Link:
- the particulate nature of matter.

KS3 Working Scientifically NC Link:
- evaluate risks.

KS4 Chemistry NC Link:
- relate properties of nanoparticulate materials to their uses
- consider the possible risks associated with some nanoparticulate materials.

Band	Outcome	Checkpoint	
		Question	**Activity**
Developing	State one example of where nanoparticle safety has been considered (Level 3).	B	Plenary 2, Homework
	Complete a risk assessment for using nanoparticle sunscreen (Level 4).		Main
Secure	Describe an example of how scientists are investigating nanoparticle safety (Level 5).	3	Plenary 2, Homework
	Write a risk assessment for the application of nanoparticle sunscreen on children (Level 5).		Main
Extending	Suggest how the safety of a given nanoparticle product could be investigated (Level 7).	4	Plenary 2, Homework
	Write a detailed risk assessment for the application of nanoparticle sunscreen on children, evaluating the overall safety of using the product (Level 8).		Main

Literacy
Students select, analyse, and evaluate information provided in two different articles, taking into account potential bias.

APP
In the student-book activity students identify independent, dependent, and control variables for experiments given.

Key Words
safety

Answers from the student book

In-text questions	**A** 20–30 nm
	B Can zinc oxide nanoparticles get through the skin and into the blood?
	C Diesel exhaust may increase the build-up of fatty deposits in arteries that can lead to heart disease.
Activity	**Spotting variables**
	Independent variable: size of pieces of zinc oxide (nanoparticles or normal-sized pieces of zinc oxide).
	Dependent variable: whether or not there was extra zinc in blood and urine samples.
	Other variables to consider: amount of sunscreen applied, other ingredients in sunscreen, length of time sunscreen used for, frequency of application. Credit other sensible suggestions.
Summary Questions	**1** Scientists are investigating nanoparticle safety because they are being used in increasing amounts, for an increasing number of different applications. (1 mark)
	2a Independent variable: type of air the mice were exposed to (polluted or not).
	Dependent variable: amount of fatty deposits in the arteries. (2 marks)
	b Other variables to consider: time of exposure to air/polluted air, existing concentration of cholesterol in mouse arteries before beginning the study, other hereditary factors that may affect the build-up of cholesterol. Credit other sensible suggestions. (2 marks)

3 Scientists carried out experiments using mice with high cholesterol. One group of mice was exposed to traffic pollution, whereas the other group was not. The scientists found that, after five weeks, the group exposed to traffic pollution had 55% more fat in the arteries, increasing the risk of heart disease. (3 marks)

4 Credit sensible suggestions (6 marks). Examples include:

Divide mice into two groups.

Apply sunscreen with zinc oxide nanoparticles to one group of mice, and sunscreen without zinc oxide nanoparticles to the other group.

Repeat several times over several days.

After a certain period of time, take urine samples from both sets of mice.

Test the urine samples to find out whether or not they contain zinc oxide nanoparticles.

The independent variable is whether or not sunscreen contains zinc oxide nanoparticles.

The dependent variable is whether or not the urine samples contain zinc oxide nanoparticles.

To make sure the test is fair the same amount of sunscreen should be applied to the mice the same number of times over the same number of days.

Starter	Support/Extension	Resources
Hazards versus risks (10 min) Ask students to consider the difference between hazards and risks and to give examples to illustrate this. Discuss that a hazard is a potential danger and a risk describes the likelihood that the hazard will occur. Students have met risk assessments before.	**Support**: You may wish to recap hazard symbols with students before beginning this activity. These were met in C1.	
Defining hazards and risks (5 min) Students match key words and phrases to their definitions using the interactive resource. Students should then use these to offer examples of different situations where hazards and risks can be named.		**Interactive**: Defining hazards and risks

Main	Support/Extension	Resources
Reported risks (40 min) Ask students to think about the potential risks and hazards associated with using nanoparticles. Allow students to pair share their ideas before opening up as a class discussion. Examples to introduce nanoparticle safety are included in the corresponding spread in the student book (sunscreens and diesel exhaust fumes). It is extremely important students understand that although nanoparticles have been investigated for health risks, research is still in the early stages. Students then read two short articles about the advantages and disadvantages of using sunscreen in the summer, prepare a risk assessment, and answer the questions that follow.	**Support**: A support sheet is available with a partially filled risk assessment for students to complete.	**Activity**: Reported risks

Plenary	Support/Extension	Resources
How likely is it...? (5 min) Hold up a bottle of bleach with the safety cap attached. Ask students to analyse the hazards and risks in this situation. (There is a severe risk of receiving chemical burns but the risk is extremely low if the lid is on, whereas the risk increases significantly if the lid is off and you do not handle it in a safe manner.)		
Other risks of nanoparticles (10 min) Give students another context in which nanoparticles are present, for example, diesel exhaust fumes are mentioned in the Student Book. Ask students to suggest the hazards and risks in this scenario before offering the answer.	**Extension**: Students should be able to spot the general pattern in the hazards of nanoparticles.	

Homework		
Students carry out research to describe how tests are carried out on a different nanoparticle product.		

1.5 Cars: pros and cons

KS3 Chemistry NC Link:
- chemical reactions.

KS3 Working Scientifically NC Link:
- select and plan the most appropriate types of scientific enquiries to test predictions, including identifying independent, dependent, and control variables.

KS4 Chemistry NC Link:
- predict the formulae of products of reactions (e.g., combustion) of alkanes
- describe and analyse the evidence for additional anthropogenic causes of climate change
- describe the potential effects of climate change
- recognise the major sources of oxides of nitrogen and particulates in the atmosphere and the problems caused by increased amounts of these.

Band	Outcome	Checkpoint	
		Question	Activity
Developing	State the products of combustion (Level 3).	A, B, 1	Starter 2, Main 1, Plenary 1, Homework
	Give one advantage and one disadvantage of cars (Level 3).	C, 3	Main 1, Plenary 2
	Complete a plan for an investigation to compare air quality at different locations (Level 4).		Main 2
Secure	Explain how combustion reactions in car engines produce exhaust gases (Level 6).	2	Starter 2, Main 1, Plenary 1, Homework
	Describe some advantages and disadvantages of cars (Level 5).	3	Main 1, Plenary 2, Homework
	Plan an investigation to compare air quality at different locations (Level 6).		
Extending	Explain combustion reactions in car engines using balanced formula equations (Level 7).		Starter 2, Main 1, Plenary 1, Homework
	Evaluate the advantages and disadvantages of cars using scientific knowledge (Level 8).	3	Plenary 2, Homework
	Plan an investigation to compare air quality at different locations, suggesting one other appropriate method (Level 7).		Main 2

Maths
Students carry out calculations using percentages in the student-book activity.

Literacy
Students organise ideas and information when writing a plan to investigate air quality at different locations.

APP
Students plan an investigation to compare the number of particulates in the air at different locations, identifying the independent, dependent, and control variables (AF4).

Key Words
hydrocarbon, particulate

Answers from the student book

In-text questions	
	A carbon dioxide and water
	B nitrogen monoxide and nitrogen dioxide
	C Diesel particulates may make asthma and chest infections worse. They may also lead to heart attacks.

Activity	**Calculating CO$_2$**
	57% of 46 million tonnes = 57 ÷ 100 × 46 000 000 = 26 220 000 tonnes
	Mass of CO$_2$ emitted by UK cars in 2005 = 46 000 000 + 26 220 000 = 72 220 000
Summary Questions	**1** diesel, hydrocarbons, carbon, water (4 marks)
	2 heptane + oxygen → carbon dioxide + water (4 marks)
	3 QWC question (6 marks). Example answers:
	Cars are convenient. They can take you wherever you want, whenever you want. However, combustion of fuels produces carbon dioxide, which contributes to global warming. This leads to climate change, causing sea levels to rise and the frequency of floods and draughts to increase. At high engine temperatures, diesel-fuelled cars produce nitrogen dioxide, which causes acid rain. Acid rain damages trees, lake life, and limestone buildings. Diesel-fuelled cars also produce particulates. These can make asthma and chest infections worse. Particulates can lead to heart disease.
	Students should offer a final conclusion based on their previous points.

Starter	**Support/Extension**	**Resources**
What is a fuel? (5 min) Ask students to recap what a fuel is and to list as many fuels as they can, especially those that can be used to power cars. Fuels were introduced in C1.	**Support**: Images of coal, oil, and gas can be shown to students as prompts if required.	
Combustion products (10 min) Demonstrate the combustion of a fuel, such as ethanol or a candle, with products passing under reduced pressure through an inverted funnel, through a U-tube containing cobalt chloride paper, and finally into a test tube of limewater. Students should be able to give the products of complete and incomplete combustion in word equations.	**Extension**: Students give balanced formula equations for complete and incomplete combustion.	

Main	**Support/Extension**	**Resources**
What else is in exhaust fumes? (15 min) Briefly ask students to suggest the advantages of cars before asking them about the disadvantages, for example, is the combustion of petrol/diesel in cars the same as the complete combustion of any other hydrocarbon? Allow time for students to pair share their ideas before giving the answer. Introduce the other products of petrol/diesel combustion (nitrous oxides and hydrocarbon particulates) and their effects on health and the environment. Students should write word equations for the reactions that occur in car engines in their books.	**Support**: Remind students of complete and incomplete combustion and the key words pure and impure. **Extension**: Encourage students to write balanced formula equations for these reactions.	
Comparing air quality (25 min) Students plan an investigation to compare the air quality at different locations and answer the questions that follow. You may wish to introduce instrumental techniques for analysing air quality, for example, gas chromatography-mass spectrometry (GCMS).	**Support**: An access sheet is available where the hypothesis is already given, and prompts are given to guide students towards writing a method.	**Activity**: Comparing air quality **Skill sheet**: Planning investigations **Skill sheet**: Hypothesis **Skill sheet**: Recording results

Plenary	**Support/Extension**	**Resources**
Recalling exhaust equations (10 min) Ask students to write the word equations to describe what happens when fuels are burnt.	**Extension**: Students write balanced formula equations as well.	
Advantages and disadvantages of cars (5 min) Interactive resource where students categorise statements as advantages or disadvantages of using cars.	**Extension**: Students evaluate these points to give a conclusion.	**Interactive**: Advantages and disadvantages of cars

Homework		
Students produce a leaflet for an environmental campaign on why people should leave the car at home or car share more often. The leaflet should describe the advantages and disadvantages of using cars.	**Extension**: Students should include balanced formula equations where appropriate.	

KS3 Chemistry NC Link:

- chemical reactions
- energetics.

KS3 Working Scientifically NC Link:

- undertake basic data analysis.

KS4 Chemistry NC Link:

- recall that crude oil is a main source of hydrocarbons as fuel
- appreciate that crude oil is a finite resource
- compare the advantages and disadvantages of hydrogen/oxygen and other fuel cells for given uses.

Band	Outcome	Checkpoint	
		Question	Activity
Developing	State one advantage and one disadvantage of a new vehicle fuel (Level 3).	B, 3	Starter 1, Starter 2, Main 1, Plenary 1, Plenary 2, Homework
	Calculate the temperature rise of water caused by burning ethanol (Level 4).		Main 2
Secure	Describe the advantages and disadvantages of new vehicle fuels (Level 5).	3	Starter 1, Starter 2, Main 1, Plenary 1, Plenary 2, Homework
	Calculate the amount of energy transferred in a given scenario (Level 5).		Main 2
Extending	Discuss the advantages and disadvantages of new vehicle fuels in relation to wider global issues (Level 7).	4	Starter 1, Starter 2, Main 1, Plenary 1, Plenary 2, Homework
	Compare the given energy content of ethanol with the value calculated experimentally, suggesting reasons for any discrepancy (Level 8).		Main 2

Maths

Students plot bar charts to display data on energy transferred by the combustion of certain fuels in the student-book activity.

Students use experimental data to carry out energy calculations.

APP

Students carry out an experiment to investigate the energy content of ethanol, presenting results appropriately (AF3), use the data obtained in calculations (AF5), and suggest possible errors in the experimental procedure (AF5).

Key Words

hydrogen fuel cell, biofuel, renewable, carbon neutral

Answers from the student book

In-text questions	**A** A non-renewable fuel is one where it is used up more quickly than it is replaced.
	B Hydrogen fuel makes one harmless waste product – water.
	Hydrogen is difficult to store, mixtures of hydrogen and oxygen are explosive/hydrogen filling stations are uncommon/production of hydrogen fuel produces carbon dioxide.
	C A fuel made from plants or animal waste.
Activity	**Fuel chart**
	Bar chart with names of fuels on x-axis and y-axis labelled 'energy released on burning fuels (kJ/kg)'.
	The scale on the y-axis should be even, with points plotted correctly.

Summary Questions	
	1 fossil, renewable, cell, water, plant, waste, biofuels (7 marks)
	2 energy transferred = 5 × 38 kJ = 190 kJ (2 marks)
	3 Disadvantages: biofuels burn producing carbon dioxide/carbon dioxide is released by the tractors that are used to grow the crops for biofuel. Advantages: biofuels are renewable/some biofuels are liquid at ambient temperatures, making them relatively easy to store and transport. (2 marks)
	4 QWC question (6 marks) Example answers: A fuel is carbon neutral when the amount of carbon dioxides (CO_2) released into the atmosphere when it is burnt is the same as the amount of CO_2 absorbed by the fuel itself. This can be argued for some biofuels, such as plant oils. Plants take in carbon dioxide during photosynthesis. However, fossil fuels are used when producing fertilisers for the crops and fossil-fuel burning tractors are used by farmers. These release CO_2 into the atmosphere. It is unclear whether biofuels like these are truly carbon neutral because it is difficult to measure exactly the amounts of CO_2 absorbed and released by plants. However, we can be sure that the use of biofuels reduces the overall CO_2 released.

Starter	Support/Extension	Resources
Methane cars (10 min) Show a video of a methane-powered car. Students discuss the advantages and disadvantages of methane-powered cars and why alternative fuels are important. Videos are readily available on the Internet. **Can we use hydrogen as a fuel?** (5 min) Discuss with students hydrogen as a fuel. Explain that, whilst it only produces water when it burns, it does have disadvantages (few filling stations, forms explosive mix with oxygen so needs to be stored safely). You can demonstrate this by igniting a hydrogen balloon with a lit splint on a metre ruler from a safe distance. Warn students of the explosion beforehand.	**Support**: This task links this topic with previous knowledge of combustion, fossil fuels, and climate change. **Extension**: Encourage students to write word and balanced formula equations for this reaction.	

Main	Support/Extension	Resources
What other fuels are available? (10 min) Introduce the idea that other fuels are available for running cars than petrol and diesel (see starters above). Introduce the concept of biofuels. Discuss that biofuels are made from plants or animal waste, and that these are renewable as they can be easily replaced. However, most biofuels still work by burning hydrocarbons, and are harvested using petrol- or diesel-powered tractors.	**Support**: Focus on the definition of carbon neutral. **Extension**: Students should be able to discuss whether a fuel is truly carbon neutral.	
The energy content of fuels (30 min) Introduce students to the idea that different fuels transfer different amounts of energy to the surroundings per kilogram. Students then carry out a practical using an ethanol spirit burner and use their results to calculate the energy content of ethanol per kilogram in the questions that follow.	**Support**: The support sheet contains a results table to fill in, with hints to guide students through energy calculations. **Extension**: You may wish to introduce students to the bomb calorimeter.	**Practical**: The energy content of fuels **Skill sheet**: Recording results

Plenary	Support/Extension	Resources
Fuel sources (10 min) Interactive resource where students locate fuel sources in a wordsearch. For each fuel source, students give an advantage and a disadvantage of using it.	**Extension**: Students explain and justify the advantages and disadvantages given.	**Interactive**: Fuel sources
Advantages and disadvantages of alternative fuels (5 min) Give the names of some alternative fuel sources. For each fuel, students should name and explain one advantage and one disadvantage for this fuel.		

Homework		
Design your own machine (vehicle/household appliance) that will run on alternative fuels. Explain the concept behind how the machine works on this fuel and analyse the advantages and disadvantages of this fuel source.		

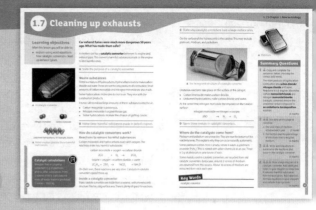

KS3 Chemistry NC Link:
- atoms, elements, and compounds
- chemical reactions
- materials.

KS3 Working Scientifically NC Link:
- interpret observations and data, including identifying patterns and using observations, measurements, and data to draw conclusions.

KS4 Chemistry NC Link:
- explain oxidation and reduction in terms of loss or gain of oxygen
- use of transition metals as catalysts
- describe the characteristics of catalysts and their effect on rates of reaction
- identify catalysts in reactions.

Band	Outcome	Checkpoint	
		Question	Activity
Developing	Name the substances that are converted by a catalytic converter (Level 3).	B, 1	Starter 2, Main 1, Plenary 1, Homework
	Use data to identify one car that has failed its emissions test (Level 3).		Main 2
Secure	Explain using word equations how catalytic converters clean up exhaust gases (Level 6).	3	Main 1, Main 2, Plenary 1, Homework
	Interpret data to identify cars that have failed their emissions tests, giving reasons (Level 6).		Main 2
Extending	Explain how catalytic converters clean up exhaust gases using balanced formula equations (Level 7).	4	Main 2, Plenary 1, Homework
	Suggest reasons why the cars identified may have failed their emissions tests (Level 8).		Main 2

Maths
Students convert between units in the students-book activity on waste material produce from metal ores and between fractions and percentages.

Students interpret numerical data provided to decide if cars in question have passed their emissions tests.

APP
Students interpret data presented in the activity regarding exhaust emissions from different cars (AF5).

Key Words
catalytic converter

Answers from the student book

In-text questions	**A** To convert harmful substances made in the engine into less harmful ones.
	B carbon monoxide, nitrogen monoxide, unburnt hydrocarbons
	C So that there is plenty of space for reactions to occur. **D** platinum, rhodium, palladium
Activity	**Catalyst calculations**
	3 t = 3 × 1000 kg = 3000 kg 3000 kg = 3000 × 1000 g = 3 000 000 g
	So mass of waste = 3 000 000 g − 15 g = 2 999 985 g

Summary Questions	**1** carbon dioxide, monoxide, monoxide, an oxidation (4 marks)
	2a total mass of rhodium = 2 t + 16 t = 18 t (1 mark)
	  b fraction of rhodium obtained from recycled sources = 2 t ÷ 18 t = $\frac{1}{9}$
	    percentage of rhodium from recycled sources = $\frac{1}{9} \times 100$ = 11% (4 marks)
	3 carbon monoxide + oxygen → carbon dioxide
	  unburnt hydrocarbon + oxygen → carbon dioxide + water
	  nitrogen monoxide → nitrogen + oxygen (3 marks)
	4 Diagram to show the following (6 marks):
	  honeycomb structure (made from a ceramic), catalyst on surface of honeycomb structure, catalysts (labelled platinum, rhodium, and palladium), label to show carbon monoxide oxidised to carbon dioxide, label to show unburnt hydrocarbons oxidised to carbon dioxide and water, and label to show nitrogen monoxide decomposed on the surface of the catalyst to make nitrogen and oxygen.
	  Balanced formula equations should also be included, for example:
	  $2\ CO(g) + O_2(g) \rightarrow 2\ CO_2(g)$
	  $C_9H_{20}(g) + 14\ O_2(g) \rightarrow 9\ CO_2(g) + 10\ H_2O(g)$
	  $2\ NO(g) \rightarrow N_2(g) + O_2(g)$
	  Allow (g) or (l) for the named hydrocarbon and H_2O.

Starter	Support/Extension	Resources
What is a catalytic converter? (5 min) Display a cross-section of a catalytic converter showing its honeycomb structure. Ask students what the image shows and where these are found.		
The contents of exhaust fumes (10 min) In small groups, students produce a list of substances they think are found in exhaust fumes. Then discuss the harmful substances found and how catalytic converters reduce the amount of these gases emitted into the atmosphere.	**Support**: This task offers students a chance to consolidate knowledge from C3 1.5.	

Main	Support/Extension	Resources
How do catalytic converters work? (15 min) Introduce the concept of the catalytic converter using a diagram. Display an image of the cross-sectional honeycomb structure on the board and make photocopies of this image for students to annotate. Discuss why catalytic converters are needed, give a description of how they work, and give word equations for the reactions that occur.	**Extension**: Students should write balanced formula equations for the reactions that take place, describing these as oxidation or reduction reactions.	
Vehicle emissions (25 min) Students work through an activity where they must interpret numerical data to decide if the cars tested have passed their emissions tests, label a diagram of the catalytic converter, and answer questions that follow.	**Support**: Students may need to be reminded that, when writing chemical formulae, Co (cobalt) is different from CO (carbon monoxide).	**Activity**: Vehicle emissions

Plenary	Support/Extension	Resources
True or false? (10 min) Interactive resource where students categorise statements on catalytic converters as true or false. Students summarise the reactions in catalytic converters using word equations on mini-whiteboards.	**Extension**: Reactions should be written as balanced formula equations.	**Interactive**: True or false?
Common catalysts (5 min) Students recall the different substances that are commonly used as catalysts in catalytic converters, and where these may be obtained.		

Homework		
Students produce a leaflet that garages can hand out to customers that explains what catalytic converters are, how they work, and why they are necessary. Word equations should be included.	**Extension**: Students should include balanced formula equations.	

KS3 Chemistry NC Link:
- earth and atmosphere.

KS3 Physics NC Link:
- calculation of fuel uses and costs in the domestic context
- energy changes and transfers.

KS3 Working Scientifically NC Link:
- apply mathematical concepts and calculate results.

KS4 Chemistry NC Link:
- compare the advantages and disadvantages of hydrogen/oxygen and other fuel cells for given uses.

KS4 Physics NC Link:
- explain, with examples, that there is no net change to the total energy of a closed system.

Band	Outcome	Checkpoint	
		Question	Activity
Developing	State the amount of fuel that hybrid vehicles use compared to vehicles fuelled solely by petrol (Level 3).		Lit, Main, Plenary 1, Homework
	State one advantage and one disadvantage of hybrid vehicles (Level 3).	B, 1	Lit, Main, Plenary 2, Homework
	Use data provided to identify the type of car that uses less fuel over a certain distance (Level 3).		Main
Secure	Explain why hybrid electric cars use less fuel than cars fuelled by petrol alone (Level 6).	2	Lit, Main, Plenary 1, Homework
	Compare the advantages and disadvantages of different types of car (Level 5).	3	Lit, Main, Plenary 2, Homework
	Calculate the distances a hybrid and a petrol-fuelled car will travel given £60 of fuel (Level 6).		Main
Extending	Use fuel consumption data to calculate the payback time of buying a hybrid vehicle (Level 7).		Main, Homework
	Compare the efficiency of different types of cars (Level 8).		Main, Homework
	Quantitatively compare the advantages and disadvantages of using different types of cars (Level 8).		Main, Homework

Maths
Students interpret numerical data about different types of vehicles and use these to quantitatively compare the types of vehicles discussed.

Literacy
Students organise ideas and adapt language to suit the general public to explain the advantages of electric and hybrid vehicles in the student-book activity and for their homework.

APP
Students select appropriate data to use in calculations, using answers to inform a conclusion (AF5).

Key Words
hybrid electric car

Answers from the student book

In-text questions	**A** A car with an internal combustion engine and a battery.
	B Advantage: no pollution as it moves/quiet. Disadvantage: travels short distance between charges/slow to charge/electricity used to charge battery may have been generated from fossil fuels. **C** a generator
Activity	**Comparing cars**
	Web pages clearly show advantages and disadvantages of electric and hybrid electric cars.
	Images of electric and hybrid vehicles required. These do not need to be labeled or annotated.
Summary questions	**1** combustion, battery, hybrid, less, less (5 marks)
	2 Electric cars do not make pollution when they move and are quiet, but are slow to charge, travel short distances between charges, and fossil fuels may have been used to generate the electricity to charge them. Petrol cars are quick to refill and travel further per tank of fuel, but make pollution and are nosiy. (4 marks)
	3 Examples of scientific points that should be included in their visual summary (6 marks):
	Hybrid cars travel further than petrol cars on a certain amount of fuel. This means hybrid cars produce less carbon dioxide and other forms of pollution while they are running. Hybrid cars are cheaper to run (lower fuel requirement). Hybrid cars may use regenerative braking, meaning that kinetic energy is used to recharge the battery when the car slows down. This cannot happen in a petrol-fuelled car. Hybrid cars can switch off their engine at a red light, so they are quieter. However, hybrid cars contain nickel-metal hydride batteries that may cause cancer. The electricity used by hybrid cars may have been generated using fossil fuels, also contributing to pollution. Hybrid cars are also slow to charge, and require charging after short distances.

kerboodle

Starter	Support/Extension	Resources
An alternative question-led lesson is also available.		**Question-led lesson**: Hybrid electric cars
What is a hybrid car? (10 min) Ask students what they know about hybrid cars. Discuss how hybrid cars combine the combustion of fuel with the use of batteries, and how this has advantages and disadvantages.	**Support**: Dispel any misconceptions at the earliest opportunity. Students may have difficulty understanding the difference between batteries in traditional vehicles and batteries in electric cars.	
What makes a vehicle move? (5 min) Show images of traditional and hybrid cars. Students spot the differences. Briefly explain how they work. The transmission is powered by a fuel-powered engine in traditional cars, and by a battery supported by fuel combustion in hybrid electric cars.		

Main	Support/Extension	Resources
Hybrid vehicles (40 minutes) Introduce the hybrid electric car, explaining the different types available, how they work, and how these differ from traditional petrol/diesel vehicles. Ask students to pair share ideas of the advantages and disadvantages of hybrid cars before giving the answer in a class discussion. Students then use the data given on the activity sheet to answer the questions that follow. Encourage students to consider the validity of the data presented.	**Support**: Prompt students to think about other factors that may influence the running costs of the car, for example, tax and insurance. **Extension**: Students give other factors affecting fuel consumption (e.g., weather and road conditions.)	**Activity**: Hybrid vehicles

Plenary	Support/Extension	Resources
Differences between a traditional and a hybrid vehicle (5 min) Interactive resource where students categorise statements as describing hybrid vehicles, traditional vehicles, or both. Students then highlight the main difference to explain why hybrid vehicles consume less fuel.	**Support**: Students work in groups. **Extension**: Students reorder statements for hybrid cars to describe how they work.	**Interactive**: Differences between a traditional and a hybrid vehicle
Advantages and disadvantages (10 min) Either give out or call out advantages and disadvantages of petrol and hybrid electric cars. Students indicate if the statements are advantages or disadvantages.	**Extension**: Students give a short explanation justifying their choice.	

Homework		
Students use activity sheet to prepare a report of hybrid cars versus traditional cars. Include a brief description of how each car works, and the advantages and disadvantages. Place emphasis on fuel consumption.	**Extension**: Discuss and compare quantitatively other hybrid vehicles, for example, series, parallel, mild, full hybrids, and PHEVs.	
An alternative WebQuest homework activity is also available on Kerboodle where students research hybrid electric cars.		**WebQuest**: Hybrid electric cars

Checkpoint lesson routes

The route through this lesson can be determined using the Checkpoint assessment.

Percentage pass marks are supplied in the Checkpoint teacher notes.

Route A (revision)

Resource: C3 Chapter 1 Checkpoint: Revision

Students work through a series of tasks that allows them to revisit and consolidate their understanding of nanoparticles, different types of vehicles, and alternative fuels. Students can keep this as a summary of the topic, and use this when revising for future assessments.

Route B (extension)

Resource: C3 Chapter 1 Checkpoint: Extension

Students design a revision poster for a KS3 revision series that must include a visual summary of the key concepts covered in this topic.

Progression to *secure*

No.	Developing outcome	Secure outcome	Making progress
1	State what nanoparticles are.	Explain what nanoparticles are.	In Task 1 students link halves of sentences together to explain what nanoparticles are.
2	State a property of nanoparticles.	Describe the properties of nanoparticles.	In Task 1 students link halves of sentences together to describe some of the properties of nanoparticles.
3	Give three properties of carbon nanotubes.	Explain how the properties of nanoparticles make them suitable for their uses.	In Task 1 students use the properties of nanoparticles to explain why nanoparticles are used to make bicycle frames and wind turbine components.
4	State one use of nanoparticles in medicine.	Describe how nanoparticles are used in medical treatments.	In Task 2 students complete a word fill, reorder statements, and link sentences together to describe three uses of nanoparticles in medicine.
5	State one example of where nanoparticle safety has been considered.	Describe an example of how scientists are investigating nanoparticle safety.	In Task 3 students are required to describe one possible method of nanoparticle safety given the context of nanoparticle sunscreens.
6	State the products of combustion.	Explain how combustion reactions in car engines produce exhaust gases.	In Task 4 students write a word equation to show the combustion of dodecane in petrol.
7	Give one advantage and one disadvantage of cars.	Describe some advantages and disadvantages of cars.	In Task 6 students draw a visual summary to compare the advantages and disadvantages of using different types of vehicles.
8	State one advantage and one disadvantage of a new vehicle fuel.	Describe the advantages and disadvantages of new vehicle fuels.	In Task 5 students read statements about new vehicles fuels to decide if they are advantages or disadvantages, true or false, correcting those that are false.
9	State the substances that are converted by a catalytic convertor.	Explain using word equations how catalytic converters clean up exhaust gases.	In Task 4 students write word equations to show how a catalytic converter converts CO, NO, and hydrocarbon particulates into less harmful substances.
10	State the amount of fuel that hybrid vehicles use compared to vehicles fuelled solely by petrol.	Explain why hybrid electric cars use less fuel than cars fuelled by petrol alone.	In Task 6 students draw a visual summary to compare the advantages and disadvantages of using different types of vehicles, in particular explaining why hybrid electric cars use less fuel than cars fuelled by petrol alone.
11	State one advantage and one disadvantage of hybrid vehicles.	Compare the advantages and disadvantages of different types of car.	In Task 6 students draw a visual summary to compare the advantages and disadvantages of using different types of vehicles.

Answers to end-of-chapter questions

1 The only statement that is true: 100 g of a nanoparticle substance has a greater surface area than 100 g of the same substance as normal-sized pieces. (3 marks)

2 biofuel, maize/sugar cane, maize/sugar cane, carbon dioxide, carbon dioxide/water, carbon dioxide/water (6 marks)

3a QuickClot became hot when in contact with blood or water. This caused burns to those using gauzes with added QuickClot. (2 marks)

b aluminosilicate nanoparticles (1 mark)

c The nanoparticles present in kaolin clay will not enter the body because they get trapped at the site of the injury. (1 mark)

4a Compound made from hydrogen and carbon atoms only. (1 mark)

b carbon dioxide and water (2 marks)

c hexadecane + oxygen → carbon dioxide + water (2 marks)

d 16 carbon atoms and 34 hydrogen atoms (2 marks)

e 141 MJ (2 marks)

5 This is a QWC question. Students should be marked on the use of good English, organisation of information, spelling and grammar, and correct use of specialist scientific terms. The best answers will fully explain how catalytic converters make car exhaust fumes less harmful (maximum of 6 marks).
Examples of correct scientific points:
One waste product in car exhaust fumes is carbon monoxide, a poisonous gas.
The catalysts in catalytic converters help oxidise carbon monoxide to carbon dioxide.
Although carbon dioxide is a greenhouse gas, it is not toxic.
Car exhaust fumes also include nitrogen monoxide, a greenhouse gas.
Catalysts in catalytic converters help decompose nitrogen monoxide on its surface, forming nitrogen and oxygen.
These gases are naturally present in the air in large quantities.
Unburnt hydrocarbons are also present in car exhaust fumes. These may increase the risk of developing cancer.
Catalysts in catalytic converters help oxidise unburnt hydrocarbons to form less harmful products – carbon dioxide and water.
Common catalysts in catalytic converters include platinum, palladium, and rhodium.

Answer guide for Maths Challenge

Developing	Secure	Extending
1–2 marks	3–4 marks	5–6 marks
• Correctly calculated emissions for one or two travel options (air = 571.2 kg, train = 178.08 kg, coach = 100.8 kg, petrol car = 126 kg, hybrid car = 41.16 kg), or a similar error made in each calculation resulting in all calculations being incorrect. • Reasonable recommendation based on data but not accompanied by supporting sentences.	• Correctly calculated emissions for two or more travel options (air = 571.2 kg, train = 178.08 kg, coach = 100.8 kg, petrol car = 126 kg, hybrid car = 41.16 kg), or a similar error made in each calculation resulting in all calculations being incorrect. • Reasonable recommendation based on data with one or two supporting sentences.	• Correctly calculated emissions for all travel options (air = 571.2 kg, train = 178.08 kg, coach = 100.8 kg, petrol car = 126 kg, hybrid car = 41.16 kg). • The data shows that taking the journey by hybrid car produces the smallest mass of carbon dioxide for the family. • However, this mass of carbon dioxide is in addition to that which would be produced anyway by coaches, trains, and aeroplanes travelling from Exeter to Newcastle. • So one possible recommendation is to travel by coach, since this results in the smallest amount of CO_2 emission for the family when using public transport.

C3 Chapter 1 Checkpoint assessment (automarked)	C3 Chapter 1 Checkpoint: Extension
C3 Chapter 1 Checkpoint: Revision	C3 Chapter 1 Progress task (Maths)

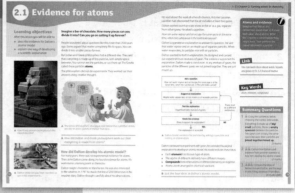

KS3 Chemistry NC Link:
- atoms, elements, and compounds.

KS3 Working Scientifically NC Link:
- interpret observations and data, including identifying patterns and using observations, measurements, and data to draw conclusions.

KS4 Chemistry NC Link:
- describe how and why the atomic model has changed over time.

Band	Outcome	Checkpoint	
		Question	Activity
Developing	State what Dalton found out about the nature of particles (Level 3).	B	Lit, Main 1, Plenary 1, Homework
	Describe how Dalton's work was influenced by other scientists (Level 4).	2	Main 1, Plenary 1, Homework
↓	Record observations from an experiment to test one of Dalton's ideas (Level 4).		Main 2
Secure	Describe evidence for Dalton's atomic model (Level 5).	2, 3	Lit, Main 1, Main 2, Plenary 1, Homework
	Explain one way of developing a scientific explanation (Level 6).	3	Plenary 1, Plenary 2
↓	Use observations from an experiment to draw conclusions about one of Dalton's ideas (Level 6).		Main 2
Extending	Explain how Dalton used his experiments as evidence in developing his atomic model (Level 7).	3	Lit, Main 2, Plenary 1, Homework
	Compare the ideas of Democritus, Lavoisier, and Dalton in developing the atomic model (Level 7).	3	Plenary 1, Homework
↓	Use observations to draw conclusions about one of Dalton's ideas, suggesting how the experiment can be adapted to find out more about particles (Level 8).		Main 2

Maths
Students arrange the discoveries of different scientists that contributed to the formulation of Dalton's atomic model in chronological order using a timeline.

Literacy
In the student-book activity students write a script for a possible conversation between Dalton and Democritus about their ideas on the atomic model.

APP
Students carry out an experiment to test one of Dalton's ideas, recording observations (AF4), interpreting and presenting this data (AF3) to draw conclusions (AF5).

Key Words
atom, element, compound

Answers from the student book

In-text questions	**A** They used creative thought.
	B Each element has its own type of atom, the atoms of different elements have different masses, compounds form when atoms of different elements join together, and atoms are rearranged in chemical reactions.
Activity	**Atoms and evidence**
	Script to include the ideas of Dalton and Democritus, including the point that Dalton found experimental evidence for atoms, while Democritus did not carry out experiments. He worked out his answers using creative thought.

Summary Questions	
	1 small, empty space, mixed up (3 marks)
	2 Dalton read about the work of Lavoisier, who had discovered that air includes two gases. The discovery got Dalton thinking about how the gases in air could be mixed up, and encouraged Dalton to carry out experiments of his own. (2 marks)
	3 QWC question (6 marks). Example answers: Democritus and Dalton both stated that everything is made from atoms. Democritus worked out his ideas using creative thought alone. Dalton collected experimental evidence to support his ideas. When developing and planning his investigation, Dalton drew on evidence from other scientists, including Lavoisier. Lavoisier had already discovered that air contains a mixture of gases. Dalton developed his model further than Democritus, for example, by pointing out that water vapour and air are made of separate particles, which mix together when water evaporates.

kerboodle

Starter	Support/Extension	Resources
How do we find out about things we cannot see? (10 min) Provide students with everyday objects hidden inside a sealed box or bag. Students try to find out as much as they can about the object without opening the sealed container. Discuss how early scientists investigated atoms despite not being able to see them.	**Support**: Students may require a reminder of what an atom is.	
Looking at atoms (5 min) Show students an image of an atom as captured by an electron microscope. Ask students to suggest what the image shows before providing the answer. Introduce the idea that most of our knowledge about atoms came about before technology was available, and ask students to suggest how this was possible.	**Support**: Encourage students to think about Greek philosophers as a starting point. **Extension**: Steer students towards the scientific process of building on previous ideas from other scientists.	

Main	Support/Extension	Resources
Who has shaped our understanding of the atom? (10 min) Introduce the story of the discovery of the atom, from the Greeks (ca. 500 BC) who coined the term 'atomos' for 'indivisible', to the contributions of Lavoisier (1700) and Dalton (ca. 1800). This can be done as a matching exercise, where students are given the scientists, dates, and a description of their contribution on sort cards. Students should then match these and present the information on a timeline in their books. (If time is short, sort cards can be stuck into exercise books.)	**Support**: Scientists and their dates can be given to students so they only focus on matching the correct descriptions. **Extension**: Students compare the ideas of scientists and explain how scientific ideas are developed by building on previous work and using peer review.	
Is there space between particles? (30 min) Students carry out two short experiments and use their observations to test whether there is space between particles. Students then answer questions that follow.	**Support**: You may wish to recap the diffusion before beginning Experiment 2 in this practical.	**Activity**: Is there space between particles?

Plenary	Support/Extension	Resources
Ordering atomic events (5 min) Students reorder sentences provided on the interactive resource to place the role of different scientists in the development of the atomic model in chronological order.	**Extension**: Students describe the work of each scientist, explaining the process of developing a scientific explanation.	**Interactive**: Ordering atomic events
Developing a scientific explanation (10 min) Students work in small groups to prepare and present a short role play that illustrates the steps required in developing a scientific explanation.	**Support**: Students may wish to use the flow chart on the corresponding student-book page as a starting point.	

Homework		
Students write a paragraph for a science history magazine about the importance of Dalton's work. This article should include a description of the experimental data Dalton used to develop his atomic model.	**Extension**: Students include how Dalton's ideas differed from those of Lavoisier and Democritus.	

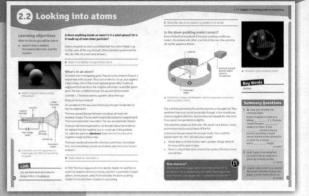

2.2 Looking into atoms

KS3 Chemistry NC Link:

- atoms, elements, and compounds.

KS3 Working Scientifically NC Link:

- present reasoned explanations, including explaining data in relation to predictions and hypotheses.

KS4 Chemistry NC Link:

- describe how and why the atomic model has changed over time
- describe the atom as a positively charged nucleus surrounded by negatively charged electrons, with the nuclear radius much smaller than that of the atom and with most of the mass in the nucleus
- recall relative charges and approximate relative masses of protons, neutrons, and electrons.

Band	Outcome	Checkpoint	
		Question	Activity
Developing	State what Dalton, Thompson, and Rutherford discovered about the atom (Level 4).	A, C, 1	Main, Plenary 1, Homework
	Make a model of an atom based on one of Dalton's, Thomson's, or Rutherford's ideas (Level 4).		Main
Secure	Explain how scientists discovered electrons and the nucleus (Level 6).	2, 3	Plenary 1, Homework
	Make a model of an atom based on one of Dalton's, Thomson's, or Rutherford's ideas, explaining key features (Level 6).		Main
Extending	Compare the findings of Dalton, Thompson, and Rutherford (Level 8).	3	Plenary 1, Homework
	Make a model of an atom based on one of the three scientists' ideas, explaining key features, including strengths and weaknesses of the model (Level 8).		Main, Plenary 2

Maths
Students calculate the mass of an electron compared with the mass of an oxygen atom's nucleus using simple division.

Literacy
Students organise their ideas when writing information cards about their atomic models, communicating and presenting this information to their audience.

APP
Students use models to describe and explain the structure of the atom (AF1), communicating their ideas in the most appropriate manner (AF3).

Key Words
electron

Answers from the student book

In-text questions	**A** As a billiard ball. **B** A tiny particle that is a part of an atom. It has a negative charge and a tiny mass. **C** In an atom there is a positively charged sphere in which negative electrons are moving around.
Activity	**How massive?** mass of oxygen atom nucleus = 16 mass of electron = 0.0005 16 ÷ 0.0005 = 32 000 The mass of an oxygen atom nucleus is 32 000 times greater than the mass of an electron.

Summary Questions	1 ball, pudding, negative, nucleus, positive (5 marks)
	2 Rutherford and colleagues fired positive particles at a piece of gold foil. Most particles went straight through the foil, through the empty space. A few particles bounced backwards from the foil, which surprised Rutherford. These particles must have bounced off a positively charged central nucleus that contains most of the mass of the atom. (4 marks)
	3 Chart should include the following (6 marks):
	Billiard ball model (Dalton): Atoms are unique to each element. An atom is like a billiard ball and cannot be broken up.
	Plum pudding model (Thomson): A positively charged sphere with negative electrons moving around in it. Deduced from Thomson's experiment with cathode rays/charged gases that glowed. Cathode rays were negative, and originated from the atom. This meant that there must be a positive part of the atom.
	Planetary model (Rutherford, Geiger, and Marsden): Atoms have a central positively charged nucleus that contains almost all of the mass. The rest of the atom is empty space, where electrons orbit the nucleus. Evidence for this model was observed when firing positive (α) particles at gold foil, when a few particles curiously bounced back off the foil, back in the original direction that the particle was fired from.

Starter	Support/Extension	Resources
Atomic key words (5 min) Students find key words that they will meet in this lesson in a wordsearch on the interactive resource. Students should be able to give definitions of words they have met before, for example, atom.	**Extension**: Encourage students to use the words on the wordsearch as clues to suggest what this lesson may be about.	**Interactive**: Atomic key words
Evidence for atoms (10 min) Students recap the evidence for the existence of atoms that they met in C1. This starter can be used as a revision exercise for the following key words: atom, particle, element, compound, mixture.	**Support**: Ensure that any misconceptions that arise during this activity are corrected.	

Main	Support/Extension	Resources
Modelling the atom (40 min) Show students an animation of the atomic structure we know today (the Bohr model). Ask students to identify the nucleus and the electrons on a diagram. This diagram can be given in the form of a printout so that students can stick this in and annotate it with properties of the nucleus and the electron (charge and relative mass). Introduce the work of Dalton, Thompson, and Rutherford towards the development of the present-day atomic model (billiard ball, plum pudding, and the gold-foil experiment). Students then use craft materials provided to make one of the three atomic models discussed this lesson, together with accompanying notes to explain their models. Students should then present their models to each other if time.	**Support**: The support sheet provides students with the key features of each model. Students should focus on Rutherford's model to avoid misconceptions as they progress to KS4. **Extension**: Introduce students to protons and neutrons, the use of α particles in Rutherford's experiment, and that α particles rebounded because of mass and because of repulsion between like charges.	**Activity**: Modelling the atom

Plenary	Support/Extension	Resources
Revisiting atomic words (10 min) Display the key words from the interactive wordsearch once more. This time, ask students to give the definition of every key word. Students should be encouraged to write sentences that use as many of these words as possible.	**Extension**: Students' sentences should chronologically retell the development of the present-day atomic model.	
Evaluating models (5 min) Students choose one model available from this lesson (either theirs or one from another group). Each student must then offer one strength and one opportunity for improvement in the model chosen.	**Explanation**: Students justify their comments using scientific knowledge.	

Homework		
Students produce a comic strip that tells the story of how scientists discovered electrons and the nucleus.		

KS3 Chemistry NC Link:

- the particulate nature of matter
- atoms, elements, and compounds
- the Periodic Table.

KS3 Working Scientifically NC Link:

- interpret observations and data, including identifying patterns and using observations, measurements, and data to draw conclusions.

KS4 Chemistry NC Link:

- show understanding that the Periodic Table allows predictions to be made about how elements might react
- predict reactions and reactivity of elements from their positions in the Periodic Table
- distinguish between metals and non-metals on the basis of their characteristic physical and chemical properties
- relate the atomic structure of metals and non-metals to their position in the Periodic Table.

Band	Outcome	Checkpoint	
		Question	Activity
Developing	Name the scientist who devised the Periodic Table (Level 3).	A, 1	Plenary 1, Plenary 2
	Name the scientists involved in the discovery of rhenium (Level 3).	C	Plenary 1, Plenary 2
	Use atomic mass data to order elements according to increasing atomic mass (Level 3).		Main
Secure	Describe how Mendeleev devised the Periodic Table (Level 5).	1	Main, Plenary 1, Plenary 2
	Describe how Tacke and Noddack discovered rhenium (Level 5).	2	Plenary 1, Plenary 2
	Use the chemical and physical properties of different elements to arrange them according to atomic masses and properties (Level 5).		Main
Extending	Explain how Mendeleev devised his Periodic Table, and why he left gaps in it (Level 7).	3	Main, Plenary 1, Plenary 2
	Compare how Tacke and Noddack discovered rhenium with the discovery of another element (Level 8).		Homework
	Use data obtained about elements to arrange them according to their properties, using this to explain how Mendeleev devised his Periodic Table (Level 7).		Main

Maths

Students use the idea of number size and scale when comparing the atomic masses of elements.

Literacy

In the student-book activity students organise ideas and information to write a script for Mendeleev, explaining his discovery of the Periodic Table.

Students also interpret meaning in scientific texts and summarise information from a range of different sources when researching different elements and how they were discovered.

APP

Students use data about different elements to draw conclusions (AF5).

Key Words

Periodic Table, catalyst

Answers from the student book

In-text questions	**A** Mendeleev **B** He left gaps for elements he thought existed but had not been discovered. **C** (Ida) Tacke, (Walter) Noddack, and (Otto) Berg
Activity	**Mendeleev's musings** Script to include the following main points about the first Periodic Table: elements arranged in order of atomic mass, elements with similar properties grouped together, gaps left for elements that Mendeleev predicted should exist but that had not yet been discovered. The script should convey Mendeleev's excitement and confidence.
Summary Questions	**1** masses, physical, oxygen, mass, similar (5 marks) **2** Tacke and Noddack extracted 1 g of a new substance from 660 kg of an ore. They thought that this substance might be one of the missing elements under manganese on the Periodic Table (that was not yet discovered). They asked Berg to do tests on the substance to confirm its identity. (This is like peer review. Tacke and Noddack asked a different scientist to check the reproducibility of their work.) (3 marks) **3** QWC question (6 marks). Example answers: Mendeleev obtained atomic mass data from Cannizzaro. Mendeleev then made a set of cards, one for each element. He tried sorting the cards in different ways. He came up with an arrangement that worked – by arranging the cards in atomic mass order. Mendeleev grouped elements with similar properties. Mendeleev left gaps for elements he predicted should exist but that had not yet been discovered. These were later confirmed when scientists discovered the missing elements.

Starter	Support/Extension	Resources
The elements song (10 min) Give students a Periodic Table and play the elements song by Tom Lehrer (it is readily available on the Internet). Ask students if there is a pattern in the song (there is not) and the patterns of the Periodic Table. Students have met the Periodic Table in C1 and C2.	**Support**: Students may require a recap of the term element before the discussion.	
Who was Mendeleev? (5 min) Introduce Mendeleev as the scientist who devised the Periodic Table. If a full Periodic Table is available, ask students to find the element that has is named in his honour (mendelevium, Md).	**Extension**: Ask students to recap patterns in the Periodic Table.	
Main	**Support/Extension**	**Resources**
Devising the Periodic Table (35 min) Introduce Mendeleev's discovery of the Periodic Table. Explain that prior to it, there was lots of information about the properties of elements, but they were not ordered into a useable fashion. Tell students how Mendeleev left gaps in the Periodic Table for missing elements he thought had not yet been discovered, and predicted the properties of these missing elements based on the patterns in the Periodic Table. Mendeleev was correct and these elements have since been discovered. Specific emphasis should be placed on the discovery of rhenium. Students then research properties of 10 elements and group these according to their patterns, to copy Mendeleev's method in devising the Periodic Table.	**Support**: The accompanying support sheet offers students partially completed information cards to use in their task.	**Activity:** Devising the Periodic Table
Plenary	**Support/Extension**	**Resources**
Mendeleev statements (10 min) Interactive resource where students decide if statements on Mendeleev and the Periodic Table are true or false.	**Extension**: Ask students why Mendeleev left gaps.	**Interactive**: Mendeleev statements
True or false? (15 min) Give students a minute to write either a true or false statement on what they have learnt today. Students take turns to read out their statement, and the class decides if it is true or false. Additional statements can be added to ensure lesson outcomes are met.	**Extension**: Students correct statements that are false, explaining their answers.	
Homework		
Write a detailed account of how Tacke and Noddack discovered rhenium. This can be done in the form of a letter or scientific paper.	**Extension**: Students choose another element's discovery and compare to the discovery of rhenium	
An alternative WebQuest homework activity is also available on Kerboodle where students research the discovery of oxygen.		**WebQuest**: Discovery of oxygen

KS3 Chemistry NC Link:

● Earth and atmosphere.

KS3 Working Scientifically NC Link:

● present reasoned explanations, including explaining data in relation to predictions and hypotheses.

KS4 Biology NC Link:

● evaluate the evidence for evolution to include fossils and antibiotic resistance in bacteria.

Band	Outcome	Checkpoint	
		Question	Activity
Developing	State what is meant by a fossil (Level 3).	A, 1	Main, Plenary 1
	State one thing that can be deduced from fossil evidence and data (Level 3).	B	Main, Plenary 1
↓	Draw diagrams to represent the stages of fossil formation (Level 4).		Main
Secure	Describe how fossils are formed (Level 5).	2	Main, Plenary 2
	Explain what fossils tell us about the age of rocks (Level 6).	3	Main, Plenary 1
↓	Draw annotated diagrams to describe in detail how fossils are formed (Level 6).		Main
Extending	Suggest why fossils are generally only found in one rock type (Level 7).	3	Starter 2, Main, Plenary 1
	Suggest how fossils can be used to provide evidence for the evolution of a species (Level 7).	3	Main, Plenary 1
↓	Draw a series of annotated diagrams to describe how fossils are formed, using this to explain other areas of science (Level 8).		Main

Literacy

Students organise ideas and scientific information when carrying out the student-book activity and when designing a poster about fossils.

Students approach the task of drawing diagrams to describe the formation of fossils by creating a structural plan beforehand.

APP

Students present the formation of fossils as a series of annotated diagrams (AF3). They use observations from fossils to support the theory of evolution (AF1) and draw conclusions (AF5).

Key Words

fossil, strata, index fossil

Answers from the student book

In-text questions	**A** Fossils are the remains, or traces, of plants or animals that lived many years ago. They have been preserved by natural processes. **B** The relative age of a rock.
Activity	**Explaining explanations** Flow diagrams should include the following stages: Asking a question – why do different rock strata contain different fossils? Suggesting an explanation – perhaps rock strata of the same age always contain fossils of the same species Testing the explanation – evidence collected by making observations in rocks of different ages and in different places.

Summary Questions	1 traces, plants, natural, sedimentary, strata (5 marks)
	2 An animal dies and is covered by mud or sand. Bacteria break down the soft tissues of the organism. The mud or sand surrounding the skeleton becomes rock. Minerals from underground water replace those in the skeleton, leaving a fossil. (4 marks)
	3 Poster should include the following scientific points (6 marks): how fossils were made different types of rocks understanding the relationship between different strata and geological ages diet of extinct species evolution of species.

Starter	Support/Extension	Resources
An alternative question-led lesson is also available. **Looking at fossils** (10 min) Pass a selection of fossils around the class and ask students to observe what they can and whether they recognise any organisms present. Ask students to suggest what fossils are and how they may have been formed. **Properties of rocks** (10 min) Ask students to recap the three types of rock. Students should give properties of each type and the conditions in which these rocks form, focusing in particular on sedimentary rock (to lead into how fossils are made).	**Extension**: Encourage students to suggest what may happen to the body of a dead animal during the formation of these rocks.	**Question-led lesson**: Lessons from fossils

Main	Support/Extension	Resources
Evidence from fossils (35 min) Introduce students to the following key points about fossils: what they are, how they are formed, and what they tell us about geological periods, including what index fossils found in different strata of sedimentary rock can tell us about the different geological time periods. The scientific method of William Smith should also be discussed. (This is presented in the student book.) These ideas can be extremely abstract to students, so you may wish to use an example to give students context, for example, by showing students a photograph of a cliff-face at Lyme Regis to exemplify strata in sedimentary rock. Explain to students how the Earth's history can be split into geological time frames and that these time frames have their own index fossils (fossils unique to that age). Students then carry out an activity where they draw a series of annotated diagrams to show how fossils are formed and answer the questions that follow.	**Support**: A support sheet is provided where students are given a series of statements about the formation of fossils to reorder as a starting point when drawing annotated diagrams.	**Activity**: Evidence from fossils

Plenary	Support/Extension	Resources
Fossil facts (10 min) Students match key words to their definitions using the interactive resource. Students should then write a short paragraph to link these words together. **Fossil analogies** (10 min) Tell students about one analogy of how fossils are formed, for example, a chest full of old photographs, with photographs at the bottom of a person aged one and newer photographs at the top. Ask students to draw parallels and describe how this analogy describes the formation of fossils.	**Extension**: Additional questions can be posed for students to explain their ideas. **Extension**: Students evaluate the strengths and weaknesses of this analogy.	**Interactive**: Fossil facts

Homework		
Students complete the activity from the lesson.		

2.5 The oldest primate

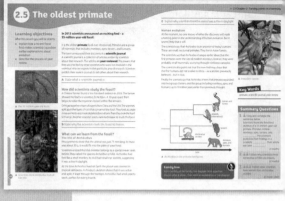

KS3 Biology NC Link:
- inheritance, chromosomes, DNA, and genes.

KS3 Working Scientifically NC Link:
- understand that scientific methods and theories develop as earlier explanations are modified to take account of new evidence and ideas, together with the importance of publishing results and peer review.

KS4 Biology NC Link:
- describe evolution as a change in the inherited characteristics of a population over time through a process of natural selection which may result in the formation of new species
- evaluate the evidence for evolution to include fossils and antibiotic resistance in bacteria.

Band	Outcome	Checkpoint	
		Question	Activity
Developing	State one thing that can be learnt from a fossil (Level 3).	C, 2	Main, Plenary 2
↓	State what is meant by a scientific journal (Level 3).	A, 1	Main, Plenary 1
Secure	Explain how a recent fossil find makes scientists question earlier explanations about evolution (Level 6).	2, 3	Main, Plenary 2
↓	Describe the role of scientific journals and the process of peer review (Level 5).	1	Main, Plenary 1
Extending	Suggest how the significance of finding the *Archicebus* fossil could be tested (Level 8).		Main, Plenary 2
↓	Compare methods of scientific communication in different sources (Level 7).		Main, Homework

Literacy
In the student-book activity, students discuss with a partner to explain what the primate family tree shows.

Students organise ideas into well-developed, structured paragraphs when comparing different methods of communication of scientific knowledge.

APP
Students explain how new scientific evidence is discussed and interpreted by the scientific community and how this may lead to changes in scientific ideas (AF1).

Key Words
primate, scientific journal, peer review

Answers from the student book

In-text questions	**A** A collection of articles written by scientists about their research.
	B So that scientists in France could use a new technique to study the fossil.
	C Its skull had relatively small eye sockets.

Activity	**Family tree** Explanation of the primate family tree should include the following key points: Lemurs, lorises, adapids, tarsiers, *Archicebus achilles*, humans, apes, and monkeys all have a common ancestor. Its descendants split into groups. One group became the monkeys, apes, and humans that we know today. The second group later split further, leading to the evolution of lemurs and lorises from the now-extinct adapids. The final group divided into two further groups – the now-extinct *Archicebus achilles*, and tarsiers.
Summary Questions	**1** humans, journal, reviewed (3 marks) **2** *Archicebus achilles* had small pointy teeth. Sharp teeth were adapted for eating insects. (2 marks) **3** QWC question (6 marks). Example answers: The first primates were not the size of modern monkeys, as previously thought. This was because the fossil of *Archicebus achilles* measured 71 mm in length. Instead the first primates were smaller mammals that scurried through rainforest canopies. The skull of *Archicebus achilles* had small eye sockets, suggesting it was active in daylight. Its teeth were sharp, suggesting that its diet consisted of insects. Scientists say that *Archicebus achilles* is an ancestor of the modern tarsier. Scientists also hypothesise that the first humans may not have evolved in Africa, as previously thought, but instead in Asia. Primates also split into two groups (tarsiers, and the group including monkeys, apes, and humans) up to 10 million years earlier than previously thought.

Starter	Support/Extension	Resources
How are fossils formed? (10 min) Students reorder sentences provided on the interactive resource to describe how fossils are formed. Students should then explain each step in detail using their scientific knowledge and understanding. **Fossils and evolution** (10 min) Ask students what fossils can tell us. For example, the small eye sockets of *Archicebus achilles* suggest it was active in daylight. Explain how fossils suggest humans evolved from primates and how modern techniques, such as DNA sequencing, provide evidence to support the theory.	**Support**: This is a review of the work covered in the previous lesson. Any misconceptions uncovered should be corrected. **Support**: Students may need a reminder of the definition of evolution.	**Interactive**: How are fossils formed?

Main	Support/Extension	Resources
Looking at scientific journals (35 min) Introduce how the *Archicebus achilles* fossil was discovered. This can be done using newspaper articles that are readily available on the Internet. Discuss the role of scientific journals and peer review in this discovery, and how it led to questions about earlier explanations of primate evolution. Students then examine the methods that different scientific journals and articles use to communicate scientific knowledge and answer the questions that follow.	**Support**: The accompanying support sheet helps students identify key sections of journal articles to help them answer questions posed.	**Activity**: Looking at scientific journals

Plenary	Support/Extension	Resources
What is in a journal? (10 min) Ask students to recap what journals are and why they are useful, and to describe the peer review process in pairs. **Fossil finds** (10 min) Scatter statements on the discovery of *Archicebus achilles* and how it caused scientists to question previous assumptions on primate evolution. In groups, students locate the statements, memorise them, and arrange them in order. They should not remove the statements from their locations.	**Extension**: Students suggest ways scientists can gather further evidence to support or refute the findings from the discovery.	

Homework		
Students should write an abstract for an imaginary article to a scientific journal OR an article for a newspaper/a website to discuss the discovery of *Archicebus achilles*.	**Extension**: Students compare the method of communication they have chosen with the other.	

Checkpoint lesson routes

The route through this lesson can be determined using the Checkpoint assessment.

Percentage pass marks are supplied in the Checkpoint teacher notes.

Route A (revision)

Resource: C3 Chapter 2 Checkpoint: Revision

Students work through a series of tasks that allows them to revisit and consolidate their understanding of atomic structure, the Periodic Table, evidence from fossils, and the role of scientific journals. Students can keep this as a summary of the topic, and use this when revising for future assessments.

Route B (extension)

Resource: C3 Chapter 2 Checkpoint: Extension

Students plan a display for the local science museum titled 'Chemistry concepts through the ages'. This display must demonstrate students' understanding of topics covered in this chapter.

Progression to *secure*

No.	Developing outcome	Secure outcome	Making progress
1	State what Dalton found out about the nature of particles.	Describe evidence for Dalton's atomic model.	In Task 1 students select statements that correctly describe evidence supporting Dalton's atomic model.
2	Describe how Dalton's work was influenced by other scientists.	Explain one way of developing a scientific explanation.	In Task 1 students complete a word fill to explain one way that scientific explanations can be developed.
3	State what Dalton, Thompson, and Rutherford discovered about the atom.	Explain how scientists discovered electrons and the nucleus.	In Task 1 students label diagrams of the plum-pudding model of the atom and the gold-foil experiment. Students then use these diagrams to explain how scientists discovered the existence of electrons and the nucleus.
4	Name the scientist who devised the Periodic Table.	Describe how Mendeleev devised the Periodic Table.	In Task 2 students rearrange statements to describe how Mendeleev devised the Periodic Table.
5	Name the scientists involved in the discovery of rhenium.	Describe how Tacke and Noddack discovered rhenium.	In Task 2 students summarise how the missing element rhenium was discovered.
6	State what is meant by a fossil.	Describe how fossils are formed.	In Task 3 students rearrange a series of diagrams to describe how fossils are formed, adding their own annotations and descriptions to each diagram.
7	State one thing that can be deduced from fossil evidence and data.	Explain what fossils tell us about the age of rocks.	In Task 3 students use their labelled diagrams to explain what fossils can tell us about the age of rocks.
8	State one thing that can be learnt from a fossil.	Explain how a recent fossil find makes scientists question earlier explanations about evolution.	In Task 3 students choose the correct endings to sentences provided to explain how the discovery of *Archicebus achilles* made scientists question earlier explanations about evolution.
9	State what is meant by a scientific journal.	Describe the role of scientific journals and the process of peer review.	In Task 4 students match halves of sentences together to describe the role of scientific journals and the process of peer review.

Answers to end-of-chapter questions

1   B, C, A, D (4 marks)
2   atoms, nucleus, positively, negatively (4 marks)
3   Ask a question: Y
    Suggest an explanation: Z
    Test the explanation: X (3 marks)
4   This is a QWC question. Students should be marked on the use of good English, organisation
    of information, spelling and grammar, and correct use of specialist scientific terms. The best
    answers will fully review Dalton's ideas in the text provided (maximum of 6 marks).
    Examples of correct scientific points:
    It is not strictly correct to state that gas particles are surrounded by heat.
    An improvement would be to state that the gas particles move around continuously
    (Brownian motion).
    The movement of particles causes friction, which can result in an increase in temperature.
    In the gas state, the particles are not touching each other, as stated by Dalton.
    Dalton was also correct to say that particles do not settle down into separate groups.
    Dalton was also correct to say that different gases have their own types of atoms.
    However, Dalton said that the greater the mass of 1 m^3 of gas, the heavier its atoms.
    We now know that gases can exist as pure gases, but also as mixtures of compounds
    and molecules.
    This means that more than one type of atom can exist in any one gas.
    Dalton's statement would be improved by stating that 'the greater the mass of 1 m^3 of gas, the
    heavier its particles.
    Particles can be used to describe both atoms and molecules.

Answer guide for Case Study

Developing	Secure	Extending
1–2 marks	3–4 marks	5–6 marks
• A poorly organised table giving one example to illustrate the following stages of developing an explanation: asking a question, suggesting an explanation, and testing the explanation. • An outline lesson plan is provided.	• A reasonably well-organised table giving one or two examples to illustrate the following stages of developing an explanation: asking a question, suggesting an explanation, and testing the explanation. • A lesson plan is provided that is designed to be exciting.	• A clearly organised table giving examples to illustrate all three stages of developing an explanation: asking a question, suggesting an explanation, and testing the explanation. • A lesson plan is provided that includes clear objectives and outcomes. • Lesson plans should also be designed to be engaging and exciting.

kerboodle

C3 Chapter 2 Checkpoint assessment (automarked)
C3 Chapter 2 Checkpoint: Revision
C3 Chapter 2 Checkpoint: Extension
C3 Chapter 2: Progress task (literacy)

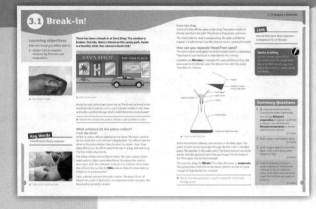

KS3 Chemistry NC Link:
- the particulate nature of matter
- pure and impure substances.

KS3 Working Scientifically NC Link:
- select, plan, and carry out the most appropriate types of scientific enquiries to test predictions.

KS4 Chemistry NC Link:
- describe, explain, and exemplify the process of filtration
- suggest suitable purification techniques given information about the substances involved.

Band	Outcome	Checkpoint	
		Question	Activity
Developing ↓	State two methods of separating mixtures (Level 3).	B, 1	Starter 1, Main, Plenary 1, Plenary 2, Homework
	Select appropriate apparatus from a list that can be used to carry out filtration and evaporation (Level 4).		Main, Plenary 2
Secure ↓	Explain how to separate mixtures by filtration and evaporation (Level 6).	2	Main, Plenary 1, Plenary 2, Homework
	Suggest and carry out a method to separate blood from sand (Level 5).		Main, Plenary 2
Extending ↓	Use particle diagrams to compare filtration and evaporation (Level 7).		Main, Plenary 1, Plenary 2, Homework
	Justify the choices of techniques used for separating blood and sand (Level 7).		Main, Plenary 2

Literacy
Students plan how to communicate scientific information to the general public as part of a media brief for the student-book activity.

Students organise scientific ideas and information when planning how to separate blood from a mixture of blood and sand in the experiment.

APP
Students plan an experiment to separate blood from a mixture of blood and sand (AF4), carry out their plan, presenting observations in an appropriate manner (AF3), and state simply whether the method used was effective (AF5). Students also suggest precautions scene of crime officers must take to reduce risk when working with body samples (AF4).

Key Words
DNA, filtration, filtrate, evaporate

Answers from the student book

In-text questions	**A** smell **B** filtration and evaporation
Activity	**Media briefing** There has been a break-in at SavaShop. The window was broken, there was blood on the sandy path, and a smell resembling vomit coming from inside. A car was stopped nearby. The driver had blood on his hands, damp patches on his coat, and smelt of vomit or rancid sweat. Officers breathalysed the driver, and have sent the blood on his hands away for DNA analysis. A doctor has taken blood from the suspect's arm to test for alcohol. Scene-of-crime officers have removed bloody sand from the path and are looking for fingerprints and hairs. The fire brigade have been called to identify the smelly liquid.

Summary Questions	1 filtration, evaporation (2 marks)
	2 Filtration separates pieces of an insoluble solid from a liquid. The pieces of solid (residue) are too big to get through tiny holes in the filter paper. The liquid (filtrate) goes through the tiny holes in the filter paper, into the container beneath. (3 marks)
	3 Particles of the smelly substance cannot get through the bag and diffuse into people's noses. (2 marks)
	4 Visual summary should include the following (6 marks):
	Blood and sand mixture was collected from the path outside the broken window.
	This can be compared with the blood collected from Ryan's hand.
	The comparison will determine whether the blood is from Ryan or someone else.
	Blood collected from Ryan's arm can also provide evidence to determine whether Ryan is over the blood alcohol limit for driving.
	This was shown to be the case from the breathalyser test.
	Ryan's breath smelt of cider.
	This suggests that Ryan had been drinking cider before driving.
	Trace evidence (for example, chemicals) found from Ryan's coat can be compared to chemicals found in SavaShop.
	This will then determine whether Ryan was or was not at the crime scene at some point.

Starter	Support/Extension	Resources
Filtration (10 min) Students complete a crossword on the interactive resource using the clues provided. This task can be used to recap the key words used in filtration, in preparation for the planning task as part of the practical. Students met separation techniques in C2.	**Support**: Spend time consolidating the filtration. **Extension**: Students give examples of other separation techniques discussed in C2.	**Interactive**: Filtration
What are mixtures? (5 min) Students recap what mixtures are and give examples of different mixtures, for example, solids in liquids (sand in water), solids (rock and sand), gases (air), and so on.	**Extension**: Students suggest techniques that could separate these mixtures.	

Main	Support/Extension	Resources
Using separation techniques to solve crimes (40 min) If students haven't worked through B3, introduce the role of forensic scientists. Ask students to consider evidence that can be collected at a crime scene, and categorise these as liquid, solid, gas, pure, or impure substances. If appropriate, provide tangible examples, for example, alcohol in blood, petrol in carpets, and so on. Students suggest different methods of separating the evidence without damaging them. This will recap C2. Students then plan and carry out the separation of blood from sand in the practical.	**Support**: A support sheet is provided where students are given a list of apparatus to choose from for planning their experiment.	**Practical**: Using separation techniques to solve crimes **Skill sheet**: Scientific apparatus

Plenary	Support/Extension	Resources
Building separation sentences (10 min) Students use the key words from the interactive crossword to form as many sentences as possible to explain how filtration works.	**Extension**: Students use the key words provided to draw an annotated particle diagram instead.	
How would you separate...? (5 min) Ask students to draw a labelled diagram to explain how a given mixture can be separated. This activity can be done on mini-whiteboards to increase class participation.	**Extension**: Students should be able to justify their answers using particle diagrams.	

Homework		
Students write a report to describe how one piece of evidence (a mixture) collected at a crime scene was separated without damaging the evidence, and how this technique works.	**Extension**: Encourage students to include particle diagrams.	

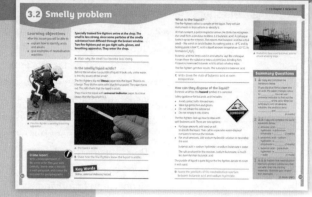

KS3 Chemistry NC Link:
- chemical reactions.

KS3 Working Scientifically NC Link:
- select, plan, and carry out the most appropriate types of scientific enquiries to test predictions.

KS4 Chemistry NC Link:
- use the names and symbols of common elements and compounds to write formulae and balanced chemical equations
- describe neutralisation as acid reacting with alkali to form a salt plus water.

Band	Outcome	Checkpoint	
		Question	Activity
Developing	Name one method of identifying acids and alkalis (Level 3).	A, 1	Lit, Starter 1, Main, Plenary 1, Homework
	State what is meant by neutralisation (Level 3).		Starter 2, Homework
	Plan an experiment to test whether unknown substances are acids or alkalis (Level 4).		Main
Secure	Explain how to identify acids and alkalis (Level 5).	1	Lit, Starter 1, Plenary 1, Homework
	Give examples of neutralisation reactions (Level 5).	D, 1–3	Starter 2, Main, Plenary 2, Homework
	Plan and carry out an experiment to test the acidity of unknown substances, interpreting results (Level 6).		Main
Extending	Suggest why acids and alkalis can have different strengths (Level 7).		Starter 1, Main
	Use balanced formula equations to represent neutralisation reactions (Level 7).		Starter 2, Main, Plenary 2, Homework
	Plan an experiment to test for the acidity of unknown solutions, considering risks, and interpreting results (Level 7).		Main

Maths
Students will interpret data from their results table and will use quantitative problem solving to calculate an amount of alkali needed for neutralisation in the practical activity.

Literacy
Students will draw inferences from results in the practical activity and will organise ideas and information when completing the student-book activity.

APP
Students will interpret results in the practical activity (AF5).

Key Words
litmus, universal indicator, hazard

Answers from the student book

In-text questions	A Some particles of the smelly substance have diffused through the broken window.
	B The fire-fighters dipped blue litmus paper into the liquid. There was a colour change from blue to red. This shows that the liquid is acidic.
	C liquid
	D sodium butanoate and water

Activity	**Crime report** Students should link their ideas in a well-organised fashion, with the use of paragraphs. They should include the points covered in Summary Question 4 of the previous lesson, as well as the following: The fire-fighters determined that the smelly liquid is acidic. An experienced police inspector recognised the smell of the liquid as being that of butanoic acid. Butanoic acid was removed by covering with sand and then calling in a specialist waste disposal unit.
Summary Questions	**1** red, pH, salt, water (4 marks) **2a** potassium, water (2 marks) **b** sodium, water (2 marks) **c** potassium butanoate (1 mark) **3** QWC question (6 marks). Example answers: In neutralisation reactions an acid is neutralised by a base, alkali or carbonate. The products are salt and water. Acids are usually corrosive. Alkalis/bases are usually toxic/harmful. Salts are often safer than the acids/alkalis that form them because they are usually not corrosive, for example, the reaction between sodium hydroxide and hydrochloric acid makes sodium chloride (a neutral salt, table salt) and water. Credit other sensible examples.

Starter	Support/Extension	Resources
What are acids and alkalis? (10 min) Ask students to name acids, alkalis, and any properties they can remember. Display the pH scale and the colours observed with universal indicator. Students explain what the image shows and how to identify acids and alkalis.	**Extension**: Students should also describe how the pH of an acid or alkali is determined by the concentration of H^+ and OH^-.	
Neutralisation reactions (5 min) Recap the meaning of neutralisation reactions. Students then identify the word and formula equations that describe neutralisation reactions from the list given on the interactive resource.	**Extension**: Students name compounds from formulae, and write balanced formula equations from word equations.	**Interactive**: Neutralisation reactions

Main	Support/Extension	Resources
Identifying acids and alkalis (40 min) Show students universal indicator paper and solution, blue and red litmus paper, and a pH probe. Ask students to explain what each can tell you in terms of a substance being an acid or alkali and its strength (pH value). Discuss how strong acids and alkalis are very corrosive and can be cleared up or made safe by neutralising with the other to produce a salt, that is normally safer, and water. Students then plan and carry out a practical to identify unknown solutions at a crime scene as acidic, neutral, or alkaline solutions, answering questions that follow.	**Support**: The accompanying support sheet offers a partially filled results table for students to use, and hints on how to interpret their observations.	**Practical**: Identifying acids and alkalis **Skill sheet**: Recording results

Plenary	Support/Extension	Resources
Acids or alkalis? (5 min) Ask students to apply what they have learnt this lesson by providing mock results from a test of unknown substances with phenolphthalein and methyl orange. Encourage students to use their results to suggest possible colours of universal indicator for the same solutions.	**Extension**: Students identify the limitation of these results (the pH of solutions cannot be found using these indicators).	
Neutralisation equations (10 min) Call out or write onto a board acids and bases undergoing neutralisation reactions. Ask students to write down the word equations for each example on a mini-whiteboard.	**Extension**: Students should write balanced formula equations.	

Homework		
Students produce a leaflet to explain methods of identifying acids and alkalis. This leaflet should explain neutralisation, giving examples as word equations.	**Extension**: Students should give examples as balanced formula equations.	

3.3 Message in a bottle

KS3 Chemistry NC Link:
- pure and impure substances.

KS3 Working Scientifically NC Link:
- select, plan, and carry out the most appropriate types of scientific enquiries to test predictions.

KS4 Chemistry NC Link:
- recall that chromatography involves a stationary and a mobile phase, and that separation depends on the distribution between the phases
- interpret chromatograms, including measuring R_f values.

Band	Outcome	Checkpoint	
		Question	Activity
Developing	Name one technique that can be used to analyse ink (Level 3).	A	Starter 1, Starter 2, Plenary 1, Plenary 2, Homework
	Plan a paper chromatography experiment to compare two ink samples (Level 4).		Main
Secure	Describe how chromatography separates dyes in ink (Level 5).	1	Starter 1, Main, Plenary 1, Homework
	Plan a chromatography experiment and interpret resulting chromatograms to compare two ink samples (Level 6).		Main
Extending	Explain how paper chromatography works (Level 7).	3	Starter 1, Main, Plenary 2, Homework
	Plan a chromatography experiment and interpret resulting chromatograms by calculating R_f (Level 8).		Main

Maths
Students will extract and interpret information from chromatograms in the practical activity.

Literacy
Students will organise ideas and information when completing the student-book activity.

APP
Students will explain how chromatography works in the practical (AF1).

Key Words
chromatography, stationary phase, mobile phase

Answers from the student book

In-text questions	**A** chromatography
	B mobile phases is the solvent (often water), stationary phase is paper
Activity	**Repeatable results?** Making further chromatograms helps to ensure that the results are repeatable, and is likely to draw attention to any mistakes that might have been made whilst making them. However, repeating the tests is unlikely to help them decide whose conclusion is correct, since the officers might still draw the same conclusions even if further chromatograms were obtained.
Summary Questions	**1** mixtures, paper, water, best, least well (5 marks) **2** The second officer's conclusion is best. It makes the point that the ink samples match while also recognising that this does not mean Ryan definitely wrote the note. (3 marks)

3 Diagram of paper chromatography apparatus drawn, as in the student book, with the following labels:

paper (stationary phase)

water/any other suitable solvent (mobile phase)

ink sample on pencil line above the level of the top of the mobile phase.

Annotations should explain the following points:

how dyes in the ink separate during chromatography

that the distance the dyes travel up the chromatography paper is dependent on how well the dye mixes with water and how strongly attracted it is to the chromatography paper

that the dye that travels the furthest is one that mixes well with water but is not strongly attracted to the chromatography paper. (6 marks)

kerboodle

Starter	Support/Extension	Resources
What is chromatography? (10 min) Ask students to explain how they can separate different dyes from an ink mixture, drawing the apparatus required on a mini-whiteboard. Discuss what the results of a chromatogram show. Students have met paper chromatography in C2. **What is being shown?** (5 min) Show students a chromatography tank, set up with a chromatogram partially completed inside, along with a chromatogram that has been prepared earlier. Ask students to name the technique that is being shown and how this technique can be used. Students have met paper chromatography in C2.	**Support**: Students can be provided with diagrams to label and annotate. **Extension**: Students explain what happens to different dye and solvent particles in paper chromatography.	

Main	Support/Extension	Resources
Using chromatography (40 min) Recap the key ideas of paper chromatography from C2 and introduce the mobile and stationary phases. Particles in soluble mixtures are carried by the mobile phase (solvent) depending on how well they dissolve and how well they are attracted to the stationary phase (paper in the case of paper chromatography). Students then plan and carry out a paper chromatography experiment to compare two ink samples, answering questions that follow.	**Support**: The accompanying support sheet provides students with a labelled diagram as a starting point for writing their method, and sentences to reorder when describing how paper chromatography works. **Extension**: You may wish to demonstrate another type of chromatography, using different stationary and mobile phases, for example, thin layer chromatography (TLC) using an organic mixture and an organic solvent.	**Practical**: Using chromatography

Plenary	Support/Extension	Resources
Setting up paper chromatography (10 min) Students rearrange sentences provided on the interactive resource to describe how a paper chromatography experiment can be set up. You may wish to identify points for further discussion, for example, why is the line on the paper drawn with pencil, not ink pen? Why does the solvent level have to be below the ink sample? **Interpreting chromatograms** (5 min) Ask students to apply what they have learnt this lesson by showing them a chromatogram on the board. Students should interpret and compare results shown on the chromatogram.	**Extension**: Students may suggest other chromatography techniques, for example, high-performance liquid chromatography (HPLC) and gas chromatography. **Extension**: Students explain how the different particles in the mixture have separated.	**Interactive**: Setting up paper chromatography

Homework		
Students design a short quiz, including answers, about chromatography. The quiz should include what chromatography is, how it can be used, and why the mixture is separated.		

3.4 Blood alcohol

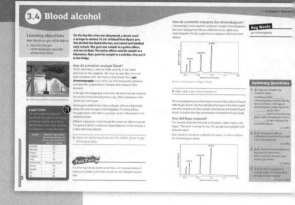

KS3 Chemistry NC Link:
- pure and impure substances.

KS3 Working Scientifically NC Link:
- interpret observations and data, including identifying patterns and using observations, measurements, and data to draw conclusions.

KS4 Chemistry NC Link:
- recall that chromatography involves a stationary and a mobile phase, and that separation depends on the distribution between the phases
- interpret chromatograms
- describe the advantages and instrumental methods of analysis (sensitivity, accuracy, and speed).

Band	Outcome	Checkpoint	
		Question	Activity
Developing	State what is meant by gas chromatography (Level 4).	A, B, 1	Plenary 2, Homework
	State if two gas chromatograms given are produced using the same sample (Level 3).	3	Main
Secure	Describe how gas chromatography separates alcohol from blood (Level 6).	2	Main, Plenary 2, Homework
	Describe the presence of different substances using gas chromatograms provided (Level 5).	3	Main
Extending	Compare similarities and differences between gas and paper chromatography (Level 8).	4	Main, Plenary 1, Homework
	Explain similarities and differences between two gas chromatograms (Level 7).	3	Main

Maths
In the student-book activity students plot an appropriate graph of a table of data on blood-alcohol levels for driving in different countries, writing a paragraph to compare the data.

Students interpret gas chromatograms given, comparing similarities and differences.

Students summarise the use of gas chromatography in tackling drink-driving for homework.

Literacy
Students rearrange statements provided to describe in detail the different stages of gas chromatography.

APP
Students interpret gas chromatograms provided to draw conclusions (AF5).

Key Words
gas chromatography

Answers from the student book

In-text questions	A The stationary phase is the polymer in the column. Helium is the mobile phase.
	B The record from gas chromatography with a peak for each substance detected in the mixture.

Activity	**Legal limits** Bar chart drawn with the names of countries on the x-axis and the maximum legal blood-alcohol concentration for drivers on the y-axis, with units (mg of alcohol in 100 cm³ of blood) and a scale from 0 to 80. Check plotted bars for accuracy.
Summary Questions	1 gas, mobile, polymer, peak (4 marks) 2 A sample of blood is heated until all substances in the mixture become gases. Helium (the mobile phase) is added to the mixture and passed through a polymer column (the stationary phase). Different substances move through the column at different speeds depending on how strongly it is attracted to the polymer. The amount of each substance in the mixture, and the time taken for each substance to pass through the column is presented on a gas chromatogram. (4 marks) 3 The chromatograms are identical. The peaks present in both gas chromatograms are the same, at the same vertical heights. This means that the results obtained by the first laboratory were correct, and that Ryan is indeed over the legal blood-alcohol concentration. (4 marks) 4 QWC question (6 marks). Example answers: In paper chromatography the mobile phase is water or another solvent. The mobile phase in gas chromatography is helium gas. In paper chromatography the stationary phase is the chromatography paper. A polymer column is the stationary phase in gas chromatography. Both types of chromatography separate substances in mixtures. Paper chromatography requires the mixture to be dissolved in one solvent. Gas chromatography relies on the ability of the mixture to turn into gas. Gas chromatography also gives the relative amounts of each substance present in a mixture.

kerboodle

Starter	Support/Extension	Resources
An alternative question-led lesson is also available. **What are breathalysers?** (10 min) Show an image of a breathalyser and ask students what they think it is. You could show a short video of it being used. Ask how ethanol (the active drug in alcohol) can be separated from blood. **Mobile and stationary phases** (5 min) Ask students to state the definitions of mobile phase and stationary phase. Students should discuss the roles of these phases in producing results for paper chromatography.	**Extension**: Students discuss how the breathalyser test differs from standard paper chromatography. **Support**: Identify and correct any misconceptions regarding these terms.	**Question-led lesson:** Blood alcohol
Main	**Support/Extension**	**Resources**
Introducing gas chromatography (40 min) Introduce gas chromatography as a technique used to separate and analyse substances that are gases or can be easily vaporised. Describe how the technique works and ask students to name the mobile and stationary phases involved. Students then label a diagram of gas chromatography, rearrange statements to describe how gas chromatography is carried out, compare two chromatograms given, and answer the questions on the activity sheet.		**Activity**: Introducing gas chromatography
Plenary	**Support/Extension**	**Resources**
Comparing chromatography (5 min) Interactive resource where students sort statements as relating to paper chromatography, gas chromatography, or both. **Gas chromatography and its uses** (10 min) In pairs, students state and describe gas chromatography. They peer-assess answers, then give examples of how or where gas chromatography is used.	**Extension**: Students explain how gas chromatography can separate substances in a mixture.	**Interactive**: Comparing chromatography
Homework		
Students write a newspaper article about how gas chromatography helps the police to tackle drink driving.	**Extension**: Students discuss similarities and differences between paper and gas chromatography.	

3.5 Body!

KS3 Chemistry NC Link:
- chemical reactions
- materials.

KS3 Working Scientifically NC Link:
- select, plan, and carry out the most appropriate types of scientific enquiries to test predictions, including identifying independent, dependent, and control variables, where appropriate.

KS4 Chemistry NC Link:
- predict reactions and reactivity of elements from their positions in the Periodic Table
- relate the reactivity of metals with water or dilute acids to the tendency of the metal to form its positive ion
- identify the conditions for corrosion and explain how mitigation is achieved by creating a physical barrier to oxygen and water or by sacrificial protection.

Band	Outcome	Checkpoint	
		Question	Activity
Developing	Name a reactive metal using the reactivity series (Level 3).	B, 2	Starter 1, Starter 2, Main 2, Plenary 1, Plenary 2
	Identify independent, dependent, and control variables when planning an investigation to compare the corrosion of different metals. (Level 4).		Main 2
Secure	Use the reactivity series to predict whether metals will react with oxygen and water vapour in the air or soil (Level 5).	B, 1, 2	Main 2, Plenary 1, Plenary 2
	Plan an investigation to compare the corrosion of different metals in detail (Level 6).		Main 2
Extending	Use the reactivity series to predict different metal reactions, giving examples as word or formula equations (Level 7).	2	Starter 2, Main 1, Main 2, Plenary 1
	Suggest improvements to an existing investigation to compare the corrosion of different metals that be used as a reference to unknown samples (Level 7).		Main 2

Maths
Some students are required to balance formula equations.

Literacy
Students organise ideas, using scientific terms confidently when discussing and planning an investigation to compare the corrosion of different metals.

APP
Students plan an investigation to compare the corrosion of different metals, identifying variables, risks, and hazards (AF4).

Key Words
metal, reactivity series, rust

Answers from the student book

In-text questions	A gold (accept copper, silver, or platinum)
	B Any two from: potassium, sodium, and magnesium

Summary Questions	**1** bottom, does not react, higher, water, hydrated (5 marks)
	2a potassium (1 mark)
	b gold and platinum (accept copper and silver) (1 mark)
	c zinc oxide (1 mark)
	3 Example answers (6 marks):
	A murder victim is buried in damp soil. This victim was wearing a gold ring, a silver necklace, and a watch made mainly from iron. The gold ring was still shiny when found. This is because gold does not react with water or oxygen in the damp soil. The silver necklace had turned black. Silver is usually unreactive but does react slowly with sulfur compounds in the air. The black product is silver sulphide. The iron watch has gone rusty. This is because iron reacts readily with water and oxygen. The product is hydrated iron oxide. Combining the level of reaction in the gold, silver, and iron suggests that these items were buried 10 years ago.

Starter	Support/Extension	Resources
Remembering reactivity (5 min) Display the reactivity series for 30 seconds. Students attempt to remember the order, then write down the correct order on mini-whiteboards. Make into a competition to encourage participation.	**Extension**: Encourage students to explain what this series of elements tells us.	
What is the reactivity series? (10 min) Ask students to describe what the reactivity series shows and how it is used by scientists. It is important at this stage to correct any misconceptions that arise about the reactivity series as appropriate.	**Extension**: Students explain the term displacement and write a word equation of an example using the reactivity series.	

Main	Support/Extension	Resources
The corrosion of metals (15 min) Introduce that metals react with substances found in their surrounding environment, for example, oxygen and water. The more reactive a metal, the quicker this will happen. Link this to the crime scenario in the student book, explaining why the gold ring is still shiny but the iron watch has rusted. A common misconception is to use rust and corrosion interchangeably. Explain that rusting is an example of metal corrosion between iron and oxygen or water.	**Support**: Students identify metals that have reacted from those that have not, based on the descriptions given in the crime scenario. **Extension**: Students should be encouraged to name products of metal corrosion.	
Comparing the corrosion of metals (25 min) Students plan an experiment to investigate the corrosion of different metals in soil and in air. Students discuss their ideas before using the prompts provided to write a method, prepare a results table, and answer the questions that follow.	**Support**: The access sheet provides a step-by-step guide to planning the investigation. The questions are also less demanding, designed to build confidence.	**Activity**: Comparing the corrosion of metals **Skill sheet**: Planning investigations **Skill sheet**: Recording results

Plenary	Support/Extension	Resources
Metal reactions (5 min) Students use the reactivity series to decide if statements provided on the interactive resource about metals and their reactions are true or false. Students should then correct the statements that are false.	**Extension**: Students explain why statements are false, and write word equations for those that are true.	**Interactive**: Metal reactions
How can the reactivity series help solve crimes? (10 min) Students communicate ideas about how the reactivity series can be used in solving crimes, for example, by suggesting how long metal items have been buried for. This task can be run as a snowball activity, with final groups feeding back ideas to the rest of the class.		

Homework		
Students carry out independent research about one piece of metal historical artefact found in the UK. Students should link the findings to their understanding of the reactivity series.	**Extension**: Encourage students to include other techniques used to recover the artefact and find out the time period from which it was made.	

KS3 Chemistry NC Link:

● materials.

KS3 Working Scientifically NC Link:

● evaluate the reliability of methods and suggest possible improvements.

KS4 Chemistry NC Link:

● explain the basic principles of addition polymerisation and condensation polymerisation
● describe and explain the separation of crude oil by fractional distillation and the production of more useful materials by cracking
● select appropriate materials given details of usage required, relating uses to properties.

Band	Outcome	Checkpoint	
		Question	Activity
Developing	State what is meant by the term biodegradable (Level 3).	C	Starter 1, Main 1, Plenary 1, Plenary 2, Homework
	Describe properties of sisal, wool, and poly(propene) (Level 4).	A, B	Main 1, Plenary 1
	Identify the aims of different experimental methods provided (Level 4).		Main 2
Secure	Describe the difference between biodegradable and non-biodegradable materials (Level 5).	2	Main 1, Plenary 1, Plenary 2, Homework
	Explain why the properties of sisal, wool, and poly(propene) make them suitable for carpets (Level 6).	1	Main 1, Plenary 1
	Suggest improvements to the different experimental methods given to test carpets (Level 6).		Main
Extending	Suggest advantages and disadvantages of using biodegradable and non-biodegradable materials (Level 7).	3	Plenary 2, Homework
	Compare the properties of sisal, wool, and poly(propene) (Level 7).		Main 1, Plenary 1
	Plan a brief method to test carpets in a different way than those already provided (Level 7).		Main 2

Literacy
In the student-book activity students organise their ideas in a structured way when writing their crime report on the evidence found in Ryan's case so far.

APP
Students suggest improvements to experimental methods provided (AF5). Some students plan and write a brief method to test how well different carpets insulate sound (AF4).

Key Words
natural, synthetic, biodegradable

Answers from the student book

In-text questions	A Any two from: insulator, soft, does not catch fire easily
	B Any two from: hard wearing, easy to clean, can be dyed with many colours
	C A biodegradable substance can be broken down by natural processes, for example, by bacteria or fungi in soil.

Activity	**Crime report**
	Additional points to include:
	Scientists used gas chromatography to ascertain that Ryan was over the blood-alcohol limit for driving.
	Tests on Ryan's blood show that his DNA matches the blood left on a ten-year-old note stating 'Buried in my garden'.
	Police officers found an old bottle of ink in a kitchen cupboard. They produced a paper chromatogram from the ink, which matched a chromatogram obtained from the ink on the note.
	Police officers found a body in one of Ryan's previous addresses. Various metal items were on the body. The changes to the metals over time, as a result of chemical reactions with oxygen from the air, and water, are consistent with the body having been buried 10 years' ago.
	The carpet that was used to wrap this body contains materials that show decomposition consistent with being buried 10 years' ago.
Summary Questions	**1** insulator, fire, properties, soft, polymer (5 marks)
	2 Biodegradable materials are made from natural sources, for example, sisal and wool. Non-biodegradable materials are made from synthetic materials, for example, poly(propene) is a polymer made from substances obtained from crude oil. (4 marks)
	3 QWC question (6 marks). Example answers:
	Carpets made from non-biodegradable materials, for example, poly(propene), are hard-wearing and easy to clean. However, these carpets cannot be broken down by natural processes, and will remain unchanged in the environment for a long time. This can cause issues when disposing of non-biodegradable carpets.

Starter	Support/Extension	Resources
Biodegradable or not? (5 min) Display an image of a biodegradable object (preferably with a biodegradable sign) on the board. Ask students to suggest what this term means.		
Looking at carpet samples (10 min) Provide carpet samples for students to feel and observe. If possible, have samples of wool, sisal, and poly(propene) carpets. Ask students to share their observations and compare the different carpet samples provided.	**Extension**: Encourage students to suggest different materials that possess the properties observed.	

Main	Support/Extension	Resources
Properties of sisal, wool, and poly(propene) (15 min) Introduce the materials that are commonly used to make carpets. Discuss their properties and ask students to make a table summarising the properties of each material and how the properties make these materials suitable for carpets. A formal explanation of the term biodegradable should be covered.	**Support**: You may wish to supply students with partially completed tables for students to fill in.	
Testing carpets (25 min) Students carry out an activity where they identify the aims of four methods used to test different carpets, evaluating these methods to identify possible improvements, and answer the questions that follow on the activity sheet.	**Support**: The accompanying support sheet offers students clues to help them identify the aim of each experiment given.	**Activity**: Testing carpets

Plenary	Support/Extension	Resources
Carpet crossword (10 min) Students complete a crossword of key words from this lesson using clues provided on the interactive resource. Students should then elaborate on the properties of wool, sisal, and poly(propene), using their knowledge to play a quick game of 'guess who' with a partner. This is where students choose one material and their partner asks questions about its properties until they can identify the material correctly.	**Extension**: Students play the game of 'guess who' using comparative terms, for example, for poly(propene), it is the longest lasting material.	**Interactive**: Carpet crossword
The advantages and disadvantages of biodegradable materials (5 min) Students explain what is meant by biodegradable, before offering advantages and disadvantages of using biodegradable materials on mini-whiteboards.		

Homework		
Students research three substances that are biodegradable and three substances that are not. Students must then use their knowledge from this lesson to explain why these materials are suitable for their uses.		

KS3 Chemistry NC Link:
- pure and impure substances
- materials.

KS3 Working Scientifically NC Link:
- interpret observations and data, including identifying patterns and using observations, measurements, and data to draw conclusions.

KS4 Chemistry NC Link:
- relate the reactivity series of metals with water or dilute acids to the tendency of the metal to form its positive ion
- describe, explain, and exemplify the processes of filtration, crystallisation, simple distillation, and fractional distillations
- recall that chromatography involves a stationary and a mobile phase and that separation depends on the distribution between the phases.

Band	Outcome	Checkpoint	
		Question	Activity
Developing ↓	Give some examples of scientific evidence (Level 3).	1, 2	Starter 1, Main, Homework
	Interpret evidence provided in a court case (Level 4).		Main
Secure ↓	Describe how scientific evidence can help solve crimes (Level 6).	2, 3	Starter 2, Main, Homework
	Interpret evidence provided in a court case, evaluating the strength of evidence given (Level 6).		Main
Extending ↓	Suggest possible strengths and weaknesses of scientific evidence (Level 7).	4	Main, Plenary 1
	Suggest further questions that would need to be answered where scientific evidence is inconclusive (Level 8).		Main

Literacy
Students organise ideas and information about Ryan's court case, presenting their ideas in a mock court case. They must take on different roles during discussion, collaborating with others in their team.

APP
Students critically interpret, evaluate, and synthesise conflicting evidence based on the evidence presented in Ryan's court case during a mock court case (AF5).

Key Words
dental record

Answers from the student book

In-text questions	**A** The ring belonged to Angela. Dental records match that of the skeleton/body.
	B damage to the shop, drink-driving, and the murder of Angela Scott
Activity	**Science solves crimes** Poster should show how scientists' work involves working to a method, taking care to avoid contamination, accuracy and precision, repeatability and reproducibility.

Summary Questions	1 evidence, DNA, note, body (4 marks)
	2 The DNA from Ryan's blood matches that of the blood on the note. The ink on the note matches the ink in Ryan's cupboard. The body was found in the garden of Ryan's former address. (3 marks)
	3 Any two from (6 marks): Filtration – to separate sample blood from sand. DNA analysis – identifies DNA from Ryan's blood sample. This matched the blood sample on the note. Chromatography – chromatograms from the note and the ink found in Ryan's kitchen cupboard matched. Metal corrosion and carpet decay – the police compared the metal jewellery obtained from the body, together with the carpet with which the body was wrapped, with known data about corrosion and decomposition. They concluded that the body was buried 10 years' ago.
	4 QWC question (6 marks). Example answers: Teeth in the buried skull can be observed directly. Dental records were made by a skilled professional and stored carefully. An experienced professional is skilled in comparing dental records to teeth. Teeth are fixed in the skull, so are definitely part of the buried body. Dental records are unique to the individual. Relatives might have forgotten exactly what Angela's ring looked like. Someone else may have been wearing Angela's ring, so the body might not belong to Angela. The person who buried the body might have placed someone else's ring with the body at the time of burial. Rings are common, and are not unique. Many people may have bought the same ring.

Starter	Support/Extension	Resources
What is evidence? (10 min) Students pair-share ideas on what evidence means and give examples of any evidence they remember about Ryan's case. Students divide the evidence into that which is scientific (DNA, fingerprints, chromatograms, and dental records) and that which is not (a confession, someone's opinion, and an anonymous phone calls). **Why is evidence cross-examined?** (5 min) Ask students to suggest reasons why it is important that evidence is checked and cross-examined. Guide students to consider that mistakes can be made and that all evidence and data should be repeatable, reproducible, and valid.	**Extension**: Students explain the difference between scientific and non-scientific pieces of evidence.	

Main	Support/Extension	Resources
The trial (40 min or more) Students summarise the key points of Ryan's case and give an explanation of how the evidence supports each point. In groups, students then carry out a mock court case acting out the roles of forensic scientist, prosecution lawyers, defence lawyers, and the judge.	**Support**: The support sheet contains questions to help students prepare for the roles they have been given.	**Activity**: The trial

Plenary	Support/Extension	Resources
Describing evidence (5 min) Interactive resource where students link the key words accuracy, validity, precision, repeatability, and reproducibility with their definitions. Students suggest why and where these are important when considering scientific evidence in a criminal case. **Techniques to gather evidence** (10 min) Assign students a technique described in this chapter that was used to gather evidence. Students summarise their technique in five minutes before reporting back to the class. Can be done as a snowballing activity.		**Interactive**: Describing evidence

Homework		
Find a newspaper article about a crime. Highlight all the pieces of evidence that are mentioned. Decide which of these are scientific evidence and suggest how these pieces of evidence may have been gathered.		
An alternative WebQuest homework activity is also available on Kerboodle where students research forensic chemists.		**WebQuest**: Forensic chemists

Checkpoint lesson routes

The route through this lesson can be determined using the Checkpoint assessment.

Percentage pass marks are supplied in the Checkpoint teacher notes.

Route A (revision)
Resource: C3 Chapter 3 Checkpoint: Revision

Students work through a series of tasks that allows them to revisit and consolidate their understanding of separation techniques, the reactivity series of metals, and the biodegradation of different materials. Students can keep this as a summary of the topic, and use this when revising for future assessments.

Route B (extension)
Resource: C3 Chapter 3 Checkpoint: Extension

Students design a documentary about a recent murder inquiry, writing out a script that will include a summary of the key concepts covered in this topic.

Progression to *secure*

No.	Developing outcome	Secure outcome	Making progress
1	State two methods of separating mixtures.	Explain how to separate mixtures by filtration and evaporation.	In Task 1 students label diagrams and reorder statements to explain how a mixture of blood and sand can be separated using filtration and evaporation.
2	Name one method of identifying acids and alkalis.	Explain how to identify acids and alkalis.	In Task 2 students complete a word fill to explain how acids and alkalis can be identified using litmus paper and universal indicator.
3	State what is meant by neutralisation.	Give examples of neutralisation reactions.	In Task 2 students are given examples of neutralisation reactions that are incorrect. Students must then write the correct word equations below.
4	Name one technique that can be used to analyse ink.	Describe how chromatography separates dyes in ink.	In Task 3 students label a diagram of paper chromatography and use it to describe how dyes in ink can be separated using this technique.
5	State what is meant by gas chromatography.	Describe how gas chromatography separates alcohol from blood.	In Task 3 students link halves of sentences together to describe how gas chromatography works.
6	Name a reactive metal using the reactivity series.	Use the reactivity series to predict whether metals will react with oxygen and water vapour in the air or soil.	In Task 4 students use the reactivity series and chemical reactivity data provided to predict if potassium, zinc, and platinum will react with oxygen and water vapour.
7	State what is meant by biodegradable.	Describe the difference between biodegradable and non-biodegradable materials.	In Task 5 students describe the difference between biodegradable and non-biodegradable materials, giving examples in the following question.
8	Describe properties of sisal, wool, and (poly)propene.	Explain why the properties of sisal, wool, and poly(propene) make them suitable for carpets.	In Task 5 students match sisal, wool, and poly(propene) to their properties and explain why these properties are suitable for making carpets.
9	Give some examples of scientific evidence.	Explain how scientific evidence can help solve crimes.	In Task 6 students complete a table that lists evidence towards Ryan's conviction. Students must then explain how each piece of evidence was used.

Answers to end-of-chapter questions

1 mixtures A, C, and E (5 marks)

2 wool, flour, paper (3 marks)

3a paper (1 mark)

  b Three, since the initial sample has split to make three spots as it moved up the paper. (2 marks)

4a four (1 mark)   **b** B (1 mark)   **c** helium (1 mark)

5a silver, gold, platinum (3 marks)   **b** potassium (1 mark)

  c iron + oxygen + water → hydrated iron oxide (2 marks)

6a $2Cu + O_2 \rightarrow 2CuO$ (2 marks)   **b** $2Ag + H_2S \rightarrow Ag_2S + H_2$ (2 marks)

  c $4Fe + 3O_2 \rightarrow 2Fe_2O_3$ (2 marks)   **d** $2Na + 2H_2O \rightarrow 2NaOH + H_2$ (2 marks)

7 This is a QWC question. Students should be marked on the use of good English, organisation of information, spelling and grammar, and correct use of specialist scientific terms. The best answers will fully explain the advantages and disadvantages of filtration and gas chromatography to separate mixtures (maximum of 6 marks).

Examples of correct scientific points:

Filtration requires relatively large amounts of the mixture to be separated.

Gas chromatography only requires very small samples.

Gas chromatography can be used to identify the substances in a mixture.

Filtration cannot identify substances.

Both techniques can be used to estimate the relative amounts of the different substances in a mixture.

Gas chromatography is more accurate in measuring amounts.

Filtration requires simple apparatus, for example, a filter funnel and filter paper.

Gas chromatography requires an expensive gas chromatography machine and a power supply.

Technical expertise is required to interpret gas chromatograms.

Answer guide for Case Study

Developing	Secure	Extending
1–2 marks	3–4 marks	5–6 marks
<ul><li>One of the following variables correctly identified:<ul><li>the material under test (independent)</li><li>whether or not the test material shows signs of degradation (dependent)</li><li>the size and shape of samples, conditions samples are kept in, time the samples are left for (control).</li></ul></li><li>Diagram includes reference to suitable place to keep samples, for example, buried in soil.</li><li>Diagram includes labels.</li><li>Results table poorly organised, or not included.</li></ul>	<ul><li>Two of the following variables correctly identified:<ul><li>the material under test (independent)</li><li>whether or not the test material shows signs of degradation (dependent)</li><li>the size and shape of samples, conditions samples are kept in, time the samples are left for (control).</li></ul></li><li>Diagram includes reference to a suitable place to keep samples, for example, buried in soil.</li><li>Diagram includes labels.</li><li>Results table includes two of the following columns (or similar): material, observations, and biodegradable/non-biodegradable.</li><li>Student makes one of the points below:<ul><li>Materials are biodegradable if they show signs of degradation having been buried in soil.</li><li>The investigation could take many weeks, since time must be allowed for the materials to degrade.</li></ul></li></ul>	<ul><li>All of the following variables correctly identified:<ul><li>the material under test (independent)</li><li>whether or not the test material shows signs of degradation (dependent)</li><li>the size and shape of samples, conditions samples are kept in, time the samples are left for (control).</li></ul></li><li>Diagram includes reference to a suitable place to keep samples, for example, buried in soil.</li><li>Diagram is clearly labelled.</li><li>Results table includes all of the following columns (or similar): material, observations, and biodegradable/non-biodegradable.</li><li>Student states that materials are biodegradable if they show signs of degradation having been buried in soil.</li><li>Student states that the investigation could take many weeks, since time must be allowed for the materials to degrade.</li></ul>

kerboodle

C3 Chapter 3 Checkpoint assessment (automarked)

C3 Chapter 3 Checkpoint: Revision

C3 Chapter 3 Checkpoint: Extension

C3 Chapter 3 Progress task (Experimental skills and investigation)

Physics ③

Preparing for Key Stage 4 success

Knowledge	
Underpinning knowledge is covered in this unit for KS4 study of:	• Non-contact forces and fields • National and global energy sources • The three Newtonian laws of motion • Speed, velocity, and acceleration • Electromagnetic radiation and matter • Contact forces, stretching, and friction • Applications for generation and detection • Waste and efficiency • Superposition, reflection, absorption, and resonance • Collisions and safety • Absorption and emission of ionising radiations • Refraction and lens action (qualitative) • Applications and effects on body tissues of radioactive materials • Magnetic effects of currents • Solar system, stability of orbital motions, satellites • Half-lives • Red-shift, the Big Bang, and universal expansion • Motors, induction, and dynamos • Amplitude and frequency modulation to transfer information • Energy of the Sun and fusion

Maths	
Skills developed in this unit. (Topic number)	• Quantitative problem solving (1.3, 1.5, 2.4, 3.5). • Use geometry to solve problems (1.5, 3.5) • Understand number size and scale and the quantitative relationship between units (2.3, 2.5). • Plot and draw graphs selecting appropriate scales for the axes (1.4). • Extract and interpret information from charts, graphs, and tables (1.7, 2.7). • Understand when and how to use estimation (2.2, 2.3). • Understand and use direct proportion and simple ratios (1.3). • Identify patterns in data (2.2, 2.8, 2.9). • Substitute numerical values into simple formulae and equations using appropriate units (1.3, 2.3, 3.1). • Carry out calculations involving $+, -, \times, \div$, either singly or in combination (1.3, 3.4, 3.5).

Literacy	
Skills developed in this unit. (Topic number)	• Planning and adapting writing style to suit audience and purpose (1.3, 1.5, 1.6, 1.7, 2.2, 2.3, 2.5). • Accessing information to ascertain meaning, using word skills and comprehension strategies (2.1, 2.4, 3.1). • Predicting, making inferences, and describing relationships (3.1). • Identifying main ideas, events, and supporting details from scientific text (1.5, 2.1, 3.5). • Take part in a debate and put forward a point of view (1.7, 2.5). • Use of scientific terms (all spreads) • Organisation of ideas and information (1.3, 1.5, 2.1, 2.2, 3.4, 3.5).

Assessment Skills	
	• QWC questions (1.1, 1.2, 1.3, 1.4, 1.5, 2.1, 2.4, 2.5, 2.6, 2.7, 2.8, 3.1, 3.2, 3.3, 3.4, 3.5) (end-of-chapter 1 Q10, end-of-chapter 2 Q10, end-of-chapter 3 Q11) • Quantitative problem solving (1.1, 1.2, 1.5, 2.4, 2.6, 2.9, 3.2, 3.3, 3.4) (end-of-chapter 1 Q9, end-of-chapter 3 Q6, Q10) • Application of Working Scientifically (end-of-chapter 1 Q5, end-of-chapter 2 Q 5)

	Key Concept	Catch-up
Chapter 1: New technology	The uses of electromagnetic waves in communication and in medicine are discussed in this chapter, offering students a recap of the **electromagnetic spectrum**, and an introduction to **electromagnetic waves**.	P1 2.1 Waves P1 2.2 Vibrations and energy transfer
	Circuits and circuit symbols are consolidated using sensor circuits in the home and in hospitals. These are topics that are essential when studying **electricity**.	P2 1.2–1.5: Electricity and magnetism
	Properties of light waves and ray diagrams are consolidated using endoscopes. These topics are essential when studying **light**, including **reflection** and **refraction**.	P1 3.1–3.4: Light
	Forces acting on a moving object are discussed when predicting projectile motion. This can be used as a scaffold towards further study of **forces and matter**.	P1 1.1–1.5: Forces
	Reaction time is revisited in this chapter, giving students further practice on the **average speed equation** and the **manipulation of mathematical equations**.	P2 3.1 Speed P2 3.2 Motion graphs
	Fuel sources are covered when discussing methods of electricity generation, which helps students understand **electromagnetic induction**, **radioactivity**, and **the National Grid**.	P2 2.1 Food and fuels P2 2.6 Energy resources
Chapter 2: Turning points in physics	Different models of the Solar System and the Universe are discussed, in context of how observations changed the way we viewed things. This serves as a foundation for understanding the **law of gravitational attraction**, **the Solar system**, and **forces**.	P1 1.1 Introduction to forces P1 1.4 Forces at a distance P1 4.1–4.3: Space
	The formation of the Universe is discussed in terms of the Big Bang. Understanding of the **Big Bang** is essential when studying **universal expansion** and **redshift**.	P1 4.1 The night sky P1 4.2 The Solar System
	Forces on moving objects are further consolidated when discussing satellites in orbit and rockets fired into space. This topic offer students further foundations towards topics in **the Solar System**, **satellites**, and **forces and matter**.	P1 1.1–1.5: Forces P1 4.2 The Solar System P1 4.4 The Moon
	The radioactivity of materials is introduced in this chapter. Students will meet these concepts again when studying **the atomic model**, **isotopes**, **radiation**, and their **effect on body tissues**.	C1 1.1 The particle model C1 2.2 Atoms
	Circuit diagrams are once again consolidated in the introduction of electromagnetic induction. This is one of the most important discoveries in physics and will be revisited in further study of **electricity** and **magnetism**.	P2 1.2 Circuits and current P2 1.3 Potential difference P2 1.6–1.8: Electricity and magnetism
	The generation, transmission, and detection of electromagnetic waves for communication are discussed. This is an important concept for understanding **wave modulation**.	P1 2.1 Waves
Chapter 3: Detection	The reflection and refraction of light and other electromagnetic waves are further consolidated in the context of telescopes. The drawing of ray diagrams is a necessity for all the topics in **light as rays**, including **reflection** and **refraction**.	P1 2.1 Waves P1 2.2 Vibrations and energy transfer P1 3.1–3.4: Light
	The use of electromagnetic waves in communication is consolidated in discussing AM and FM waves, as well as the detection of waves by satellites. These are important concepts towards further study of the **electromagnetic spectrum** and **wave modulation**.	P1 2.1 Waves P1 2.2 Vibrations and energy transfer
	Atomic structure is further examined with the introduction of further subatomic particles, for example, the Higgs boson. This is important for understanding **atomic structure** and the **changes in the atomic model** over time.	C1 2.1 Elements C1 2.2 Atoms

kerboodle

P3 Unit pre-test	P3 Practical project hints: writing frame	
P3 Big practical project (foundation)	P3 End-of-unit test (foundation)	
P3 Big practical project (higher)	P3 End-of-unit test (foundation) mark scheme	
P3 Big practical project teacher notes	P3 End-of-unit test (higher)	
P3 Practical project hints: graph plotting	P3 End-of-unit test (higher) mark scheme	
P3 Practical project hints: planning		

Answers to Picture Puzzler
Key Words

parachute, Lewis Hamilton, aerial, Neptune, Earth, turtle

The key word is **planet**.

Close Up

face of a phosphorescent watch

1.1 Your phone

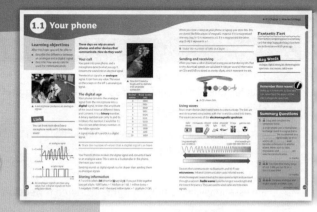

KS3 Physics NC Link:
- sound waves
- light waves.

KS3 Working Scientifically NC Link:
- apply sampling techniques.

KS4 Physics NC Link:
- recall that electromagnetic waves are transmitted through space where all have the same velocity
- give examples of some practical uses of electromagnetic waves.

Band	Outcome	Checkpoint	
		Question	Activity
Developing	Give examples of a digital and an analogue signal (Level 4).	1, 2	Main, Plenary 1, Plenary 2, Homework
	State the types of electromagnetic waves used for communication (Level 4).	1, 2	Starter 2, Main, Plenary 1, Homework
	Sample an analogue signal (Level 3).		Main
Secure	Describe the difference between an analogue and a digital signal (Level 6).	1, 2	Main, Plenary 2, Homework
	Describe how waves can be used for communication (Level 5).	2	Main, Plenary 1, Homework
	Reproduce a wave using sampling (Level 5).		Main
Extending	Suggest reasons to explain the difference in quality of analogue and digital signals (Level 7).		Main, Plenary 2
	Explain how electromagnetic waves transfer phone signals (Level 8).	2	Main, Plenary 1
	Analyse the quality of digital signals when the rate of sampling is varied (Level 8).		Main

Maths
Students extract information from a graph of an analogue wave, sampling this to give a digital signal.

Literacy
Students create their own mnemonic to remember the order of waves in the electromagnetic spectrum in the student-book activity.

APP
Students interpret analogue and digital signals provided (AF5).

Key Words
analogue, digital, bit, electromagnetic spectrum, microwave, radio wave

Answers from the student book

In-text questions	**A** 2
	B 8
Activity	**Remember those waves!**
	Credit sensible suggestions for mnemonics, for example, Red Monkeys In Venice Use eXtra Grapes.
Summary Questions	**1** analogue, digital, electromagnetic, infrared (4 marks)
	2 There are 1 000 000 000 bytes in 1 GB and 1 000 000 bytes in 1 MB.
	Therefore there are 1 000 000 000 ÷ 1 000 000 = 1000 MB in 1 GB.
	A 500 GB hard drive will hold 500 × 1000 = 500 000 songs (2 marks)

3 QWC question (6 marks). Example answers:

When you speak into a microphone the sound wave is converted to an electrical signal.

The electrical signal is an analogue signal.

An analogue signal can have any value.

Your mobile phone converts the analogue signal to a digital signal.

A digital signal is made of 1s and 0s.

Each 1 or 0 is called a bit (binary digit).

The digital signal is coded into an electromagnetic wave.

The wave is transmitted through the air to another phone.

The other phone decodes the signal and converts it back to an analogue signal.

The analogue signal is sent to a loudspeaker and you hear a sound.

Starter	Support/Extend	Resources
Measuring digital and analogue (5 min) Demonstrate the digitisation of technology using props, for example, show old style telephones, early brick-like mobile phones, phones with infrared technology, ones with Bluetooth, wifi, and finally 3G and 4G phones. Students put the devices in chronological order and discuss similarities and differences between them.		
The electromagnetic spectrum (5 min) Introduce the electromagnetic (EM) spectrum to the class, describing how certain waves can be used in communication. Ask students to use the EM spectrum to identify the types of waves used in radio, TV, phones, remote controls, photography, and optical fibres.	**Support**: Use a mnemonic to remember the order of waves, for example, Red Monkeys In Venice Use eXtra Grapes. **Extension**: Students use their existing knowledge to justify their answers.	

Main	Support/Extend	Resources
Digital and analogue (40 min) Introduce analogue and digital signals in communication using a simple example such as a phone call. Discuss how the different waves in the EM spectrum are used in communication. Ensure students are confident that analogue signals take any value but digital signals have fixed values before starting the activity. Show students how analogue waves can be sampled, and discuss advantages of sampling over recording continuous values. In the activity students sample analogue signals into digital data and answer questions that follow.	**Support**: Remind students of the different waves that make up the EM spectrum. When sampling the analogue signal, if the signal falls in the middle of two values, students should round up to the next integer as a rule of thumb.	**Activity**: Digital and analogue

Plenary	Support/Extend	Resources
How do mobile phones work? (10 min) Students reorder statements provided on the interactive resource to explain how your voice is transmitted to another person via a mobile phone.	**Extension**: Students compare this to how a signal is transmitted from a broadcasting station to a digital radio.	**Interactive**: How do mobile phones work?
Comparing analogue and digital signals (5 min) Students should give examples of digital and analogue signals using mini-whiteboards, describing the similarities and differences between them.	**Support**: Provide a list of points for students to classify as similarities or differences. **Extension**: Students explain how sampling techniques affect the quality of sound in digital signals.	

Homework		
Students find three devices at home that use analogue or digital signals. They describe how these devices process data and the EM waves used. Students use this information to explain whether the devices they have chosen use analogue or digital signals.		

KS3 Physics NC Link:
- calculation of fuel uses and costs in the domestic context
- current electricity.

KS3 Working Scientifically NC Link:
- make and record observations and measurements using a range of methods for different investigations; and suggest possible improvements.

KS4 Physics NC Link:
- design and use circuits to explore changes in resistance – including for LDRs
- explain that mechanical processes become wasteful when they cause a rise in temperature so dissipating energy in heating the surroundings.

Band	Outcome	Checkpoint	
		Question	Activity
Developing	State the equation for efficiency (Level 3).		Main
	Name the component that detects light levels (Level 3).	B, 1	Main, Homework
	Record experimental observations using the results table given (Level 3).		Main
Secure	Describe what is meant by efficiency (Level 5).	1	Starter 2, Main, Homework
	Describe how an LDR detects light (Level 6).	3	Main, Homework
	Design a suitable results table and use this to record data obtained from an investigation (Level 5).		Main
Extending	Compare quantitatively the efficiency of a range of devices (Level 7).	2	Main, Plenary 1, Homework
	Suggest different ways to use an LDR (Level 7).	3	Main, Homework
	Record observations in a suitable results table and suggest possible improvements to the experimental procedure (Level 7).		Main, Plenary 2

Maths
Students calculate the efficiency of appliances throughout this lesson, and use percentage efficiency to calculate energy dissipated in the student-book activity.

Literacy
Students organise scientific information and adapt their language to suit a general audience when writing a leaflet on increasing efficiency in the home for homework.

APP
Students record results from the experiment in a suitable results table (AF3), suggesting possible improvements to the method (AF5).

Key Words
efficient,
light-emitting diode (LED),
light-dependent resistor (LDR),
sensor, sensing circuit

Answers from the student book

In-text questions	**A** 10%
	B light-dependent resistor (LDR)
Activity	**How efficient?**
	Energy used to light the room = 45% of 100 J = 0.45 × 100 = 45 J
	Energy to heat the room = 100 J − 45 J = 55 J

Summary Questions	
	1 lighting, heating, LDR, sensing (3 marks)
	2 An LED is much more efficient than an incandescent light bulb because an LED lights the room more than heating it. (2 marks)
	3 The resistance of the LDR changes in different light levels. If the light level is high, the resistance of the LDR is low. (2 marks)
	4 QWC question (6 marks). Example answers:
	An LDR senses light levels. It can be used to sense when it is day or night.
	If the light level is high the resistance of the LDR is low.
	Two LDRs can be used in a sensing circuit.
	An LDR inside the house and one outside it can form part of a sensing circuit.
	An LDR near a lightbulb could sense when it is on and turn it off during the day.
	This means that the lightbulb would be on for less time.
	The number of kWh/units of electricity used would be fewer. The cost of your electricity bill would be less.

kerboodle

Starter	Support/Extend	Resources
Automatic controls (5 min) Ask students to list devices in their home that include automatic controls, for example, automatic lights, the kettle turning off, radiators, thermostats, and chargers for mobile devices. Ask students to suggest how they think these devices work.		
The meaning of efficiency (10 min) Explain what is meant by efficiency and ask students to suggest examples of pairs of devices that are efficient/not efficient, for example, well-maintained and badly-maintained cars or incandescent and energy-saving lightbulbs. Give the equation for efficiency and ask students to explain why machines can never be 100% efficient (due to energy dissipation).	**Extension**: Students suggest implications of using energy-efficient devices, for example, they may cost more to buy but have lower running costs due to lower fuel consumption.	

Main	Support/Extend	Resources
Investigating the efficiency of lightbulbs (40 min) Introduce how the efficiency of different appliances can be calculated before relating this to specific examples, such as lightbulbs. Students should appreciate that incandescent bulbs are extremely inefficient as a lot of the electrical energy is transferred as heat to the surroundings. Discuss ideas of increasing efficiency and reducing fuel costs by using LEDs and LDRs in sensor circuits before moving onto the practical investigation. In this practical students carry out an investigation to measure the power, temperature, and light intensity of different bulbs and the resulting resistance of the LDR in the sensor circuit. Students then answer the questions that follow.	**Support**: You may wish to recap the law of conservation of energy, and the definitions for power, resistance, and light intensity before starting the practical. The accompanying support sheet contains a partially filled results table for students to use.	**Practical**: Investigating the efficiency of lightbulbs **Skill sheet**: Recording results

Plenary	Support/Extend	Resources
Efficiency statements (5 min) Students choose the correct words to complete sentences provided on the interactive resource that relate to efficiency.	**Extension**: Encourage students to offer other sentences for the rest of the class to complete.	**Interactive**: Efficiency statements
The scientific method (10 min) Students compare results with other groups in the class, explaining possible differences in results, and suggesting improvements to the experimental procedure.	**Support**: Structure the discussion so that students are only looking for similarities and differences in data between different groups.	

Homework		
Students research ways to use machines/appliances efficiently in the home and design a leaflet suitable for homeowners to advise them on how they can reduce the amount of money spent on fuel with simple changes.		

KS3 Physics NC Link:
- light waves
- current electricity.

KS3 Working Scientifically NC Link:
- evaluate data, showing awareness of potential sources of random and systematic error.

KS4 Physics NC Link:
- design and use circuits to explore changes in resistance – including for thermistors.

Band	Outcome	Checkpoint	
		Question	Activity
Developing	Give the name of the circuit component that detects changes in temperature (Level 3).	A, 1	Lit, Plenary 1, Plenary 2, Homework
	State ways that sensors can be used in hospitals (Level 4).	1	Lit, Plenary 1, Homework
	Name the most accurate method of measuring temperature used in the experiment (Level 4).		Main
Secure	Describe how a thermistor detects changes in temperature (Level 5).	2	Lit, Main, Plenary 1, Plenary 2, Homework
	Describe how sensors can be used in hospitals (Level 5).	2	Lit, Main, Plenary 1, Homework
	Compare the accuracy of the different methods of measuring temperature used in the experiment (Level 6).		Main
Extending	Explain in basic terms how a thermistor works (Level 8).		Main, Homework
	Compare two ways in which sensors are used in hospitals (Level 7).	3	Main, Plenary 2
	Evaluate the qualitative and quantitative data obtained using different methods of measuring temperature (Level 8).		Main

Literacy
Students write a summary of how technology is used in hospital equipment for a press release in the student-book activity.

Students adapt writing style to write a leaflet for patients, reassuring them about hospital sensors, for homework.

APP
Students use models to mimic conditions in the hospital in order to investigate different ways of monitoring temperature (AF1). Students present results in appropriate tables (AF3) and evaluate the accuracy and precision of the methods used and of the data obtained (AF5).

Key Words
thermistor

Answers from the student book

In-text questions	**A** thermistor
	B small changes in potential difference
Activity	**Press release**
	Summary should include the following points:
	You can monitor temperature with a thermistor, or pulse rate using light and infrared.
	You can monitor heart rate by using electrodes that detect a change in potential difference.
	Ventilators pump air into the lungs of patients who struggle to breathe.
	You can use a defibrillator to start the heart of a patient when it has stopped and a pacemaker to keep it going.

Summary Questions	1 thermistor, infrared, potential difference, pacemaker, defibrillator (5 marks) 2 Connect a thermistor in a circuit with a cell and an ammeter. The resistance of the thermistor will decrease when the temperature increases. The current will increase as the temperature increases. (3 marks) 3 QWC question (6 marks). Example answers: Measuring pulse rate and heart rate both involve sensors. Electrodes are used to measure heart rate and electromagnetic waves (light and infrared) are used to measure pulse rate. As the heart beats, electrodes detect a change in potential difference, whereas for pulse rate, a sensor is placed on the end of a patient's finger. This sensor emits light and infrared. Blood with high oxygen content absorbs more infrared than visible light. The sensor detects the changes in blood oxygen content by monitoring infrared absorption and converts this change into a pulse rate.

Starter	Support/Extend	Resources
Monitoring temperature (5 min) Ask students for situations where it is important to monitor temperature continuously and how this could be done. Explain how sensors like thermistors are used. Students apply ideas from the previous lesson with the LDR. **Incubators** (10 min) Students suggest requirements for newborn babies in incubators. What conditions should be monitored inside the incubator? What sorts of circuits can do this? Students then discuss requirements for helpless patients (those in intensive care) and suggest how sensors could be used to provide for their needs. Be aware that this topic may be a sensitive one for some students.	**Extension**: Students discuss which is better – a temperature monitor or an automatic control to maintain temperature between fixed limits. **Support**: Prompt students towards requirements of these patients. Show students a thermistor, discuss its name, and ask students how it is similar to an LDR. (A thermistor is essentially a temperature-dependent resistor.)	

Main	Support/Extend	Resources
Monitoring temperature (40 min) Show students a thermistor and ask them what it may do. You may wish to tell students its name and say it is similar to an LDR as clues. Explain how they can be used in hospitals and introduce other common sensors. Students then calibrate a thermistor using a thermometer, use the thermistor to monitor the temperature of a model incubator, and answer the questions that follow on the practical sheet. You may wish to show students a video of a baby in an incubator so they have a clearer idea of why continuous monitoring is important. Students discuss other methods to monitor temperature, evaluating the accuracy and precision of each technique.	**Support**: A support sheet is available with a suggested results table. **Extension**: Explain to students the basic principle of how a thermistor works (semiconductors with more delocalised electrons to carry charge at higher temperatures). Students should be encouraged to draw a calibration curve if time.	**Practical**: Monitoring temperature **Skill sheet:** Recording results

Plenary	Support/Extend	Resources
Technology in hospitals (10 min) Students link together the different sensors used in hospitals with what they monitor. Students should then describe in full how each technique works. **Methods for measuring temperature** (5 min) Students use what they have learnt this lesson to reconsider how best to monitor temperature continuously, justifying their answers.	**Extension**: Students compare the use of thermistors in hospitals to that of another sensor, suggesting how other sensors can also be improved.	**Interactive**: Technology in hospitals

Homework		
Students produce a patient leaflet to describe how sensors are used around the hospital. This leaflet should be used to reassure patients about the use of technology in hospitals.	**Extension**: Students write a basic explanation of how each sensor works.	

KS3 Physics NC Link:
- sound waves
- light waves.

KS3 Working Scientifically NC Link:
- interpret observations and data, including identifying patterns and using observations, measurements, and data to draw conclusions.

KS4 Physics NC Link:
- recall that different substances may absorb, transmit, refract, or reflect electromagnetic waves
- give examples of some practical uses of electromagnetic waves.

Band	Outcome	Checkpoint	
		Question	**Activity**
Developing	State one way in which optical fibres are used (Level 3).	1	Main, Homework
	State the types of electromagnetic wave used to see inside the human body (Level 3).	B, 1	Main, Plenary 1, Plenary 2
↓	Choose a suitable technique to diagnose symptoms in a given patient (Level 4).		Main
Secure	Describe how optical fibres work (Level 5).	1, 2	Main, Homework
	Describe some techniques for seeing inside the human body (Level 5).	3	Main, Plenary 1, Plenary 2
↓	Choose a suitable technique to diagnose symptoms in a given patient, justifying their answer (Level 6).		Main
Extending	Use a ray diagram to explain how optical fibres work (Level 7).		Main, Homework
	Compare the use of different waves in the EM spectrum for seeing inside the human body (Level 7).	4	Main, Plenary 1
↓	Evaluate the risks and benefits of using one of the techniques discussed to diagnose symptoms, giving an overall conclusion (Level 8).		Main

Maths
Students use protractors correctly when measuring angles and drawing ray diagrams to show total internal reflection (TIR).

Literacy
Students write crossword clues for scientific vocabulary in the student-book activity. They summarise uses of optical fibres and TIR in a poster for homework.

APP
Students draw conclusions from observations given (AF5).

Key Words
endoscope, critical angle, total internal reflection, optical fibre, X-ray, gamma ray, magnetic resonance imaging (MRI)

Answers from the student book

In-text questions	**A** The angle at which the angle of refraction is 90°.
	B visible light, X-rays, gamma rays
Activity	**Crossword clues** Credit sensible suggestions for crossword clues, for example: visible light – used in an endoscope X-rays – used to see broken bones gamma rays – used to see internal organs ultrasound – used to see a fetus or internal organs (the latter is done by using this wave on the end of an endoscope)

Summary Questions	1 bigger, reflected, endoscope, X-rays, gamma rays (5 marks)
	2 The angle of incidence must be bigger than the critical angle. The ray of light must be hitting the boundary from inside the medium/glass. (2 marks)
	3a MRI scanners can be used to investigate how the brain works. This technique relies on the use of extremely powerful magnets to produce images. (2 marks)
	b Gamma rays can be used to check for kidney function. The patient drinks a special chemical that is taken in by the kidneys and emits gamma rays (medical tracer). A detector is then used outside the body, detecting the gamma rays emitted and producing an image. (2 marks)
	4 QWC question (6 marks). Example answers:
	Visible light is used in endoscopes. Light is reflected within optical fibres. X-rays are used to take images of bones. Bones absorb more X-rays than soft tissues, so the X-rays that pass through a body can build an image of the bones inside. Gamma rays are used to investigate kidney function. A medical tracer is ingested and is absorbed by the kidney. Detectors detect the gamma rays emitted. Ultrasound is emitted from a transmitter. It reflects off objects and is detected by a receiver. This can be used to monitor soft tissues. MRI scanners use powerful electromagnets to see how organs like the brain work.

Starter	Support/Extend	Resources
An alternative question-led lesson is also available. **What's wrong?** (10 min) Ask students to suggest ways that a doctor can diagnose what is wrong with a patient without operating. If appropriate, present a student as a patient with imaginary symptoms. **Optical fibres** (10 min) Demonstrate optical fibres by shining an LED light in one end and allowing students to use the other end as a light. Ideally, the optical fibre should be over 2 m in length. Students suggest possible uses of optical fibres. They may already know some uses in communication (e.g., fibre optic broadband).	**Extension**: Students discuss advantages and disadvantages of the methods suggested, for example, ease/speed of use and reliability.	**Question-led lesson**: Your hospital – seeing inside

Main	Support/Extend	Resources
Patient diagnosis (40 min) Introduce the different EM waves that can be used by doctors to see inside the body without operating. Discuss the risks and benefits of these techniques. It is important at this stage that students understand total internal reflection (TIR) in the use of optical fibre endoscopes. Demonstrate TIR using optical fibres or the TIR of light through a stream of water. Students then read a summary of five different diagnosis techniques and answer the questions that follow. Before starting the activity, you may wish to discuss with students their experiences, for example, having X-rays taken for broken bones or at the dentist. If possible, include X-ray images or ultrasound footage to make the lesson more relevant. Be aware that this topic may be sensitive for some students.	**Support**: Recap reflection, refraction, and the EM spectrum if necessary. The support sheet lists uses of the EM spectrum to help students answer the questions.	**Activity**: Patient diagnosis

Plenary	Support/Extend	Resources
X-rays (5 min) Students reorder sentences provided on the interactive resource to describe how X-rays can be used in hospitals to assess broken bones. **Summary of diagnosis techniques** (10 min) Students work in groups to present a 30-second infomercial that summarises the different diagnosis techniques available in hospitals.	**Extension**: Students consider why some diagnosis methods are available in doctors' surgeries, while others are only available in hospitals (cost, risks, etc.).	**Interactive**: X-rays

Homework		
Students produce a poster to summarise the uses of optical fibres and TIR. (This poster should not be limited to medical uses.)	**Extension**: Include a clearly labelled ray diagram of TIR.	

KS3 Physics NC Link:

- describing motion
- forces and motion.

KS3 Working Scientifically NC Link:

- evaluate data, showing awareness of potential sources of random and systematic error.

KS4 Physics NC Link:

- explain the vector-scalar distinction as it applies to displacement, velocity, and speed
- recall Newton's First Law and relate it to observations showing that forces can change direction of motion as well as its speed
- explain that force is rate of momentum change and explain the dangers caused by large decelerations and the forces involved.

Band	Outcome	Checkpoint	
		Question	**Activity**
Developing	State one way in which technology is used in sport (Level 3).	1	Starter 1, Plenary 1
	State the name of the time taken for a person to react to a signal (Level 3).	B	Plenary 1
	Give the definitions of random and systematic error (Level 4).		Plenary 2
Secure	Describe how technology is used in sport (Level 5).	3	Starter 1, Main
	Describe what is meant by reaction time (Level 5).	2	Main
	Identify sources of random and systematic errors in given scenarios (Level 5).		
Extending	Explain the advantages of using technology in timing for sport (Level 7).	4	Main
	Explain the impact of reaction time on the timing of different sport races (Level 8).	4	Main
	Suggest ways to minimise random and systematic errors for given scenarios (Level 7).		Plenary 2

Maths
Students demonstrate understanding of proportion when discussing effects of reaction times on sprints compared to marathons. Students quantitatively compare this in the extension task of the activity sheet.

Literacy
Students interpret ideas provided in scientific text and use scientific terms correctly when explaining the difference between accuracy and precision.

APP
Students discuss possible sources of error in using technology for timing sports events (AF4).

Key Words
projectile motion, reaction time, uncertainty

Answers from the student book

In-text questions	**A** The speed and the direction of motion. **B** reaction time
Summary Questions	**1** speed, reaction, time, force (4 marks) **2** Reaction time is the time taken for a signal to be sent from the ear to the brain, where it is interpreted, and then for the brain to send signals to the relevant part(s) of the body to produce a response to a given signal. (2 marks)

3 A stopwatch depends on the reaction time of the person holding it. They have to see the ball touch the ground before reacting, which takes time. A light gate does not involve reaction times. When the ball interrupts the light beam, the timer stops. The time given is therefore more accurate. (4 marks)

4 QWC question (6 marks). Example answers:
Light gates are used to time races. This occurs in a variety of sports such as athletics, swimming, and racing. These are important as they eliminate human reaction time. A beam of light is fired from one light gate to another on the other side of the track. Finishers interrupt the beam, which sends an electric signal to the timer, giving an accurate time for the race. Formula one is another sport that uses technology. Drivers wear special helmets and clothing that have been designed to absorb shock, and are fire-proof. Cars are designed to increase contact time in a collision to minimise injury (crumple zones). Cameras also take photos at high speeds (hundreds per second) to help decide photo finishes in races.

kerboodle

Starter	Support/Extend	Resources
Olympic timings (10 min) Show students a video about the importance of timing in sport, for example, 'Science of the Summer Olympics – Measuring a champion' from NBC Learn is an excellent resource. Students list and describe ways of using technology for timing in different sports after watching this video. This video also discusses the importance of accuracy and precision.	**Support**: Give students a list of methods for measuring time to match against the sports in the video. **Extension**: Students suggest the advantages and disadvantages of using different timing methods for different events.	
Why do champions win? (10 min) In groups, students select a sport and write down reasons why champions win. They use their list to discuss the impact of speed and reaction times on winning. Open up to a class discussion.	**Support**: Provide a set of reasons for students to rank in a diamond nine.	

Main	Support/Extend	Resources
Reaction times (35 min) Introduce reaction times and their importance in timing sport events. Point out to students how athletes take time to react, and how significant reaction times are in short-distance races. You could show video clips of different sporting events to demonstrate this, in slow motion if possible. Alternatively, use an interactive reaction timer. These are readily available on the Internet. Students then read information about data obtained in 100-m races to discuss the effect of reaction time on athletes' performances, answering questions that follow. If time, allow students to calculate their reaction time using a video of Usain Bolt's 100-m race and a stopwatch. Difference between official race time and stopwatch reading is roughly twice their reaction time. Good Internet connection will be necessary for this part of the activity.	**Support**: Students may require a reminder of the factors affecting reaction time before the start of this activity.	**Activity**: Reaction times

Plenary	Support/Extend	Resources
Sport events (10 min) Students use the clues provided on the interactive resource to complete a crossword based on the key words in this lesson.	**Extension**: Students add their own key words and clues.	**Interactive**: Sport events
Accuracy versus precision (10 min) Recap the definition of accuracy and precision. Students describe the accuracy and precision of scenarios in sports. They give the definition of random and systematic errors, identifying possible sources of these errors in the given scenarios.	**Extension**: Students suggest ways to minimise errors.	

Homework		
Students research another way (other than timing races in athletics) where technology is used in sport. This can be done as an information poster or leaflet. An alternative WebQuest homework activity is also available on Kerboodle where students research technology used for timing in sport.	**Extension**: Challenge students to find out about crumple zones in cars and how this relates to safety in Formula 1.	**WebQuest**: Timing in sport

1.6 Your planet

KS3 Physics NC Link:
- calculation of fuel uses and costs in the domestic context.

KS3 Working Scientifically NC Link:
- interpret observations and data, including identifying patterns and using observations, measurements, and data to draw conclusions.

KS4 Physics NC Link:
- list and describe the main energy sources available for use on Earth (including fossil fuels, nuclear fuel, biofuel, wind, the tides, and the Sun) and distinguish between renewable and non-renewable sources.

Band	Outcome	Checkpoint	
		Question	Activity
Developing	State how the demand for electricity is changing (Level 3).	1	Lit, Starter 1, Main
	State ways to meet future electricity demands (Level 4).	B, 2	Main, Plenary 2, Homework
	Use graphical data to state the countries that have the highest and lowest oil use per person (Level 3).		Main
Secure	Explain why demand for electricity is increasing (Level 5).	A, 1	Lit, Starter 1, Main, Plenary 1
	Describe how future demand for electricity could be met (Level 5).	2	Main, Plenary 2, Homework
	Describe the general relationship between oil use and average income per person (Level 5).		Main
Extending	Suggest reasons why the demand for electricity is increasing in different countries (Level 7).		Lit, Main, Plenary 1
	Evaluate advantages and disadvantages of different methods of electricity generation (Level 8).	3	Main, Plenary 2, Homework
	Calculate and compare the oil consumption of different countries using the data provided (Level 8).		Main

Maths
Students interpret information from graphs and tables, identifying patterns given in numerical form to draw conclusions and answer questions.

Literacy
In the student-book activity students write a summary for 'an electricity journey' that lists everything the student uses electricity for in a day.

APP
Students interpret numerical data provided in graphs and tables and evaluate the different methods of electricity generation (AF5).

Key Words
nuclear fusion

Answers from the student book

In-text questions	**A** Any from: bigger population, more developed countries, or more devices that use electricity. **B** Two from: wind, waves, tides, falling water (hydroelectric), geothermal. **C** nuclear fusion
Activity	**How many?** Students' entries should include all the devices they use or encounter in a day that require electricity, for example, electric light, phone, radio, alarm, shower, toaster, kettle, car, traffic lights, laptop/computer/tablet, MP3 player, projector, power packs, oven, and TV.

Summary Questions	**1** increasing, increasing, increasing, don't (4 marks)
	2 Any two from (4 marks):
	Wind, wave, tidal, falling water (hydroelectric) – these turn the turbines directly.
	Geothermal – water is pumped underground. The Earth heats the water to steam that drives a turbine.
	Nuclear fusion – hydrogen atoms fuse together to make helium, releasing large amounts of energy.
	Solar cells – absorb light from the Sun, produce a potential difference directly.
	3 Credit sensible suggestions for the rules of a snakes and ladders game. Example answers (6 marks):
	Ladders for:
	An increase of renewable fuel sources, because carbon dioxide emission is less than for fossil fuels overall, and these fuel sources will not run out.
	Using nuclear fusion, because a lot of energy is released in the reaction, with no greenhouse gases produced.
	Snakes for:
	Using fossil fuels, as these add to pollution and contribute to climate change.
	Using nuclear fusion, as this is extremely difficult to set up, and a working fusion reactor for electricity generation has yet to be achieved.

Starter	Support/Extend	Resources
What have you used yesterday? (10 min) Students list everything they used the day before that requires electricity to run. How does this list compare to students 30 years ago? Ask students to suggest how the demand for electricity is changing based on their answer to the previous question.	**Extension**: Students categorise equipment as necessities or luxury items.	
Demand graphs (10 min) Students sketch a graph showing demand for electricity varying during one day in their home. The graph should show peaks (morning/evening) and troughs (at night). Students should then explain the shape of the graphs they have drawn.	**Support**: Ask students if they use electricity when asleep compared to when watching TV.	

Main	Support/Extend	Resources
The demand for electricity (35 min) Discuss with students the general trend (increase) in the demand for electivity over the last 30 years. Explain why this is the case on a global scale. Introduce the different methods of electricity generation that can meet demand. Ask students for advantages and disadvantages of each method. Ensure students understand that nuclear fusion is in its experimental stage. You may wish to show students photographs of the 'doughnut' from the JET reactor for added context. Students then use numerical data presented in graphs and tables to interpret oil usage in different countries and how this relates to other factors (climate, average annual income of population). Students use their own knowledge and the data provided to answer questions about electricity demand and generation, suggesting reasons for patterns identified in the data.	**Support**: Discuss with students what the data provided show, and how the graph can be linked to the table before allowing students to begin the activity. **Extension**: The main differences between nuclear fission and fusion can be explained briefly, where appropriate.	**Activity**: The demand for electricity

Plenary	Support/Extend	Resources
The demand for electricity (10 min) Students categorise possible reasons for the increasing demand for electricity using the interactive resource.	**Extension**: Students think of other reasons, particularly relating to other countries.	**Interactive**: The demand for electricity
Future demand (10 min) Students write a paragraph on one method of generating electricity. Include a brief description, one advantage, one disadvantage, and a conclusion. Students peer mark their answers, and share some with the rest of the class.	**Support**: Limit methods to ones that are easy to explain, for example, fossil fuels.	

Homework		
Students complete the activity sheet and write a report on how each country on the activity sheet can meet its demand for electricity, using the data provided.		

Checkpoint lesson routes

The route through this lesson can be determined using the Checkpoint assessment.

Percentage pass marks are supplied in the Checkpoint teacher notes.

Route A (revision)
Resource: P3 Chapter 1 Checkpoint: Revision

Students work through a series of tasks that allows them to revisit and consolidate their understanding of the topics within this chapter. Students can keep this as a summary of the topic, and use this when revising for future assessments.

Route B (extension)
Resource: P3 Chapter 1 Checkpoint: Extension

Students design exam questions and an accompanying mark scheme that must include a visual summary of the key concepts covered in this topic.

Progression to *secure*

No.	Developing outcome	Secure outcome	Making progress
1	Give examples of a digital and an analogue signal.	Describe the difference between an analogue and a digital signal.	In Task 1 students label analogue and digital signals and use these to describe similarities and differences between them.
2	State the types of electromagnetic waves used for communication.	Describe how waves can be used for communication.	In Task 1 students match different electronic devices to the types of electromagnetic waves they use.
3	State the equation for efficiency.	Describe what is meant by efficiency.	In Task 2 students describe the term efficiency using the context of two lightbulbs.
4	Name the component that detects light levels.	Describe how an LDR detects light.	In Task 3 students use a resistance–light graph to describe how changing light levels affect the resistance in an LDR.
5	Give the name of the circuit component that detects changes in temperature.	Describe how a thermistor detects changes in temperature.	In Task 3 students complete a word fill to describe how a thermistor detects temperature.
	State ways that sensors can be used in hospitals.	Describe how sensors can be used in hospitals.	In Task 3 students complete a table to describe how different sensors are used in hospitals.
6	State one way in which optical fibres are used.	Describe how optical fibres work.	In Task 3 students use the key terms provided to describe how optical fibres work.
7	State the types of electromagnetic wave used to see inside the human body.	Describe some techniques for seeing inside the human body.	In Task 3 students match different techniques for looking inside the human body with their descriptions.
8	State one way in which technology is used in sport.	Describe how technology is used in sport.	In Task 4 students complete a table to describe how different types of technology are used in sport.
9	State the name of the time taken for a person to react to a signal.	Describe what is meant by reaction time.	In Task 4 students describe reaction time in the context of a 100-m race.
10	State how the demand for electricity is changing.	Explain why demand for electricity is increasing.	In Task 5 students suggest three possible reasons for the increase in electricity demand.
11	State ways to meet future electricity demands.	Describe how future demand for electricity could be met.	In Task 5 students select possible ways to meet the increasing demand for electricity from statements provided.

Answers to end-of-chapter questions

1 radio waves, visible light, X-rays, infrared (4 marks)
2 LDR – used to detect light   thermistor – used to detect temperature
   LED – an efficient lightbulb   endoscope – used to see inside people   (4 marks)
3 0.2 seconds (1 mark)
4a Any two from: endoscopy/X-rays/gamma rays/ultrasound/MRIs
 b Design helmets/protective clothing for the driver and having design features on the car to increase contact time during a collision. (2 marks)
5a How does the number of layers of plastic film affect the potential difference produced by a solar cell? (1 mark)
 b Column headers: Number of layers of plastic film, Potential difference (V) (1 mark)
 c A bar chart should be drawn because the number of layers of plastic film is a discrete variable. (2 marks)
6a The complete diagram should include the following points (4 marks):
   existing light ray continues in a straight line through the first surface
   reflected through 90° at the second surface
   continues in a straight line through the third surface
 b Waves entering a surface along the normal are not refracted. Waves approaching the second surface at an angle greater than the critical angle are totally internally reflected. (2 marks)
7 Sketch graph should show the resistance decreasing with temperature in a curve (credit $\frac{1}{x}$ or exponential decay). This is because in a thermistor, the resistance decreases with an increase in temperature. (2 marks)
8a analogue (1 mark)   b digital (1 mark)   c digital (1 mark)   d analogue (1 mark)
9 lightbulb – 20 J, 20% (2 marks)   kettle – 1500 J, 75% (2 marks)
   television – 5000 J, 50% (2 marks)   car – 300 J, 25% (2 marks)
10 This is a QWC question. Students should be marked on the use of good English, organisation of information, spelling and grammar, and correct use of specialist scientific terms. The best answers will fully explain how thermistors and heaters can be used to keep the temperature of a greenhouse constant (maximum of 6 marks). Examples of correct scientific points:
   A heater increases the temperature inside the greenhouse.
   A thermistor detects temperature.
   Its resistance goes down as temperature increases.
   A sensing circuit can be used, containing a thermistor, to detect when the temperature inside the greenhouse is too low.
   This can then switch on the heater to warm the greenhouse.
   The thermistor can detect when the optimum temperature is reached.
   The sensing circuit can then turn off the heater.

Answer guide for Big Write

Developing	Secure	Extending
1–2 marks	3–4 marks	5–6 marks

• Display boards include some examples of technology from two the following categories: homes, hospitals, sport, and electricity generation.
• Display describes briefly some of the ways technology has affected our lives.
	• Display boards include some examples of technology from three of the following categories: homes, hospitals, sport, and electricity generation.
	• Display describes the impact of the following technologies:
	  o LEDs
	  o endoscopes/scanning
	  o electronic timing
	  o renewable resources.
	• Display describes at least one of the uses above in detail.
		• Display boards include at least one example of technology from all of the following categories: homes, hospitals, sport, and electricity generation.
		• Display describe the impact of the following technologies:
		  o LEDs/LDRs
		  o endoscopes/X-rays/gamma rays/MRI
		  o electronic timing
		  o renewable resources.
		• Display describes at least three of the uses above in detail.
		• Display explains how at least one of the uses above works.

kerboodle

P3 Chapter 1 Checkpoint assessment (automarked)	P3 Chapter 1 Checkpoint: Extension
P3 Chapter 1 Checkpoint: Revision	P3 Chapter 1 Progress task (Maths)

2.1 Discovering the Universe 1

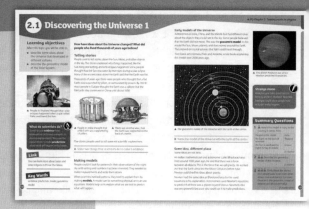

KS3 Physics NC Link:

- forces
- space physics.

KS4 Physics NC Link:

- give examples of forces that act without contact across an empty space, linking these to the gravity, electric, and magnetic fields involved
- explain the difference between planetary orbits and orbits of meteors
- explain for circular orbits how the force of gravity can lead to changing velocity of a planet but unchanged speed.

Band	Outcome	Checkpoint	
		Questions	Activities
Developing	State some ideas about the Universe that developed in different cultures (Level 4).	1	Lit, Starter 1, Main, Plenary 1
↓	State what is meant by geocentric (Level 3).	2	Starter 2, Main, Plenary 2
Secure	Describe some ideas about the Universe that developed in different cultures (Level 6).	1	Lit, Starter 1, Main, Plenary 1
↓	Describe the geocentric model of the Solar System (Level 5).	2	Starter 2, Main, Plenary 2
Extending	Compare ideas about the Universe that developed in different cultures (Level 7).	3	Main, Plenary 1
↓	Suggest an observation that could not be explained by the geocentric model (Level 8).		Main, Homework

Literacy
Students extract and summarise a range of information from different sources about the beliefs of different cultures regarding the Earth and the Solar System, discussing ideas in a presentation.

APP
Students use models to describe the beliefs of different cultures regarding the Earth and the Solar System (AF1).

Key Words
evidence, prediction, model, geocentric model

Answers from the student book

In-text questions	**A** make observations, take measurements
	B geocentric
Activity	**Strange moon** Eclipses can be demonstrated using light sources and round objects. Demonstrate how the shadow produced when an object blocks a light source can be cast over a celestial body, for example, the Moon. There is no light for the moon to reflect, meaning that we will not see the Moon during an eclipse.

Summary Questions	
	1 geocentric model – Greece the Earth on the back of a tortoise – India the Sun is swallowed by a god during a solar eclipse – Thailand (3 marks) **2** The Earth is at the centre. The Sun, Moon, planets, and stars move around the Earth (on crystal spheres that allow light to be transmitted). (2 marks) **3** QWC question (6 marks). Example answers: Stories and scientific explanations both tried to explain what we see. Scientists collect evidence. Evidence can be obtained by measurements or observations. Scientists use evidence to develop the explanation. They use the explanation to make predictions about what will happen in the future. If the predictions come true then it supports the explanation. You cannot make predictions with stories. Stories do not depend on evidence. Stories are often rooted in beliefs.

kerboodle

Starter	Support/Extend	Resources
Beliefs about the Universe (10 min) Describe one theory from the corresponding student-book spread about the Universe. Ask students for ideas about what they think. If students know that the story is untrue, ask them to justify this by comparing the story with known observations/explanations today. Be aware that sensitivity is required when discussing different religious beliefs. **Geo- words** (5 min) Show students a list of words with the prefix 'geo-' on the board. Ask students what these words have in common, and what the prefix may mean.	**Support**: Choose a belief that is far-fetched by today's standards, for example, Apollo pulling the Sun along in his chariot. **Extension**: Students should explain what the geocentric model of the Solar System is based on other words given.	

Main	Support/Extend	Resources
The Solar System in different cultures (40 min) Introduce different ideas about the Solar System that developed in different cultures, focusing on the geocentric model. Students then work in groups to make a model of one of these beliefs (flat Earth, world turtle, or geocentric model). Students have 30 minutes to research and create their models before giving a two-minute presentation to the rest of the class. Students should complete the grid summarising the three different beliefs during the presentations.	**Support**: You may wish to read the corresponding spread in the student book with students to support weaker readers. Further prompts may be required to help students find the relevant information. **Extension**: Encourage students to evaluate the models created by others.	**Activity**: The Solar System in different cultures

Plenary	Support/Extend	Resources
The Solar System in other cultures (5 min) Students match each country to how its people believed the Solar System was constructed using the interactive resource. Students should then be asked to describe each model given. **The geocentric model** (10 min) Ask students true or false questions relating to the geocentric model. Questions may relate to the name or description of the model. Ask students to show their answers using thumbs up/thumbs down, coloured cards, or a traffic light system.	**Extension**: Students compare one model with another. **Extension**: Students should add further questions to ask the rest of the class.	**Interactive**: The Solar System in other cultures

Homework		
Students carry out further research on the geocentric model, writing down three interesting facts that were not covered in the lesson.	**Extension**: Students focus on observations that could not be explained using the geocentric model.	

2.2 Discovering the Universe 2

KS3 Physics NC Link:

● space physics.

KS3 Working Scientifically NC Link:

● present reasoned explanations including explaining data in relation to predictions and hypotheses.

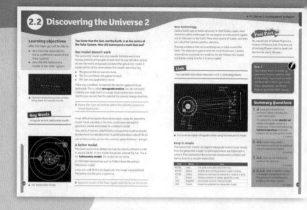

Band	Outcome	Checkpoint	
		Questions	**Activities**
Developing	State some observations that led to our present model of the Solar System (Level 4).	1, 2	Main, Plenary 1
↓	Name our present model of the Solar System (Level 3).	B	Main, Plenary 2
Secure	Describe how observations led to a different model of the Solar System (Level 6).	1, 2	Main, Plenary 1
↓	Describe the heliocentric model of the Solar System (Level 5).	3	Starter 2, Main, Plenary 2
Extending	Compare similarities and differences between different models of the Solar System (Level 7).		Main, Plenary 1
↓	Explain the importance of evidence in developing the heliocentric model (Level 7).	4	Main, Plenary 2

Maths
Students show their understanding of number size and scale when presenting the developments of the geocentric and heliocentric models on a scaled timeline.

Literacy
In the student-book activity students find out about words beginning in 'geo'.
Students collate scientific information from a range of sources to write a presentation about the development of the heliocentric model from the geocentric model.

APP
Students use the geocentric and heliocentric models of the Solar System to explain observations in the night sky (AF1). Students research these models and present their ideas to the rest of the class (AF3).

Key Words
retrograde motion, heliocentric model

Answers from the student book

In-text questions	**A** retrograde motion **B** heliocentric model
Activity	**Geo-?** geography – relating to maps and images of the Earth geometry – relating to measurements (of the Earth) Words beginning with 'helio-' are related to the Sun, for example, heliocentric, heliosphere.
Summary Questions	**1** did not, Galileo (2 marks) **2** The geocentric model has the Earth at its centre. The Sun and planets orbited the Earth. This did not explain Galileo's observation that objects (moons) orbited Jupiter. (2 marks) **3** The heliocentric model has the Sun at the centre. Planets orbit the Sun. (2 marks)

4 Timeline should include (6 marks):

Over 2000 years ago – Plato and Aristotle wrote books explaining the geocentric model. This model was hypothesised due to several observations: the ground did not seem to move, the Sun and Moon did appear to move, and the stars also appeared to move.

Around 200 BC – Greek astronomer Aristarchus hypothesised the heliocentric model. This was ignored.

Around 1000 years ago – an Indian mathematician and astronomer called Bhaskaracharya said there was a force between all objects called gravity.

140 AD – Ptolemy published his modified version of the geocentric model. This model was made to explain retrograde motion, the apparent backward motion of planets at various points throughout the year.

1543 – Copernicus published a book with the heliocentric model.

Around 500 years ago – Newton published his ideas about gravity, using equations as evidence for his and Bhaskaracharya's ideas.

1609 – Galileo used a telescope to observe the moons of Jupiter. This provided evidence that supported the heliocentric model.

Starter	Support/Extend	Resources
How are observations about the Solar System made? (5 min) Ask students to suggest how observations about the Solar System are made, leading the discussion towards the use of telescopes and how Galileo was the first person to use the telescope for celestial observations. Observations of the Solar System can be presented in the form of a timeline. **Geocentric versus heliocentric** (10 min) Students recap what is meant by the geocentric model of the Universe. Ask students to discuss whether this is the model we use today. Why/why not? Encourage students to give examples (moons orbiting other planets, retrograde motion).	**Extension**: You may wish to introduce some of the different types of telescopes available (light, radio waves, etc.).	

Main	Support/Extend	Resources
Understanding the Universe (40 min) Review the geocentric model before introducing the heliocentric model. You may wish to use animations or ask students to volunteer in a role play depicting the two models for consolidation. Students then carry out a research task using the student book (and other available resources) on the geocentric and heliocentric models. Students answer questions posed on the activity sheet and add further information of their own in order to discuss their findings in a presentation. It is important that students have covered the contents of the two corresponding spreads in the student book prior to beginning this activity.	**Support**: The accompanying support sheet gives students a writing frame to complete about the two models of our Solar System. Students may then read their completed writing frames for the presentation.	**Activity**: Understanding the Universe

Plenary	Support/Extend	Resources
From geocentric to heliocentric (5 min) Students reorder statements provided on the interactive resource to describe how observations led to the geocentric model being discarded in favour of the heliocentric model. **The heliocentric model** (10 min) Students work in groups to perform a role play that describes the heliocentric model of the Solar System. There should be added commentary to the role play.	**Extension**: Students should compare similarities and differences between the different models of the Solar System. **Extension**: Students can start by modelling the geocentric model before explaining the evidence for the shift towards the heliocentric model.	**Interactive**: From geocentric to heliocentric

Homework		
Students write a short article in the school magazine explaining the meaning of retrograde motion and how this led to the change from the geocentric to heliocentric model. The article should contain a model/analogy to explain retrograde motion, as well as a description of the heliocentric model.		

2.3 The Big Bang

KS3 Physics NC Link:
- space physics.

KS3 Working Scientifically NC Link:
- present observations and data using appropriate methods, including tables and graphs.

KS4 Physics NC Link:
- explain the redshift of light from galaxies that are receding (qualitative only), that the change of speed with galaxies' distances is evidence of an expanding universe, and hence explain the link between the evidence and the Big Bang model.

Band	Outcome	Checkpoint	
		Questions	Activities
Developing	State the age of the Solar System (Level 3).	B, 2	Main
	Name the theory of how the Universe started (Level 3).	A	Main, Plenary 2
↓	Present key events following the Big Bang visually (Level 4).		Main
Secure	Describe the timescale of the Universe (Level 6).	1, 2, 4	Main, Plenary 1
	Describe what is meant by the Big Bang (level 5).	3	Main, Plenary 2, Homework
↓	Present and describe key events following the Big Bang (Level 5).		Main
Extending	Explain why atoms could not be formed immediately after the Big Bang (Level 7).		Main, Plenary 1
	Explain ways in which the Big Bang theory is supported by evidence (Level 8).		Main, Plenary 2, Homework
↓	Present and describe key events following the Big Bang, focusing on one event in detail (Level 7).		Main

Maths
Students convert units of time to equivalents in length, presenting major events leading from the Big Bang to the beginning of the human race on a scaled timeline.

Literacy
Students collate information from different sources, interpreting meaning from scientific text, and adapting their language to suit the audience when presenting a summary of this information on a poster.

APP
Students describe evidence to support the Big Bang theory (AF1) and present major events in the development of the Universe on a poster and on a timeline (AF3).

Key Words
Big Bang, analogy

Answers from the student book

In-text questions	**A** the Big Bang
	B 5 billion years

Summary Questions	
	1 Big Bang, formation of the Solar System, first living things, dinosaurs died out (4 marks)
	2 Age of the Earth = 5 billion years
	Age of the Universe = 14 billion years
	So the Earth is $\frac{5}{14}$ of the age of the Universe. (2 marks)
	3 The beginning of the Universe and expansion of space and time from something smaller than an atom. (2 marks)
	4 Timeline should include the following events (measurements given assume a timeline that is 14 cm in length is drawn) (6 marks):
	14 billion years ago (0 cm) – the Big Bang. Space and time expanded from something smaller than an atom.
	13.85 billion years ago (0.15 cm) – the first stars began to appear
	5 billion years ago (9 cm) – our Solar System was formed
	4 billion years ago (10 cm) – first signs of life on Earth
	Between 65–200 million years ago (13.8–13.935 cm) – dinosaurs on Earth
	Half a million years ago (13.9995 cm) – start of human life
	Students may wish to zoom in on the sections with dinosaurs and humans for clarity.

Starter	Support/Extend	Resources
What is a billion? (5 min) Ask students what a billion means to them. Students may have met million before but they may not have met billion. Help students appreciate the scale of a billion by writing one billion in full. You may wish to give examples of one billion, for example, one million seconds = 11.5 days but one billion seconds = 31.7 years. Take care that 1 billion = 1×10^9 and not 1×10^{12}.	**Extension**: Encourage students to write these large numbers using standard form.	
How did the universe begin? (10 min) Ask students to discuss their ideas of how the Universe began. Allow students to pair-share their ideas before opening up as a class discussion. Some students may have learnt about the Big Bang before but others may not.		

Main	Support/Extend	Resources
The timescale of the Universe (40 min) Students carry out an activity where they read the information provided about the Big Bang theory and present the information in a different and eye-catching way on a poster. Other resources, for example, textbooks and the Internet, may be provided if available for students to carry out further research on one area of interest.	**Support**: You may wish to read the text provided as a group to help weaker readers access the material given.	**Activity**: The timescale of the Universe

Plenary	Support/Extend	Resources
How the Universe began (5 min) Students arrange the main events in the evolution of the Universe into sequence using the interactive resource.	**Extension**: Students explain why one event cannot happen without another before it.	**Interactive**: How the Universe began
What is the Big Bang? (10 min) Students line up in a traffic light system to show how confident they are at answering this question. Those that are confident (green) should explain to those who are less sure (amber and red). Ask students to line up again after five minutes. Encourage students to provide evidence to support the Big Bang theory, for example, cosmic microwave background radiation (CMBR).	**Support**: Provide students with a list of key words from this lesson that they can use to answer the question posed.	

Homework		
Students write a poem to describe the Big Bang.	**Extension**: Students write a poem about how CMBR or redshift supports the Big Bang theory.	

2.4 Spacecraft and satellites

KS3 Physics NC Link:

- describing motion
- forces
- forces and motion
- balanced forces
- space physics.

KS3 Working Scientifically NC Link:

- make predictions using scientific knowledge and understanding.

KS4 Physics NC Link:

- explain that motion in a circle involves constant speed but changing velocity (qualitative only)
- relate linear motion to other relative motions, such as the Earth's relative to the Sun
- explain the concept of equilibrium and identify, for equilibrium situations, the forces that balance one another
- explain for circular orbits how the force of gravity can lead to changing velocity of a planet but unchanged speed, and relate this association to the orbits of communications satellites around the Earth.

Band	Outcome	Checkpoint	
		Questions	**Activities**
Developing	Name the orbits a satellite can take (Level 4).	B, 1	Main, Plenary 2, Homework
	State some uses of satellites (Level 4).	1	Starter 1, Plenary 2, Homework
	Predict the orbit of a given satellite based on its use (Level 4).		Main
Secure	Describe how to get a satellite into orbit (Level 6).	2	Main, Plenary 1
	Describe some uses of satellites (Level 5).	3	Plenary 2, Homework
	Predict with justification the orbit of a given satellite based on its use (Level 6).		Main
Extending	Compare the orbits of different satellites (Level 7).	3	Main, Homework
	Compare the different uses of satellites (Level 7).	3	Main, Homework
	Provide detailed explanations of the orbits of satellites given their uses (Level 7).		Main

Maths

In the student-book activity students convert between units of time to calculate the number of times the ISS orbits the Earth each day.

Students calculate the radius and circumference of different orbits, and the speed, distance, and time in orbit for satellites. These calculation require some rearrangement of the relevant equations.

APP

Students predict the orbit taken by different satellites based on the information given (AF5).

Key Words

geostationary orbit, low Earth orbit (LEO), polar orbit

Answers from the student book

In-text questions	**A** force of the gases on the rocket, force of the Earth on the rocket (gravity) **B** geostationary
Activity	**How many?** There are 24 × 60 minutes in one day = 1440 minutes The ISS orbits 1440 ÷ 90 = 16 times a day
Summary Questions	**1** geostationary orbit – satellite television polar orbit – mapping the Earth's surface low Earth orbit – International Space Station (3 marks) **2** The satellite must be launched at the right speed, to the right height. The force of gravity keeps the satellite in orbit. (2 marks) **3** QWC question (6 marks). Example answers: Both types of satellites orbit the Earth. Both types of satellites can be used to monitor the Earth. Geostationary orbits are always above the same place on Earth. Geostationary satellites are used for satellite television. The orbit of a geostationary satellite is much bigger than low Earth orbit (LEO) satellites. A geostationary satellite is about 36 000 km from the Earth. A LEO has an orbit below 1000 km from Earth. LEOs can be used to see the whole of the Earth's surface. The ISS is an example of a satellite in LEO. Some LEO satellites go over the North and South Poles in polar orbit. These are useful for mapping.

Starter	Support/Extend	Resources
An alternative question-led lesson is also available. **Using satellites** (5 min) Students list the applications they know of that require satellite technology, for example, communication, navigation, and the gathering of information weather (forecasts, tracking, and so on). **Into orbit** (10 min) Tell students a fantastic fact about sending things into orbit, for example, that fruit flies were the first living things to go into outer space. Ask students to suggest how scientists can launch objects into space.	**Support**: Prompt students in the discussion by using terms like satellite dish and GPS. **Extension**: Extend discussion to include the impact of sending too many satellites into space.	**Question-led lesson**: Spacecraft and satellites

Main	Support/Extend	Resources
Satellites (40 min) Introduce students to the uses of satellites, how these can be launched into orbit, and the three different types of satellite orbits (geostationary, LEO, and polar). Students then watch two short demonstrations to model a rocket launch, and how a satellite stays in orbit, before carrying out an activity where they compare different orbits of satellites before using their knowledge and the information provided to predict the orbits taken by different satellites based on their uses.	**Support**: Allow extra time to guide students through the demonstrations. Use prompt questions (e.g., What does the bung represent in this case?) **Extension**: Ask students to give a quick evaluation of the demonstrations shown.	**Activity**: Satellites

Plenary	Support/Extend	Resources
Launching a satellite (10 min) Students reorder sentences provided on the interactive resource to describe how to get a satellite into orbit. **Satellite uses and their orbits** (5 min) Issue students with mini-whiteboards on which they must write geostationary on one side and LEO on the other. Give different uses of satellites and ask students to hold up their mini-whiteboards as appropriate, as fast as they can. Pick on students randomly to describe how the satellite is used for a certain purpose.	**Extension**: Give alternative scenarios to explain, for example, what happens if the speed of the rocket when it is fired is too high or low? **Extension**: Ask students to justify why a certain orbit must be used for a particular use of satellite, for example, why can a TV satellite not be in LEO?	**Interactive**: Launching a satellite

Homework		
Students prepare two contrasting stories or comic strips about a day in the life of someone with satellite technology, and another without. This should cover different uses of satellite technology and the orbits in which the satellites are situated.		

2.5 Mission to the Moon

KS3 Physics NC Link:
- forces
- forces and motion
- space physics.

KS3 Working Scientifically NC Link:
- evaluate risks.

KS4 Chemistry NC Link:
- give examples of forces that act without contact across empty space, linking these to gravity, electric, and magnetic fields involved
- recall that fusion in stars involves pairs of hydrogen nuclei forming helium, emitting radiation and increasing the particle kinetic energy.

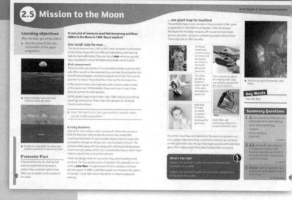

Band	Outcome	Checkpoint	
		Questions	Activities
Developing ↓	State one risk and one benefit of the space programme (Level 4).	1	Starter 1, Main, Plenary 1, Plenary 2, Homework
	Identify risks for given hazards in a space mission (Level 4).		Main
Secure ↓	Describe some of the risks and benefits of the space programme (Level 6).	2, 3	Starter 1, Main, Plenary 1, Plenary 2, Homework
	Complete a risk assessment for a space mission (Level 6).		Main
Extending ↓	Explain risks and benefits of the space programme (Level 7).	3	Main, Plenary 1, Plenary 2, Homework
	Write a detailed risk assessment for a space mission (Level 7).		Main

Literacy
Students retrieve information from a range of sources and use the ideas identified to evaluate risks and benefits of space travel.

APP
Students identify risks and benefits of space travel (AF4).

Key Words
risk, solar flare

Answers from the student book

In-text questions	**A** The probability that something will happen and the consequences if it should.
Activity	**What's the risk?** For example: A cyclist can reduce the probability of being in an accident by watching other traffic carefully, by travelling at a safe speed, or by obeying traffic rules. If a cyclist is involved in an accident, the severity of consequences can be reduced by wearing a helmet or protective clothing.
Summary Questions	**1** Risks: rocket exploding, radiation Benefits: smart-phone technology, baby milk (4 marks) **2** Credit sensible suggestions, for example, the Moon landings accelerated the development of computers, modern hospitals use computers for imaging and diagnosing disease. (2 marks)

3 QWC question (6 marks). Students should offer at least three risks and three benefits of the space programme. Examples answers:

Any three risks from:

During take-off the astronauts lie on top of an enormous rocket that can explode.

The spacecraft can combust as it re-enters the atmosphere due to intense friction between the body of the spacecraft and the atmosphere.

If the parachute fails to open in time the spacecraft would land on Earth at higher speeds than anticipated, causing a crash.

Solar flares can stop all on-board computers working while the spacecraft is in space.

Any three benefits from:

Without the Apollo missions and the space programme we would not have many of the technological devices that we take for granted today.

In 1963 half the computers in the world were developed for the Moon missions.

The liquid-cooled suits used by racing car drivers and fire-fighters are based on the Apollo astronauts' spacesuits.

The shock-absorbing materials used in sports shoes were developed for spacesuits.

Baby-milk formulas are based on protein-rich drinks developed for astronauts.

Computer programs for swiping credit cards use software designed for the Apollo missions.

Water filters use technology designed to recycle astronauts' urine.

Starter	Support/Extend	Resources
Space missions (5 min) Students categorise statements about space missions provided on the interactive resource as advantages and disadvantages. This activity serves as a starting point for further discussion. **Ideas on space exploration** (10 min) Show students a video clip from a film about space exploration. These are readily available on the Internet. Ask students to discuss what they know already about space exploration, and identify examples of incorrect science given in the video. (For example, many films depict sound travelling through space.)	**Extension**: Encourage students to justify their choices. **Support**: Time should be spent correcting misconceptions as appropriate.	**Interactive**: Space missions

Main	Support/Extend	Resources
Space travel (40 min) Introduce students to the different risks and benefits of the space programme. This can be done using the student book. Review the definitions of the key words risk and hazard, starting from a familiar scenario, for example, travelling to school. Students then carry out an activity where they read the opinions of four different people on the space programme and complete a risk assessment for a space mission. Students answer questions that follow.	**Support**: The accompanying support sheet offers students a partially completed grid for their risk assessment.	**Activity**: Space travel

Plenary	Support/Extend	Resources
Risks and benefits of space travel (5 min) Students pair-share ideas for a class discussion on the risks and benefits of space travel. **The most important factor** (10 min) Issue students with nine cards. For each card, one side should have a benefit of space travel, and the other side, a risk. Students then sort the cards to show all the benefits of space travel and rank these in a diamond nine. Repeat for the risks of space travel.	**Extension**: Encourage students to justify their choices throughout the activity.	

Homework		
Students find out about one space mission and present risks and benefits of this mission in a table, with a short evaluation afterwards about whether they think this mission was worth it.		

2.6 Radioactivity 1

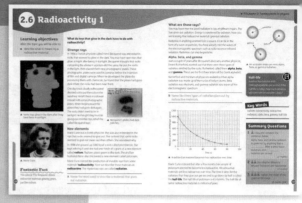

KS4 Physics NC Link:

- recall that some nuclei may emit alpha, beta, or neutral particles and electromagnetic radiation as gamma rays
- explain that radioactive decay is a random process, the concept of half-life, and how the hazards associated with radioactive material differ according to the half-life involved, and to the differences in the penetration properties of alpha particles, beta particles, and gamma rays.

Band	Outcome	Checkpoint	
		Questions	**Activities**
Developing ↓	State the term given to a material that gives out radiation (Level 3).	A, 1	Starter 1, Starter 2, Plenary 1, Plenary 2, Homework
Secure ↓	Describe what is meant by a radioactive material (Level 6).	1, 2	Starter 2, Main, Plenary 1, Plenary 2, Homework
Extending ↓	Explain how the radioactivity of a sample changes with time (Level 8).	3	Maths, Main, Plenary 1, Plenary 2, Homework

Maths
Students draw, interpret, and carry out calculations involving half-life.

Literacy
Students summarise information from a range of sources about different scientists who contributed towards the discovery of radioactivity.

APP
Students draw graphs to show the activity of a radioactive sample and demonstrate half-life (AF3).

Key Words
radium, radioactivity, radioactive, radiation, alpha, beta, gamma, half-life

Answers from the student book

In-text questions	**A** radioactive
	B alpha, beta, and gamma
Activity	**Half-life**
	After two days:
	radiation emitted per second = 2000 ÷ 2 = 1000 alpha particles per second
	After four days:
	radiation emitted per second = 1000 ÷ 2 = 500 alpha particles per second
Summary Questions	**1** radioactive, less (2 marks)
	2 radiation – waves or particles emitted by radioactive materials
	radioactive – (a description of) a material that gives out radiation (2 marks)
	3 QWC question (6 marks). Example answers:
	The graph shows a general decrease in the number of waves/particles emitted per second.
	For example, from 1000 waves/particles emitted per second at 0 s to 60 waves/particles emitted per second at 80 s.
	The graph is in the shape of a downward curve.
	This curve is known as exponential decay.
	The decrease in the number of particles emitted is fast at first, and then slows down.
	For example, at 20 s, 500 particles are emitted per second.
	At 40 s, 500 ÷ 2 = 250 particles are emitted per second.
	Credit alternative examples given with numerical data.

Starter	Support/Extend	Resources
Existing knowledge about radioactivity (5 min) Show students images of glowing green items. You may wish to show students video clips of glowing green items that are often found in cartoons. Ask students what they think these items are and what they know about them. **Reviewing hazard symbols** (5 min) Ask students to draw as many hazard symbols as they can remember before displaying these on the board. Ask students to name and describe each symbol in turn. In particular, the radioactivity symbol should be covered as this will form the focus for this lesson.		

Main	Support/Extend	Resources
Discovering radioactivity (40 min) Formally introduce the definitions of the key words radioactivity and radioactive material. Explain how there are three types of radiation emitted by radioactive substances – alpha, beta, and gamma, and that the radioactivity of sources decreases with time. A good way to model the decrease of radioactivity in a radioactive source with time is to issue each student with a die. At the start of the demonstration, every student stands up to represent a radioactive atom. Every time that a student rolls a certain number, for example, a six, they sit down. This is an effective and visual way of showing the random nature of radioactive decay. Students then carry out an activity where they read an information sheet about Becquerel, Curie, and Rutherford. Students can carry out further research on one of these scientists if resources are available (textbooks, the Internet) and complete a fact file for one of these scientists. Students then answer the questions that follow.	**Support**: You may wish to read the information sheet as a group to help weaker readers. **Extension**: GCSE textbooks can be offered to students during their research, and the concept of half-life can also be discussed.	**Activity**: Discovering radioactivity

Plenary	Support/Extend	Resources
What is radioactivity? (10 min) Students complete the sentences provided on the interactive resource to describe radioactivity.	**Extension**: Ask students to explain why the radioactivity of a material decreases with time. Students should include an explanation of half-life in their answers.	**Interactive:** What is radioactivity?
Sketch graphs (10 min) Students draw a sketch graph on mini-whiteboards to show how the radioactivity of a radioactive material changes with time. They should use these graphs to describe radioactivity to each other.	**Extension**: Students explain the shape of the sketch graph.	

Homework		
Students design a poster about one radioactive element of their choice, including the properties of the element, how it was discovered, who discovered it, and when it was discovered. The poster should also include a brief description of the term radioactivity. The poster can be presented in the form of a fact file, ready for display.		

2.7 Radioactivity 2

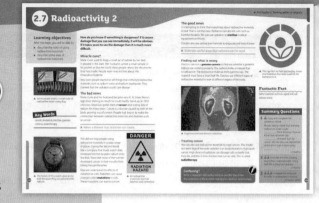

KS3 Working Scientifically NC Link:
- evaluate risks.

KS4 Physics NC Link:
- give examples of practical use of alpha particles, beta particles, and gamma rays
- describe and distinguish between uses of nuclear radiations for exploration of internal organs, and to control or destroy unwanted tissue
- explain why radioactive material, whether external to the body or ingested, is hazardous because of damage to the tissue cells.

Band	Outcome	Checkpoint	
		Questions	Activities
Developing	State one risk of using radioactive materials (Level 3).	A, 1	Main, Plenary 1, Homework
	State one use of radioactive materials (Level 3).	B, 1	Lit, Main, Plenary 2, Homework
	Give the risks of using a radioactive technique in medicine and an everyday activity using probability (Level 4).		Main
Secure	Describe the risks of using radioactive materials (Level 6).	2	Lit, Main, Plenary 1, Homework
	Describe some uses of radioactive materials (Level 5).	3	Main, Plenary 2, Homework
	Explain why radioactive techniques are used in medicine despite the associated risks (Level 6).		Main
Extending	Explain how to reduce the risks of using radioactive materials (Level 8).		Main, Plenary 1, Homework
	Compare different uses of radioactive materials (Level 7).	3	Main, Plenary 2
	Evaluate the risks and benefits of using radioactive techniques to suggest appropriate treatment of patients in different scenarios (Level 8).		Main

Maths
Students calculate probability in quantitative problem solving.

Literacy
In the student-book activity students extract and summarise information to write clear and concise explanations linking the terms radioactive, radiation, and radiotherapy.

Students identify meaning in scientific texts and summarise the information provided by answering questions.

APP
Students identify evidence supporting or refuting the use of radioactivity techniques in medicine (AF1) and draw conclusions from data provided (AF5).

Key Words
cancer, mutation, sterilise, gamma camera, radiotherapy

Answers from the student book

In-text questions	**A** cancer
	B In sterilising medical equipment and food, and to diagnose and treat diseases.

Activity	Confusing?
	Credit sensible suggestions, for example, doctors use radioactive materials that give out radiation in a cancer treatment called radiotherapy.
Summary Questions	**1** cure, cause, radiotherapy (3 marks)
	2 Long half-life means that the radioactive material remains highly radioactive for a long time. This increases the time the radioactive material has to damage body cells and cause diseases such as cancer. (2 marks)
	3 QWC question (6 marks). Example answers:
	Radioactive materials emit radiation. Radiation can damage cells. It can also cause mutations in cells. This can cause cancer.
	However, radiation can also be used to kill cells, for example, harmful bacteria. Radiation is used to sterilise medical equipment and food. Doctors can use radiation to destroy cancer cells during radiotherapy.

Starter	Support/Extend	Resources
A risky business? (5 min) Ask students to recap the story of Marie Curie and how she, together with husband Pierre, discovered the radioactive elements radium and polonium. Then tell students about how the Curies became ill. This can be used as an introduction to the risks of radioactive materials.		
Risk assessments (5 min) Ask students to recap the difference between risks and hazards before asking them to write one entry on the risk assessment of a simple task (e.g., sharpening a pencil) on a mini-whiteboard.	**Support**: Students may require a reminder of the headers required in a risk assessment table.	

Main	Support/Extend	Resources
Uses and risks of radioactive materials (40 min) Introduce the risks and benefits of using radioactive materials. This should include the effect of radiation on healthy cells, as well as its effect on tumour cells. The use of radioactive material in medical tracers and scans, and the irradiation of food and medical equipment should also be mentioned. Students then carry out an activity where they interpret information given about medical uses of radioactive materials and answer questions that follow. This activity requires students to analyse scientific text and numerical data, forming their own conclusions about why radioactive techniques continue to be used in medicine despite their risks.	**Support**: You may wish to read the information together as a class to help weaker readers access the information provided.	**Activity**: Uses and risks of radioactive materials

Plenary	Support/Extend	Resources
The correct treatment? (10 min) Students categorise statements given on the interactive resource as being true or false. Students should then correct the statements that are false and justify their changes. This activity then leads onto a discussion of ways that the risks of radiation exposure can be minimised. This can be done as a diamond nine if time.	**Extension**: Encourage students to suggest further statements to add to the interactive resource.	**Interactive**: The correct treatment?
Uses of radioactive materials (10 min) Students are presented with a list of possible uses of radioactive materials on the board. They should correctly identify these uses (using thumbs up/down, coloured cards, or traffic lights) and give further descriptions of each one.	**Extension**: Encourage students to compare the uses of radioactive materials, rather than to give a description.	

Homework		
Students write a short letter for the opinions column of a newspaper, in response to the article 'Radiation – good or bad?' In this letter students should evaluate the risks and benefits of radioactive materials and present a conclusion. An alternative WebQuest homework activity is also available on Kerboodle where students research radioactivity in medicine.	**Extension**: Students write a letter supporting the use of radioactive materials by countering risks with safety precautions that can be taken.	**WebQuest**: Radioactivity and medicine

2.8 Electromagnetism 1

KS3 Physics NC Link:
- current electricity
- magnetism.

KS3 Working Scientifically NC Link:
- use appropriate techniques, apparatus, and materials during laboratory work, paying attention to health and safety.

KS4 Physics NC Link:
- explain the difference between direct and alternating voltages
- explain how to show that a current can create a magnetic effect and describe the directions of the magnetic field around a conducting wire
- recall that a change in the magnetic field around a conductor can give rise to an induced e.m.f. across its ends, which could drive a current, generating a field that would oppose the original change; hence explain how this effect is used in a alternator to generate a.c., and in a dynamo to generate d.c.

Band	Outcome	Checkpoint	
		Questions	Activities
Developing ↓	Name the process used to generate electricity (Level 3).	A, 1	Main, Plenary 1, Plenary 2
	Carry out an experiment to induce an electric current (Level 4).		Main
Secure ↓	Describe how to generate electricity using electromagnetic induction (Level 6).	2, 3	Main, Plenary 1, Plenary 2, Homework
	Carry out an experiment to induce an electric current, describing trends shown by the results (Level 5).		Main
Extending ↓	Suggest how to change the amount of current produced in electromagnetic induction (Level 7).		Main, Plenary 1, Plenary 2
	Carry out an experiment to induce an electric current, describing trends shown, and use this to predict further results (Level 7).		Main

Maths
Students identify numerical patterns from experimental results, and use these patterns to predict further ammeter readings.

Literacy
Interpret scientific diagrams and instructions to carry out an experimental method.

APP
Students collect data from an electromagnetic induction experiment (AF4), present this in a table (AF3), and analyse results to draw a conclusion (AF5).

Key Words
electromagnetism, electromagnetic induction, peer review, alternating current

Answers from the student book

In-text questions	**A** electromagnetic induction
Activity	**Peer review** Students must include the importance of publishing in journals for communication of scientific ideas, and the importance of peer review to verify if results are correct and reproducible.

Summary Questions	**1** moving, stationary (2 marks)
	2 As you wind up the torch, the coil of wire moves. This means that the coil of wire is moving relative to the stationary magnet inside the torch. A potential difference is produced, causing a current to flow in a complete circuit. (3 marks)
	3 QWC question (6 marks). Example answers: You need a magnet and a (coil of) wire to generate electricity. A potential difference, and hence current in a complete circuit, is induced when a magnet is moved inside a coil of wire. Alternatively, the (coil of) wire can be moved inside a magnetic field. This is called electromagnetic induction. Electricity is generated in power stations using this method. The direction of magnetic movement determines the direction of the current. If the magnet spins, or is moved in two directions, an alternating current is induced.

kerboodle

Starter	Support/Extend	Resources
Revisiting electromagnets (5 min) Ask students to describe what electromagnets are. Electromagnets were introduced in P2. This can lead onto ideas about electromagnetic induction later on in the lesson. **Revisiting power stations** (10 min) Recap stages in electricity generation in a power station. This was introduced in P2. You may wish to use an animation or a short video to trigger students' memory. Animations and videos are readily available on the Internet. This activity can then be used to introduce electromagnetic induction in the generator.	**Support**: Provide prompt questions as required. **Extension**: Ask students to explain how electromagnets work.	

Main	Support/Extend	Resources
Electromagnetic induction (40 min) Introduce electromagnetic induction as the use of a magnetic field to cause a potential difference, which in turn induces a current in a complete circuit. The concept is simple–move a coil of wire and a magnet relative to each other to generate a potential difference. This can be linked back to what happens in a generator in a power station. Students then carry out an experiment where they investigate the difference in the induced current when using different numbers of turns in the coil of wire. A preliminary investigation of moving an uncoiled copper wire between magnets in a metal yoke is included in the experimental method. Although this is the case, you may wish demonstrate this experiment before asking students to follow the rest of the method to save time.	**Support**: Demonstrate the preliminary experiment. This will help students familiarise themselves with the apparatus required. **Extension**: Students should consider using magnets of different strengths if time.	**Practical:** Electromagnetic induction

Plenary	Support/Extend	Resources
Generating electricity (5 min) Students complete the sentences on the interactive resource using the words provided to explain how current is induced in electromagnetic induction. **What's inside a generator?** (10 min) Ask students to answer the following question 'What is inside a generator in a power station that causes electricity to be generated?' Students can then peer mark their answers using a mark scheme.	**Extension**: Students add other ways in which the current induced can be increased. **Extension**: Students should describe how the current induced can be increased.	**Interactive**: Generating electricity

Homework		
Students pretend they are Faraday, who has recently discovered electromagnetic induction. Students should write a letter/report/journal article to describe his experiment and findings.		

2.9 Electromagnetism 2

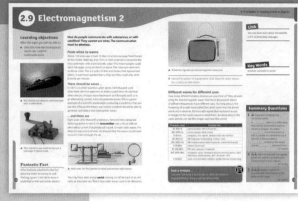

KS3 Physics NC Link:
- energy and waves
- light waves.

KS3 Working Scientifically NC Link:
- interpret observations and data, including identifying patterns and using observations, measurements, and data to draw conclusions.

KS4 Physics NC Link:
- explain the relationship between velocity, frequency, and wavelength
- describe the main groupings of the spectrum; that these range from long to short wavelengths and from low to high frequencies; and that our eyes can only detect a limited range.

Band	Outcome	Checkpoint	
		Questions	Activities
Developing	Name one piece of equipment used to detect electromagnetic waves (Level 4).	A, 1	Plenary 1, Plenary 2
	Use data provided to state some electromagnetic waves that are used in communication (Level 4).		Main
Secure	Describe how electromagnetic waves are used for communication (Level 5).	2, 3	Main, Plenary 1, Plenary 2
	Deduce the type of electromagnetic wave used given data on frequency (Level 6).		Main
Extending	Compare the frequency of electromagnetic waves with their uses (Level 7).	3	Main, Plenary 1
	Interpret frequencies of different waves to compare how they are used in communication (Level 7).		Main

Maths
In the student-book activity students calculate the time taken to send one verse of 'Happy Birthday' using Morse code.

Students compare frequencies of different waves used in communication, convert between Hz and MHz, and rearrange the wave speed equation to find wavelength.

Literacy
Students summarise a range of information from different sources and organise this into well-developed, linked ideas in a poster.

APP
Students interpret data provided to draw conclusions (AF5).

Key Words
wireless, transmitter, aerial

Answers from the student book

In-text questions	**A** aerial
Activity	**Just a minute…** There are 16 words in a verse of Happy Birthday. It would take 16 ÷ 8 = 2 minutes to send this verse by Morse code.

Summary Questions	
	1 carrier, wireless, transmitter, aerial (4 marks)
	2 A transmitter in a circuit with an alternating current produces radio waves.
	A detector in the form of a loop of wire (an aerial) can be used to receive the radio signal, feeding this to the electronic device to provide an output.
	For example, radio waves are used in radio broadcasting.
	Other types of EM waves can also be used, for example, IR in remote controls, or microwaves in satellite communications. (4 marks)
	3 Poster should be informative and eye-catching. It should contain information about how EM waves are used in a selection of the following (6 marks):

submarines	avalanche beacons
mines	television
navigation	microwave ovens
time signals	astronomy
heart rate monitors	mobile phones
radio broadcasting	communication satellites.

kerboodle

Starter	Support/Extend	Resources
Forms of communication (10 min) Ask students how methods of communication have evolved over the years, from letters and Morse code to emails and texts. Lead the discussion into wireless communication and uses of the different parts of the electromagnetic (EM) spectrum. **The EM spectrum** (10 min) Students have met the EM spectrum before, in P3 Chapter 1. Ask students to share what they remember about the different waves in the spectrum, and how they are used. Students may remember a mnemonic they have made for remembering the order of waves in the EM spectrum.		

Main	Support/Extend	Resources
Communications (35 min) Introduce the different uses of the EM spectrum in communication and how these waves are transmitted and received. Students then complete an activity where they fill in a partially completed diagram of the EM spectrum, use the information in the diagram to deduce the types of EM waves used in different methods of communication given frequency data, and design a poster to illustrate the variety of uses of EM waves in communication. Students will likely need to complete their posters for homework.	**Support**: Information in the student book may be explored as a class to help weaker readers.	**Activity**: Communications

Plenary	Support/Extend	Resources
Electromagnetic communication (10 min) Students use the clues provided to complete a crossword on the interactive resource that covers key concepts of the lesson. This crossword includes the types of EM waves used in communication and how these EM waves are used. **How are EM waves used for communication?** (10 min) Ask students a series of true or false questions to describe how EM waves are used in communication. Questions may also include how EM waves are transmitted and received by different devices. Ask students to show their answers using thumbs up/thumbs down, coloured cards, or a traffic light system.	**Extension**: Students use their activity sheets to compare frequencies for different uses of EM waves. **Extension**: Students may suggest their own questions to pose to the rest of the class.	**Interactive**: Electromagnetic communication

Homework		
Students complete their posters and questions for homework.		

Checkpoint lesson routes

The route through this lesson can be determined using the Checkpoint assessment.

Percentage pass marks are supplied in the Checkpoint teacher notes.

Route A (revision)
Resource: P3 Chapter 2 Checkpoint: Revision

Students work through a series of tasks that allows them to revisit and consolidate their understanding of the major turning points in astrophysics, electromagnetism, and radioactivity. Students can keep this as a summary of the topic, and use this when revising for future assessments.

Route B (extension)
Resource: P3 Chapter 2 Checkpoint: Extension

Students design a poster for A-Level students starting the topic 'Turning points in physics' that includes a summary of the key concepts covered in this topic.

Progression to *secure*

No.	Developing outcome	Secure outcome	Making progress
1	State some ideas about the Universe that developed in different cultures.	Describe some ideas about the Universe that developed in different cultures.	In Task 1 students link three ideas about the Universe that developed in ancient cultures with their descriptions.
2	State what is meant by geocentric.	Describe the geocentric model of the Solar System.	In Task 1 students describe similarities and differences between the geocentric and heliocentric models.
3	State some observations that led to our present model of the Solar System.	Describe how observations led to a different model of the Solar System.	In Task 1 students identify from a list of possible statements the observations that led to a shift from the geocentric model to the heliocentric model.
4	Name our present model of the Solar System.	Describe the heliocentric model of the Solar System.	In Task 1 students describe similarities and differences between the geocentric and heliocentric models.
5	State the age of the Solar System.	Describe the timescale of the Universe.	In Task 2 students label a scaled timeline with some of the major events that occurred since the Big Bang.
6	Name the theory of how the Universe started.	Describe what is meant by the Big Bang.	In Task 2 students complete a word fill to describe what is meant by the Big Bang.
7	Name the orbits a satellite can take.	Describe how to get a satellite into orbit.	In Task 3 students describe the conditions necessary to send a satellite into orbit.
8	State some uses of satellites.	Describe some uses of satellites.	In Task 3 students identify the orbits required by four different satellites, describing how these are used.
9	State one risk and one benefit of the space programme.	Describe some of the risks and benefits of the space programme.	In Task 3 students complete a table to describe some of the risks and benefits as a result of the space programme.
10	State the term given to a material that gives out radiation.	Describe what is meant by a radioactive material.	In Task 4 students complete a word fill to describe radioactive materials.
11	State one risk of using radioactive materials.	Describe the risks of using radioactive materials.	In Task 4 students are given a list of statements about the uses and risks of radioactive materials. They must correct the statements that are false.
12	State one use of radioactive materials.	Describe some uses of radioactive materials.	In Task 4 students are given a list of statements about the uses and risks of radioactive materials. They must correct the statements that are false.
13	Name the process used to generate electricity.	Describe how to generate electricity using electromagnetic induction.	In Task 5 students label a diagram of the apparatus required for electromagnetic induction and use this to describe how electricity can be generated.
14	Name one piece of equipment used to detect electromagnetic waves.	Describe how electromagnetic waves are used for communication.	In Task 5 students reorder statements to describe how electromagnetic waves can be used for communication.

Answers to end-of-chapter questions

1 geocentric model – the Earth is at the centre of the Universe.

   heliocentric model – the Sun is at the centre of the Universe.

   Big Bang theory – the Universe began when all of space and time expanded. (3 marks)

2 14 billion years (1 mark)

3 alpha, beta, gamma (1 mark)

4a geocentric (1 mark)   **b** polar (1 mark)   **c** low Earth (1 mark)

5a The needle on the ammeter moves to the right. (1 mark)

 b The needle on the ammeter will not move. (1 mark)

 c Any two from: size of bar magnet, strength of bar magnet, metal used for the coils of wire.

 d Bar chart – because the number of turns in a coil is a discrete variable. (2 marks)

6a Radiation can cause mutations in cells of microorganisms that cause them to die. Because of this we can use radiation to kill bacteria and sterilise medical equipment. (2 marks)

 b Patients drink a radioactive material as a medical tracer. These must have short half-lives to reduce the risk of cell damage or mutation that can lead to cancer. (2 marks)

7 Communication with submarines underwater can be carried out using waves of frequencies 30–300 Hz. Signals are added to the carrier wave that represent sound or images and an aerial detects the wave, transforming the signals back to sound or images. (2 marks)

8 The Universe is expanding, with the distance between galaxies increasing. This means that the Universe originated from one point billions of years ago.

   Credit alternative evidence, for example, cosmic microwave background radiation, which is radiation left over in the Universe from the time of the Big Bang. (1 mark)

9 The radiation emitted per second will decrease for both samples. This decrease will be much quicker for Sample A than Sample B. After 10 days the radiation emitted per second will be 12.5 waves/particles per second for Sample A, and 100 waves/particles per second for Sample B. (4 marks)

10 This is a QWC question. Students should be marked on the use of good English, organisation of information, spelling and grammar, and correct use of specialist scientific terms. The best answers will fully explain why doctors need to balance risk and benefit when they use a gamma camera (maximum of 6 marks).

   Examples of correct scientific points: For doctors to use this technique, patients are required to swallow radioactive material. The radioactive tracer emits radiation. This is picked up by the gamma camera so an image can be formed on a screen. On the one hand, this technique can be used to diagnose disease, saving many lives. However, radiation can also damage cells. Mutations in cells can lead to cancer. The risks can be reduced by using material that has a short half-life. Risks can also be reduced by using small quantities of radioactive material.

Answer guide for Big Write

Developing	Secure	Extending
1–2 marks	3–4 marks	5–6 marks
• Timeline identifies two or three of the discoveries in the 20th century. • Includes descriptions of some of the ways these discoveries changed how people lived, although the description is limited. • Little or no attempt has been made to write an illustrated story.	• Timeline identifies the discovery of the Big Bang, radioactivity, electromagnetic induction, and electromagnetic waves. • Includes descriptions of the ways these discoveries changed how people lived, for example, radiotherapy and electricity generation. • A brief illustrated story has been written.	• Timeline describes in detail the impact of the discoveries of the Big Bang, radioactivity, electromagnetic induction, and electromagnetic waves, and how these discoveries have changed our lives. Examples include the use of electromagnetic waves in communication, the development of new materials as a result of the space programme, and the use of radioactive materials in medicine. • A detailed story has been written with appropriate illustrations to accompany the story.

P3 Chapter 2 Checkpoint assessment (automarked)	P3 Chapter 2 Checkpoint: Extension
P3 Chapter 2 Checkpoint: Revision	P3 Chapter 2 Progress task Handling information

3.1 Detecting planets

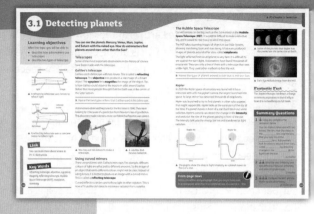

KS3 Physics NC Link:

- light waves
- space physics.

KS3 Working Scientifically NC Link:

- make and record observations, suggesting possible improvements.

KS4 Physics NC Link:

- describe and explain superposition in water waves and the effects of reflection, transmission, and absorption of waves at material interfaces
- use the ray model to show how light travels and to illustrate specular reflection and the apparent position of images in plane mirrors
- use the ray model to illustrate refraction and explain the apparent displacement of an image in a refracting substance (qualitative only)
- recall that electromagnetic waves are transverse
- recall that different substances may absorb, transmit, refract, or reflect electromagnetic waves.

Band	Outcome	Checkpoint	
		Questions	Activities
Developing	State one use of telescopes (Level 3).	1	Starter 1, Plenary 1, Plenary 2, Homework
	Name the two types of telescope (Level 3).	A	Plenary 2, Homework
	Make a simple refracting telescope (Level 4).		Main
Secure	Describe how astronomers use telescopes (Level 5).	1	Starter 1, Plenary 1, Plenary 2, Homework
	Describe two types of telescope (Level 6).	2	Main, Plenary 1, Plenary 2, Homework
	Make a refracting telescope and describe images formed (Level 5).		Main
Extending	Draw a ray diagram to explain how one type of telescope works (Level 8).		Main, Homework
	Compare two types of telescope (Level 8).	2, 3	Main, Plenary 1, Homework
	Make a refracting telescope and compare it to a reflecting telescope (Level 7).		Main

Literacy
Students identify meaning in scientific text and summarise information from the student book in order to answer questions about the two types of telescope.

APP
Students make connections between abstract ideas when explaining how telescopes work (AF1) and draw conclusions about the different types of telescope based on the advantages and disadvantages for each telescope (AF5).

Key Words
refracting telescope, objective, reflecting telescope, eyepiece, magnify, Hubble Space Telescope (HST), exoplanet, intensity

Answers from the student book

In-text questions	**A** reflecting and refracting
	B exoplanet

136

Activity	**Front-page news** Credit sensible headline and accompanying text to introduce the discovery of the first exoplanet. For example: Planet X! Astronomers have found evidence of a planet around a star that is not our Sun. This is the first exoplanet they have discovered, and it is too early to know if it is like our planet, or whether there is life on it.
Summary Questions	1 objective, eyepiece, exoplanets, intensity (4 marks) 2 Similarities: both focus light from afar to form an image/both produce images that are upside down/both can be used to observe distant bodies. Differences: one uses reflection, the other refraction/one uses mirrors, the other lenses/refracting telescopes only work with light, whereas reflecting telescopes can focus all types of EM radiation. (2 marks) 3 QWC question (6 marks). Students are required to give at least three similarities and three differences between the two telescopes. Example answers: Both are telescopes. Both have mirrors. Both can be used to look for exoplanets. HST produces images whereas Kepler does not. HST looks at celestial bodies other than exoplanets whereas Kepler's only purpose is to look for exoplanets. HST takes photographs whereas Kepler looks for a change in light intensity as an exoplanet moves in front of a star.

Starter	Support/Extend	Resources
Looking for exoplanets (10 min) Ask students to suggest ways they think scientists look for exoplanets. Focus ideas onto using the telescope. Discuss types of telescopes available (from refracting and reflecting telescopes, to the Hubble Space Telescope (HST) and the Kepler space observatory).		
Reflection versus refraction (10 min) Review ideas of refraction and reflection, in particular recapping the drawing of ray diagrams. Make curved mirrors and lenses available to students so that they can experiment with how these objects produce an image. Students should compare the processes involved and the type of image produced by each object (virtual or real).	**Support**: Give students partially drawn ray diagrams to complete. **Extension**: Students experiment with two lenses to form an image (like in a refracting telescope).	

Main	Support/Extend	Resources
Telescopes (35 min) Introduce the two different types of telescope (reflecting and refracting), and how scientists have used these when observing the Universe. (To give students an idea of context, you may wish to use the Hubble Space Telescope website for images.) Students carry out a short activity where they make a simple refracting telescope to observe objects around the classroom, before answering questions that follow.	**Support**: Extra time may be required to recap reflection and refraction in detail before starting this activity.	**Activity**: Telescopes

Plenary	Support/Extend	Resources
Reflecting and refracting telescopes (10 min) Students match halves of sentences together to summarise the key points of this lesson using the interactive resource.	**Extension**: Students form further sentences for the rest of the class to complete.	**Interactive**: Reflecting and refracting telescopes
Truth continuum (10 min) Give statements relating to key points of this lesson, which may be true or false. Students arrange themselves on a truth continuum depending on how confident they are that the answer is true or false. Statements can range from the names of the two types of telescope to images of possible ray diagrams for these telescopes.	**Extension**: Invite students to offer their own statements to test the rest of the class.	

Homework		
Students design a poster to compare the two types of telescope. The poster should include advantages and disadvantages of each telescope and how scientists can use these telescopes to answer questions about the Universe. Students may wish to include examples of different telescopes, for example, the HST.	**Extension**: Students draw ray diagrams of each type of telescope discussed.	

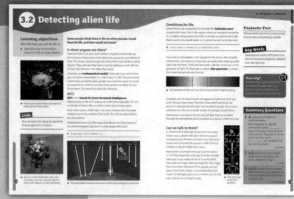

KS3 Physics NC Link:

- light waves
- space physics.

KS4 Physics NC Link:

- recall that different substances may absorb, transmit, refract, or reflect electromagnetic waves
- give examples of some practical uses of electromagnetic waves.

Band	Outcome	Checkpoint	
		Questions	Activities
Developing ↓	State the conditions required for life like that on Earth to exist (Level 4).	B, 1	Main, Plenary 1, Homework
Secure ↓	Describe how astronomers search for life on other planets (Level 6).	1	Main, Plenary 1, Homework
Extending ↓	Explain different techniques astronomers use to search for possible habitable planets (Level 8).	3	Main, Plenary 1, Homework

Maths

In the student-book activity students calculate the total time taken for 20 light messages to be relayed from Earth to Proxima Centauri.

Some students also carry out simple calculations to work out the earliest date an extra-terrestrial signal can be sent to Earth for us to receive it successfully.

Literacy

Students interpret meaning in scientific text given on the information sheet, summarising this information to answer the questions that follow.

APP

Students use appropriate scientific and mathematical conventions to communicate abstract ideas (AF3).

Key Words

mathematical models, SETI (Search for Extra-Terrestrial Intelligence), habitable zone, line spectrum

Answers from the student book

In-text questions	**A** Search for Extra Terrestrial Intelligence.
	B A region where an exoplanet would be at a suitable temperature (for liquid water to exist on the planet).
Activity	**How long?**
	Proxima Centaur is 4 light years away from Earth.
	Each message will take 4 years to travel from Earth to Proxima Centauri (and vice versa).
	Total time taken = 20 × 4 = 80 years
Summary Questions	**1** radio, water, oxygen (3 marks)
	2 X-rays are absorbed by the atmosphere. (1 mark)

3 QWC question (6 marks). Example answers:

Liquid water is essential for life on Earth.

Astronomers use computers to estimate the habitable zone around other stars. This is the region where an exoplanet would be at a suitable temperature for liquid water to exist.

Astronomers also use line spectra of light reflected from exoplanets to determine if the unique spectra for water is present for a certain exoplanet. These line spectra work like bar codes. Black lines appear on line spectra when frequencies are missing (absorbed by the substances present in the exoplanet's atmosphere).

SETI has also been used by astronomers as a way of detecting radio signals from space.

Astronomers have also put telescopes that detect other waves in the EM spectrum into orbit around the Earth.

kerboodle

Starter	Support/Extend	Resources
Messages for aliens (10 min) Students work in small groups to decide on a message that they would send to an alien, before suggesting ways this message could be sent.	**Support**: Provide students with prompt questions, for example, 'What can travel through a vacuum?' and 'What language would aliens understand?'	
Introducing light years (10 min) Introduce relative distances in our Solar System, compared with distances further afield, for example, to Proxima Centauri, our nearest star. This will lead to introducing distances measured in light years.	**Extension**: Ask students the question 'How is it we're looking back in time when we look at the Andromeda galaxy, 2.5 million light years away?'	

Main	Support/Extend	Resources
Detecting aliens (35 min) Introduce students to the different techniques astronomers use to detect extra-terrestrial life forms. These should include looking for radio signals (SETI), line spectra of oxygen and water, and using mathematical models to find habitable zones. Students then read an information sheet about different ways astronomers have tried to communicate with possible extra-terrestrial life forms since 1972, summarise this information in a table, and answer the questions that follow. If extra time is available, you may wish to visit the SETI website for its weekly 10-minute broadcasts, which could be used as discussion material.	**Support**: Students may require a brief recap of the requirements of life on Earth, as covered previously in B2. **Extension**: You may wish to introduce the Drake equation used to calculate the probability of life in the Universe.	**Activity**: Detecting aliens

Plenary	Support/Extend	Resources
Detecting aliens (10 min) Students match up key terms from this lesson with their definitions provided on the interactive resource. Students should then use these key terms to write a short paragraph to describe how astronomers search for life on different planets. This can be done by giving students criteria for success so they can mark their answers afterwards against a mark scheme.	**Extension**: Encourage students to write the mark scheme instead.	**Interactive**: Detecting aliens
Messages to space (10 min) Show students images of the Pioneer Plaque and the Voyager Golden Record Cover. These images are readily available on the Internet. Ask students to suggest what these images show before asking students why they think these pieces of information are seen to be important enough to be conveyed to life on other planets.	**Extension**: Students suggest other pieces of information that they would put on the plaque/cover instead, justifying their suggestions.	

Homework		
Students design a section of a lesson in a textbook to describe how astronomers search for life on other planets. The material in this text book should be aimed at KS3 students.	**Extension**: Students should explain at least three of these techniques.	
An alternative WebQuest homework activity is also available on Kerboodle where students research the search for extra-terrestrial life.		**WebQuest**: Searching for aliens

3.3 Detecting position

KS3 Physics NC Link:
● light waves
● space physics.

KS3 Working Scientifically NC Link:
● make and record observations and measurements using a range of methods for different investigations; and evaluate the reliability of methods and suggest possible improvements.

KS4 Physics NC Link:
● describe the main groupings of the spectrum – radio, microwave, infra-red, visible, ultra-violet, X-rays, and gamma-rays
● recall that different substances may absorb, transmit, refract, or reflect electromagnetic waves
● give examples of some practical uses of electromagnetic waves in each of the main groups of wavelength.

Band	Outcome	Checkpoint	
		Questions	Activities
Developing	State what GPS stands for and give examples of its uses (Level 3).	A	Starter 1, Plenary 1, Homework
	State one method to find distances in space (Level 3).	1	Starter 2, Main, Plenary 1, Plenary 2, Homework
	Record measurements of distances from one place to another using the map provided (Level 4).		Main
Secure	Describe how GPS works (Level 6).	2	Main, Plenary 1, Homework
	Describe how you can find the distance to planets and stars (Level 6).	1–3	Main, Plenary 2, Homework
	Interpret distances recorded to find a mystery location using trilateration (Level 5).		Main
Extending	Evaluate advantages and disadvantages of GPS (Level 7).		Main, Homework
	Compare different ways to find distances in space (Level 8).	3	Main, Plenary 2, Homework
	Explain how the method of finding a particular location on a map is a model of how GPS works (Level 8).		Main

Maths
In the student-book activity students calculate the uncertainty in distances given an uncertainty in time.

Students use geometry to pinpoint exact locations on a map using trilateration.

Literacy
Students describe how three methods of finding distances work, organising ideas into well-developed paragraphs that include scientific terminology.

APP
Students collect measurements of distance on a map (AF4), present these in a table (AF3), and explain how this activity models the technique of GPS (AF1).

Key Words
Global Positioning System (GPS), line of sight, radar, parallax

Answers from the student book

In-text questions	A Global Positioning System
	B Radio

Activity	**How close?** distance = speed x time uncertainty in distance = speed of EM wave $\times$ uncertainty in time = $(3 \times 10^8) \times (3 \times 10^{-8}) = 9$ m
Summary Questions	**1** time, position, radar, parallax (4 marks) **2** Satellites that orbit the Earth use time to work out distance/position of an object. For example, a mobile phone detects radio waves sent from three satellites. The time taken for the device to receive each signal can be used to calculate the distance from each satellite. This triangulates the mobile phone's position and a fourth satellite can be used to confirm it (trilateration). (4 marks) **3** QWC question (6 marks). Example answers: Radar is used to find distances by measuring the time it takes a radio wave to reflect from an object. This is similar to the use of sonar, except that radar uses radio waves (a part of the EM spectrum) instead of sound. This technique is used by astronomers to find distances within our Solar System. For example, a pulse of radio waves will take 2.5 s to reflect from the Moon, and over 5.5 h to reflect from Pluto. Parallax relies on the (apparently) different locations of distant objects relative to the Earth. This technique uses visible light reflected from distant bodies. Mathematics (knowledge of angles) is required to calculate distances using known distances such as the Earth–Sun distance. Astronomers use parallax to calculate distances beyond our Solar System.

Starter	Support/Extend	Resources
Using GPS (10 min) Introduce what is meant by GPS (Global Positioning System) and how it uses signals from satellites to work out accurate locations. Students should then list the devices they use or know of that use GPS (phones, satnavs, and so on).	**Extension**: Encourage students to suggest how they think GPS works.	
Planets and stars (5 min) Ask students how they measure distances on Earth, from small distances (between one student and another) to larger ones (between different continents). Ask students if these methods will work for measuring distances across space and ask students to suggest other options.	**Support**: Prompt students towards the use of light and EM spectrum using the unit of distance in space, light years.	

Main	Support/Extend	Resources
Detecting position (40 min) Introduce the use of radio waves (GPS and radar) and how scientists and mathematicians use parallax to find distances on Earth and beyond. In particular, students should be introduced to how GPS systems use trilateration to pinpoint one location on Earth using the distances from at least three satellites. Students then carry out an activity based on the London Underground map to model how the GPS system works, before answering questions that follow.	**Support**: A review of the speed equation may be required before starting this activity. The support sheet contains step-by-step instructions for Task 2. **Extension**: Make this activity more challenging by using a map of the UK or a star map instead.	**Activity**: Detecting position

Plenary	Support/Extend	Resources
Summarising GPS (5 min) Students match halves of sentences together using the interactive resource to summarise key points about GPS. Ask further questions for students to answer, using the sentences made to exemplify their points, for example, can GPS be used underwater?	**Extension**: Students should pose further questions about GPS to the rest of the class.	**Interactive**: Summarising GPS
Distances to stars (10 min) Students pair-share, then discuss as a class, ideas about methods of finding distances in space (radar and parallax).	**Support**: Present a list of key words to explain the methods.	

Homework		
Students design a poster to describe how GPS, radar, and parallax work. Encourage students to include diagrams where possible.	**Extension**: Students compare advantages and disadvantages of using each method.	

3.4 Detecting messages

KS3 Physics NC Link:
- sound waves
- light waves.

KS3 Working Scientifically NC Link:
- understand and use SI units and IUPAC (International Union of Pure and Applied Chemistry) chemical nomenclature.

KS4 Physics NC Link:
- recall that electromagnetic waves are transverse and are transmitted through space where all have the same velocity
- give examples of some practical uses of electromagnetic waves in each of the main groups of wavelength
- explain the concept of modulation and how information can be transmitted by waves through variations in amplitude or frequency, and that each of these is used in its optimum frequency range.

Band	Outcome	Checkpoint	
		Questions	Activities
Developing ↓	Name the two types of modulated wave (Level 3).	A	Starter 1, Plenary 2, Homework
	Convert numerical data provided into SI units (Level 4).		Main
Secure ↓	Describe how a radio wave carries a signal (Level 6).		Main, Plenary 1, Plenary 2, Homework
	Give answers in SI units when using the wave speed equation (Level 5).		Main
Extending ↓	Explain the difference between AM and FM signals (Level 8).		Main, Plenary 1, Plenary 2, Homework
	Use SI units when using rearrangements of the wave speed equation (Level 7).		Main

Maths

In the student-book activity, students convert frequencies between Hz, kHz, and MHz.

Students also carry out calculations using the wave speed equation provided. Some students rearrange this equation for further calculations.

APP

Students process data, using calculations to identify the relationship between frequency and wavelength (AF5).

Key Words

carrier wave, modulation, diffraction

Answers from the student book

In-text questions	**A** amplitude modulated (AM) and frequency modulated (FM)
Activity	**How many hertz?** Radio 1 has frequency of 99.1 MHz. There are 1 000 000 Hz in 1 MHz. 99.1 MHz = 99.1 × 1 000 000 = 99 100 000 Hz There are 1 000 Hz in 1 kHz. 99 100 000 Hz = 99 100 000 ÷ 1000 = 99 100 kHz
Summary Questions	**1** diffraction – the spreading out of waves around an obstacle carrier wave – the radio, micro-, or infrared wave that carries a signal modulating – changing the amplitude or frequency of a wave (3 marks)

2 AM is amplitude modulation. It means changing the amplitude to represent 1 s and 0 s.
FM is frequency modulation. This means changing the frequency of the carrier wave. (2 marks)
3 QWC question (6 marks). Example answers:
A microphone converts sound waves into an electrical signal.
This signal is converted into a digital sequence of 1s and 0s.
A radio transmitter adds the digital signal of the sound to the carrier wave.
The frequency of this carrier wave is 99.1 MHz (for Radio 1).
The transmitter then changes either the amplitude or the frequency of the carrier wave (modulation).
Radio 1 is an FM station so it is the frequency that is modulated.
The carrier wave is broadcast and travels across the country as a radio wave.
A radio set is tuned to the same frequency as the carrier wave.
The radio set converts the radio signal back into sound.
The loudspeaker plays the radio programme.

Starter	Support/Extend	Resources
An alternative question-led lesson is also available. **Analogue radios** (10 min) Show students an example of an old analogue radio. Information on this radio must show a range of frequencies (kHz and/or MHz) and initials of bands (AM, FM). Ask students to discuss and suggest what these abbreviations may mean. **SI units** (10 min) Ask students to list as many SI units as they can remember. Students should match SI units to what they measure. This activity should lead to the SI unit for frequency, Hertz (Hz).	**Support**: Students focus on the prefixes k (kilo) and M (mega). **Extension**: Point out SW/MW/LW (short, medium, and long wave) on the radio for further discussion. **Support**: Give students a list of SI units and their measurements to match up. **Extension**: Ask students to suggest why SI units were invented.	**Question-led lesson**: Detecting messages
Main	**Support/Extend**	**Resources**
Radio broadcasts (35 min) Introduce how radio broadcasts work. This should include a brief description of radio waves as carrier waves, AM and FM modulation, the diffraction of radio waves, and the wave speed equation (wave speed = frequency × wavelength). Students then carry out an activity where they will find frequencies of six radio stations using an analogue radio, find the wavelengths of their signals using the wave speed equation, and answer the questions that follow. It is a common misconception for students to confuse radio waves with sound waves. Radio waves are EM waves that are used as carrier waves containing digitalised conversions of sound waves. Misconceptions should be corrected as appropriate.	**Support**: The support sheet gives students hints for unit conversions between Hz, kHz, and MHz, as well as a step-by-step guide to calculating wavelengths given the frequency and wave speed. **Extension**: Challenge students to use standard form in calculations where possible.	**Activity**: Radio broadcasts
Plenary	**Support/Extend**	**Resources**
Broadcasts (10 min) Students reorder sentences provided on the interactive resource to describe how a radio programme is broadcast and played on the radio, summarising the key points of this lesson. **The chain game** (10 min) Students initially pair-share ideas about how radio broadcasts and transmitted, before combining together into groups of four or six. Pick groups at random to sequentially give the steps to describe how radio shows are broadcast and received.	**Extension**: Encourage students to explain details of selected steps in the sequence, for example, the two types of modulation covered. **Extension**: Encourage students to include an explanation of different frequencies and why they are necessary.	**Interactive**: Broadcasts
Homework		
Students design a cartoon to explain the steps involved in broadcasting a radio show. Students may also be required to complete questions on their activity sheet.	**Extension**: Students draw annotated diagrams of AM and FM to explain the difference between them.	

3.5 Detecting particles

KS3 Physics NC Link:
● particle model.

KS3 Working Scientifically NC Link:
● understand that scientific methods and theories develop as earlier explanations are modified to take account of new evidence and ideas, together with the importance of publishing results and peer review.

KS4 Physics NC Link:
● describe how and why the atomic model has changed over time
● describe the atom as a positively charged nucleus surrounded by negatively charged electrons, with the nuclear radius much smaller than that of the atom and with almost all of the mass in the nucleus.

Band	Outcome	Checkpoint	
		Questions	Activities
Developing	State one method scientists use to investigate what the Universe is made of (Level 3).	A, 1	Main, Plenary 1, Homework
	Name one type of particle detector (Level 3).	B	Main, Plenary 1, Plenary 2, Homework
	State Rutherford's hypothesis about the structure of the atom (Level 3).		Main
Secure	Describe how physicists investigate what the Universe is made of (Level 6).	1, 2	Main, Plenary 1, Homework
	Describe how particles can be detected (Level 6).	2	Main, Plenary 1, Homework
	Describe the stages of developing a new theory (Level 6).		Main
Extending	Compare different techniques scientists use to investigate what the Universe is made of (Level 7).	2	Main, Plenary 1
	Suggest ways in which scientists use existing knowledge to make further scientific discoveries (Level 7).		Main
	Explain the importance of peer review when developing new theories in science (Level 7).		Main

Literacy
Students read a piece of scientific text to identify key ideas and summarise information by answering questions that follow.

APP
Students describe ideas that refute previous scientific theories (AF1). Students also explain how scientific evidence is peer reviewed and how this may lead to changes in scientific ideas (AF1).

Key Words
accelerator, Large Hadron Collider (LHC), semiconductor, quark, Higgs boson

Answers from the student book

In-text questions	**A** bubble or cloud chamber
	B semiconductor

Summary Questions	1 tracks, accelerating (2 marks)
	2 In the past, people used detectors like bubble chambers and cloud chambers. When particles pass through these chambers they leave a distinctive trail. Scientists could work out the type of particle from the type of track it made. These days, scientists use particle accelerators with detectors made from semiconductors. A very strong electric field accelerates charged particles inside tunnels, and particles produced from the subsequent high-speed collisions are detected by semiconductors. These detect the mass and charge of the particles produced. (4 marks)
	3 QWC question (6 marks). Example answers: The muon was discovered in 1936. The muon did not fit with the existing model that everything was made of protons, neutrons, and electrons. Scientists developed a new model where there were particles smaller than protons, neutrons, and electrons. New families of particles were discovered, one of which was called quarks. Another of the new particles discovered is the Higgs boson, discovered in 2012. This is the particle that gives everything mass. This particle was discovered at the Large Hadron Collider (LHC). This is a particle accelerator that uses very strong electric fields to accelerate charged particles (protons and electrons) so they collide with each other. New particles formed from these collisions are detected using a semiconductor detector.

kerboodle

Starter	Support/Extend	Resources
What's in the tin? (10 min) Give students food tins without their labels attached. Students should be encouraged to find out what is inside each tin without the need to open them (by shaking, rolling, lifting, and comparing them with similar food tins). Ask students to summarise their findings after five minutes, before linking this with how scientists use existing knowledge and patterns from observations to determine the unknown.	**Support**: Suggest a list of actions or provide a list of possible answers as prompts. **Extension**: Students justify their conclusions using observations.	
What are atoms made of? (5 min) Ask students to review what atoms are made of. They should give the answer protons, neutrons, and electrons. Introduce how, in 1936, muons were discovered. Ask students to pair-share ideas and suggest how these particles may have been found.	**Extension**: Ask students further questions about the properties of protons, neutrons, and electrons, in particular their charges.	

Main	Support/Extend	Resources
Rutherford's experiment (40 min) Ask students to describe the present (Rutherford's) atomic model and how it was developed. Students met this in C3. Introduce students to the fact that other (smaller) particles have since been discovered, for example, the muon, in 1936. Describe how cloud chambers, bubble chambers, and particle accelerators are used to detect the presence of other/new particles, most notably the Higgs boson, discovered at the LHC in 2012. Students then carry out an activity where they read information given about the scientific method used by Rutherford, and how this links to the discovery of other particles, before answering questions that follow.	**Support**: A support sheet is available with shorter, less demanding text. Alternatively, you may wish to read the main text provided as a class to support weaker readers.	**Activity**: Rutherford's experiment

Plenary	Support/Extend	Resources
What is inside? (10 min) Split students into three groups (Rutherford's experiment, cloud and bubble chambers, and particle accelerators). You may wish to split these groups further to facilitate discussion and collaboration. Ask students to describe the topic given to their group in one minute.	**Support**: Run this as a set of structured questions – can students answer simple statements about the topic?	
Investigating the Universe (5 min) Interactive resource where students complete a crossword on the key words from this topic.	**Extension**: Students list several things they have learned about, and at least one thing they would like to find out more about	**Interactive**: Investigating the Universe

Homework		
Students are given one subatomic particle to research and to write a short paragraph about, summarising their findings. Students should include the date of its discovery, the name(s) of its discoverer(s), and how it was discovered.	**Extension**: Encourage students to explain how this particular method of discovery works.	

Checkpoint lesson routes

The route through this lesson can be determined using the Checkpoint assessment.

Percentage pass marks are supplied in the Checkpoint teacher notes.

Route A (revision)
Resource: P3 Chapter 3 Checkpoint: Revision

Students work through a series of tasks that allows them to revisit and consolidate their understanding of key concepts in this chapter. Students can keep this as a summary of the topic, and use this when revising for future assessments.

Route B (extension)
Resource: P3 Chapter 3 Checkpoint: Extension

Students design a revision poster for a KS3 revision series that includes the key concepts covered in this chapter.

Progression to *secure*

No.	Developing outcome	Secure outcome	Making progress
1	State one use of telescopes.	Describe how astronomers use telescopes.	In Task 1 students link three different types of telescopes (Galilean, HST, and Kepler) with a description of how they are used.
2	Name the two types of telescope.	Describe two types of telescope.	In Task 1 students label diagrams of reflecting and refracting telescopes, using these to describe how these two types of telescopes work.
3	State the conditions required for life like that on Earth to exist.	Describe how astronomers search for life on other planets.	In Task 2 students complete a word fill using the key terms given to describe how astronomers use mathematical models, line spectra, and powerful telescopes to search for alien life.
4	State what GPS stands for and give examples of its uses.	Describe how GPS works.	In Task 3 students reorder statements to describe how GPS works.
5	State one method to find distances in space.	Describe how you can find the distance to planets and stars.	In Task 3 students carry out a simple experiment to test parallax in the classroom, before using this and their own knowledge to decide if a series of statements about parallax, radar, and GPS are true or false. Students then correct the statements that are false.
6	Name the two types of modulated wave.	Describe how a radio wave carries a signal.	In Task 4 students use a diagram of how signals are changed when transmitting a radio wave to describe how a radio wave carries a signal from a radio station to a household radio.
7	State one method scientists use to investigate what the Universe is made of.	Describe how physicists investigate what the Universe is made of.	In Task 5 students work through a table of statements to decide if these describe the use of cloud and bubble chambers or particle accelerators.
8	Name one type of particle detector.	Describe how particles can be detected.	In Task 5 students work through a table of statements to decide if these describe the use of cloud and bubble chambers or particle accelerators.

Answers to end-of-chapter questions

1. exoplanet – Kepler Space Telescope
   Higgs boson – Large Hadron Collider
   position of a plane – radar (3 marks)
2a. Y (1 mark)   **b** amplitude (1 mark)
3. quark, proton, atom, molecule (1 mark)
4. A planet is a body in our Solar System that orbits our Sun but an exoplanet is a body that orbits a star outside our Solar System. (2 marks)
5a. Eyepiece and objective lenses correctly labelled. (The objective lens is the larger of the two.) (1 mark)
   b It is very difficult to make lenses that are very big. They would also be too heavy to send into space. (2 marks)
6a. 93.2 MHz = 93.2 × 1 000 000 = 93 200 000 Hz (1 mark)
   b Sound waves are longitudinal waves that can be converted into an electrical signal and added to a carrier wave. A carrier wave, for example, a radio wave, is a transverse wave and digital signals are added to it by a radio transmitter, changing the amplitude or the frequency of the carrier wave. (2 marks)

7 Muons were detected using their characteristic tracks made in cloud chambers. The Higgs boson was detected using a detector made from semiconducting material at the Large Hadron Collider (LHC). (4 marks)

8a C, D, B, E, A (1 mark)

b The larger the exoplanet, the larger the change in intensity of radiation detected by the Kepler observatory. This is because the larger the exoplanet, the more light it can block out from the star, causing a bigger intensity change. (2 marks)

9 X-rays are absorbed by the atmosphere so the Chandra telescope would be useless on the ground as X-ray readings would be zero. (2 marks)

10a speed (m/s) = distance (m) ÷ time (s)

time (s) = distance (m) ÷ speed (m/s) = $6\,000 \div 300\,000\,000 = 2 \times 10^{-5}$ s (3 marks)

b distance Earth–Moon–Earth (m) = speed (m/s) × time (s) = $300\,000\,000 \times 2.5 = 7.5 \times 10^{8}$ m

distance between the Earth and the moon = $(7.5 \times 10^{8}) \div 2 = 3.75 \times 10^{8}$ m (3 marks)

c It is difficult to aim the radio wave correctly so that it hits the object under investigation. The signal would be too feint by the time that it returned to be detectable. (2 marks)

11 This is a QWC question. Students should be marked on the use of good English, organisation of information, spelling and grammar, and correct use of specialist scientific terms. The best answers will fully explain how an alien astronomer can work out that there is life on Earth (maximum of 6 marks). Examples of correct scientific points:

Computers can be used to estimate the habitable zone around our Sun.

This is the region where a planet would be at a suitable temperature for liquid water to exist.

Line spectra can also be used.

This is light reflected from planets that creates a unique series of lines on a spectrum of light, similar to a bar code.

Black lines appear on the line spectrum when frequencies are missing (because these are absorbed by the substances present in the planet's atmosphere).

This can be compared with known line spectra of substances required for life, for example, water.

Telescopes can also be used to detect radio waves and other EM waves emitted from Earth. Extremely powerful telescopes may be able to see Earth directly.

Answer guide for Big Write

Developing	Secure	Extending
1–2 marks	3–4 marks	5–6 marks
• Design correctly uses telescopes for planets, exoplanets, and stars, and particle accelerators for very small particles. • Language used is appropriate but lacks clarity. • Appropriate key words are used but not explained. • Images are not included.	• Design correctly describes the use of different telescopes for observing planets, exoplanets, and stars. • Design correctly describes what happens in a particle detector during particle collisions. • Language used is appropriate and clear. • Appropriate key words are used and explained. • Illustrations are included but are not appropriate or explained.	• Design correctly describes the use of different telescopes for observing planets, exoplanets, and stars in an imaginative way. • Design correctly describes what happens in a particle detector during particle collisions. • Language used is appropriate, clear, and used in a way that helps understanding. • Appropriate key words are used and explained clearly and concisely. • Annotated/labelled diagrams are used to illustrate ideas discussed in a visual way.

kerboodle

P3 Chapter 3 Checkpoint assessment (automarked)
P3 Chapter 3 Checkpoint: Revision
P3 Chapter 3 Checkpoint: Extension
P3 Chapter 3 Progress task (Literacy)

Index

Great Clarendon Street, Oxford, OX2 6DP, United Kingdom

Oxford University Press is a department of the University of Oxford.
It furthers the University's objective of excellence in research,
scholarship, and education by publishing worldwide. Oxford is a
registered trade mark of Oxford University Press in the UK and in
certain other countries

British Library Cataloguing in Publication Data
Data available

978-0-19-839261-3

10 9 8 7 6 5 4 3

Paper used in the production of this book is a natural, recyclable
product made from wood grown in sustainable forests.
The manufacturing process conforms to the environmental
regulations of the country of origin.

Printed in Great Britain

Acknowledgements
The publisher and the authors would like to thank the
following for permissions to use their photographs:

Cover image: Shaskin/Shutterstock